Academic Inquiry 3

Academic Inquiry 3

Essays and Integrating Sources

Sarah Leu
Heike Neumann

SERIES EDITOR Scott Roy Douglas

OXFORD
UNIVERSITY PRESS

Oxford University Press is a department of the University of Oxford. It furthers the University's objective of excellence in research, scholarship, and education by publishing worldwide. Oxford is a registered trade mark of Oxford University Press in the UK and in certain other countries.

Published in Canada by
Oxford University Press
8 Sampson Mews, Suite 204,
Don Mills, Ontario M3C 0H5 Canada

www.oupcanada.com

First Edition published in 2018

Library and Archives Canada Cataloguing in Publication
Leu, Sarah, author
Essays and integrating sources / Sarah Leu, Heike Neumann ;
series editor, Scott Roy Douglas.

(Academic inquiry ; 3)
Includes index.
ISBN 978-0-19-902541-1 (softcover)

1. Report writing. 2. Essay–Authorship. 3. English language–Rhetoric. I. Neumann, Heike, 1971-, author II. Title. III. Series: Academic inquiry (Series) ; 3

LB2369.L48 2017 808'.042 C2017-906847-4

Cover image: © iStock/Jacob Ammentorp Lund (Top and bottom)

Cover design: Laurie McGregor
Interior design: Laurie McGregor

Oxford University Press is committed to our environment. Wherever possible, our books are printed on paper which comes from responsible sources.

Printed and bound in Canada

1 2 3 4 — 21 20 19 18

To Luis Ochoa and Irmgard Neumann
—Heike

To my favourite plurilingual users of English: Tom, Nico, and Finn
—Sarah

SCOPE and SEQUENCE

		1	2	3	4	5	6
		Communications	Sociology	Tourism and Hospitality Management	Biology	Environmental Science	Business
	Topic	Media Literacy	Technological Innovation in Society	Travel	Immunity	Climatology	Corporate Social Responsibility
Exploring Ideas	Introduction: Activating Background Knowledge	Categorizing Media	Completing a Question Diagram	Completing a T-Chart	Completing a Graphic Organizer	Analyzing a Problem	Evaluating Corporate Social Initiatives
	Fostering Inquiry	Writing an Inquiry Question	Investigating an Idea	Comparing and Contrasting Characteristics	Analyzing Causes and Effects	Finding Solutions	Building an Argument
	Structure	Summary	Expository Essay	Compare-and-Contrast Essay	Cause-and-Effect Essay	Problem–Solution Essay	Persuasive Essay
	Language Tip	Using Reporting Verbs	Showing Relationships among Ideas	Using Compare-and-Contrast Connectors	Using Cause-and-Effect Connectors	Hedging	Signalling Stance
Academic Reading	Vocabulary Skill	Choosing the Right Synonym	Understanding Your Dictionary	Learning to Use New Words Using a Dictionary	Using Vocabulary Learning Strategies	Understanding Collocation	Correcting Grammar Using Your Dictionary
	Academic Word List	10 Word Families from the Academic Word List in Each Unit					
	Mid-frequency Vocabulary	10 Word Families up to the 8K Frequency Level in Each Unit					
	Pre-reading	Annotating a Text	Previewing Images and Subtitles to Make Predictions	Writing a Definition Based on Prior Knowledge to Make Predictions	Completing a KWL Chart to Make Predictions	Assessing Knowledge of Key Vocabulary	Establishing Opinions to Compare with Those Expressed in a Source Text
	Reading 1	"Our Media-Saturated Culture"	"Technology and Societal Change"	"Tourism"	"Immunity"	"Climate Change"	"Business Ethics"
	Reading 2	"Filtering Decisions"	"Technology and Jobs: More of One and Less of the Other?"	"Weed Your Way Around the World"	"Asking for an Outbreak of Preventable Diseases"	"Is Geoengineering the Solution to Saving the Earth?"	"Two Faces of Apple"
	Critical Thinking	Bloom's Taxonomy: *Knowledge*	Bloom's Taxonomy: *Comprehension*	Bloom's Taxonomy: *Application*	Bloom's Taxonomy: *Analysis*	Bloom's Taxonomy: *Synthesis*	Bloom's Taxonomy: *Evaluation*

		1	2	3	4	5	6
	Topic	Media Literacy	Technological Innovation in Society	Travel	Immunity	Climatology	Corporate Social Responsibility
Process Fundamentals	**Before You Write**	Summary Outline	Brainstorming	Venn Diagram	Flow Chart	Webbing	Planning for Your Audience
	Integrating Information from an Outside Source	APA and MLA Citations	Selecting Information from Sources	Sentence Patterns for Integrating Source Material, Part 1	Sentence Patterns for Integrating Source Material, Part 2	Citing Indirect Sources	Refuting a Source
	Preventing Plagiarism	Acknowledging Sources	Acknowledging Ideas	Taking Ownership	Editing and Revising Responsibly	Using Internet Sources Responsibly	Collaborating Responsibly
	Thesis/Topic Skill	Recognizing an Author's Purpose and Thesis	Writing a Thesis Statement That Answers a Question	Writing Topic Sentences	Writing a Cause-and-Effect Thesis Statement	Writing a Problem–Solution Thesis Statement	Writing a Debatable Thesis Statement
	Introductions	Introducing a Summary	Anecdote or Scenario	Thought-Provoking Question	Strategies for Introducing Cause and Effect	Example	Turnaround
	Conclusions		Look to the Future	Synthesizing Main Ideas	Thought-Provoking Comment	Warning	Call to Action
Writing Fundamentals	**Composition Skill**	Paraphrasing	Developing Body Paragraphs with the Question Technique	Achieving Essay Unity	Revising	Achieving Coherence	Acknowledging Opposing Views
	Sentence and Grammar Skill	Understanding Clauses and Avoiding Sentence Fragments	Using the Passive Voice	Increasing Sentence Variety and Avoiding Run-Ons and Comma Splices	Using Adverbials	Using Conditional Sentences	Using Quantifiers with Countable and Non-countable Nouns
Unit Outcome	**Writing Assignment**	Summary	Expository Essay	Compare-and-Contrast Essay	Cause-and-Effect Essay	Problem–Solution Essay	Persuasive Essay
	Evaluation	Summary Rubric	Expository Essay Rubric	Compare-and-Contrast Essay Rubric	Cause-and-Effect Essay Rubric	Problem–Solution Essay Rubric	Persuasive Essay Rubric
	Unit Review	Self-Assessment and Vocabulary Checklists					
	Learning Strategies (placement varies)	Activating Prior Knowledge	Getting Help	Organizing Ideas	Creating Mental Connections	Noticing	Monitoring Your Work

Contents

UNIT 1 COMMUNICATIONS

UNIT 2 SOCIOLOGY
Technological Innovation in Society 35

UNIT 3 TOURISM AND HOSPITALITY MANAGEMENT

UNIT 4 BIOLOGY
Immunity 107

UNIT 5 ENVIRONMENTAL SCIENCE

UNIT 6 BUSINESS
Corporate Social Responsibility 185

Note to Instructors

Taking an inquiry-based approach, this series fosters academic writing skills that contribute to student success in post-secondary studies. Each unit is based on an academic discipline and opens with an introduction to theme-related content that prepares students to think about ideas within that discipline. At the heart of each unit, students develop personalized Unit Inquiry Questions to guide their study; these questions are inspired by each student's personal interest and curiosity. The process promotes higher-order thinking skills, encourages student curiosity, and resists simple yes or no answers. The Unit Inquiry Questions put an active learner-centred focus on content and prime students for dynamic engagement with unit materials, concepts, and skills.

Student writing skills are developed using a language-through-content approach to composition instruction, with each unit focused on one rhetorical writing pattern and one academic discipline. At the core of each unit is an authentic reading, such as an excerpt from an undergraduate textbook that students might typically encounter in a post-secondary setting. These readings provide a springboard for the inclusion of informative content in student writing and promote effective writing skills. Within each of the core academic readings, students are exposed to key vocabulary from the Academic Word List (AWL) along with pertinent mid-frequency vocabulary (MFV); these words are introduced to students in pre-reading activities and recycled throughout the unit to foster a greater depth and breadth of lexical usage in student writing.

Additionally, the rich contextual framework within each unit provides an opportunity for the recycling of skills and the spiralling of concepts. Each unit also emphasizes the fundamentals of the writing process as well as key composition and grammar skills, according to the demands of the unit content and writing assignments. These fundamentals are supported by special skills boxes focusing on thinking critically, developing learning strategies, and preventing plagiarism. Furthermore, all the process and writing fundamentals are accompanied by focused activities, opportunities for meaningful writing practice, and multiple writing models to provide comprehensible input to students as they gather ideas to answer their Unit Inquiry Questions and complete their own writing projects.

The final writing assignment in each unit is based on students' personalized Unit Inquiry Questions and the rhetorical pattern explored in the unit. Numerous opportunities for controlled writing output are provided throughout the unit until the final assignment is written as a culmination of the language and content knowledge gained throughout the unit. The final writing assignment is supported with evaluation and review activities to reinforce student learning and mastery of the unit outcomes.

Robustly supporting the content in the student books, the *Academic Inquiry* companion website (teacher's resource) is a rich source of supplementary materials. Online, teachers can find teaching notes, pacing guides, adaptable practice materials for each unit's learning objectives, answer keys, additional sample writing models, editing activities, and printable versions of the evaluation rubrics. Teachers will also find extension activities in the form of genre-based academic writing tasks (such as journal entries, lab reports, and case studies) and integrated tasks (such as surveys, short presentations, and posters). Finally, teachers have access to writing prompts suitable for timed exam purposes. Teachers can contact their local Oxford University Press sales and editorial representative for access to the password-protected teacher's resource.

Note to Students

Writing for academic purposes can seem like a difficult task; however, it doesn't have to be impossible. *Academic Inquiry* breaks down the task of academic writing into manageable parts. Each unit has carefully structured activities. You develop your academic writing skills step by step until you have the confidence to handle academic writing tasks on your own.

This textbook series takes an inquiry-based approach to learning. Each unit focuses on a core academic discipline, and you are encouraged to decide for yourself what specific area within that discipline you want to write about. This approach puts you in control of your learning. You find answers to your own questions. You develop your own writing topics.

Each unit opens with an opportunity to explore ideas connected to a topic within a specific academic discipline. Then you develop a question about that topic. It is a meaningful question based on your own curiosity. Throughout the unit, you have opportunities to find answers to this question—your Unit Inquiry Question.

Next, you work on expanding your vocabulary. New vocabulary supports your ability to express your ideas effectively and precisely. The new vocabulary is introduced in the context of academic readings, similar to those found in college and university settings. These readings also help you find ideas for your writing.

After you have read and responded to the readings in each unit, you have the opportunity to explore the unit topic in greater detail. You brainstorm and develop your chosen writing topic. You consider ways to prevent plagiarism. You make connections to your Unit Inquiry Question. You cover the structure and elements of quality academic writing, as well as critical thinking skills, learning strategies, vocabulary, and grammar points.

The key to developing these skills is extensive writing practice. Throughout each unit, you revisit and revise your own writing on a number of occasions. You see examples of good academic writing. You have the opportunity to review and rework your Unit Inquiry Question. You then complete the final unit assignment related to your Unit Inquiry Question. The end of each unit includes a writing rubric and self-assessment checklist connected to what you have learned in that unit. These tools help promote your understanding of the elements of effective academic writing.

The *Academic Inquiry* series guides you through the academic writing process. In each unit, you explore academic writing skills one at a time within the context of an academic discipline. In doing so, you will find the process of academic writing to be much less challenging. This style of writing is about communicating your ideas, which takes hard work and practice. However, developing the ability to express yourself clearly and effectively makes all that hard work and practice worthwhile. *Academic Inquiry* will empower you to use your skills and knowledge of the process in your future college and university studies.

Acknowledgements

The authors would like to acknowledge everyone at Oxford University Press who helped with this series and contributed to its publication. In particular, the authors thank the editorial team for their insightful suggestions and tireless dedication to excellence in English language teaching materials.

Oxford University Press Canada would like to express appreciation to the instructors and coordinators who graciously offered feedback on *Academic Inquiry* at various stages of the developmental process. Their feedback was instrumental in helping to shape and refine the book.

Carolyn Ambrose-Miller, Niagara College
Mélanie Barrière, Université de Sherbrooke
Erminia Bossio, Sheridan College
Devon Boucher, Thompson Rivers University
Kim Cechetto, Fanshawe College
Dara Cowper, Centennial College
Susan A. Curtis, University of British Columbia
Jason Doucette, Saint Mary's University
Cynthia Eden, University of Guelph
Giacomo Folinazzo, Niagara College
Sean Henderson, Wilfrid Laurier University
Gilmour Jope, University of the Fraser Valley
Barbara Kanellakos, Dalhousie University
Kristibeth Kelly, Fanshawe College
Kasie Kelos, Seneca College
Daryaneh Lane, University of Waterloo
Fiona Lucchini, Bow Valley College (retired)
Jonathon McCallum, Mohawk College
Angela Meyer Sterzik, Fanshawe College
Kristopher Mitchell, Dalhousie University
Anne Mullen, Université Laval
Thomas O'Hare, Université de Montrèal
Sophie Paish, Dalhousie University
Cyndy Reimer, Douglas College
Shawna Shulman, York University
Ardiss Stutters, Okanagan College
Elham Tavallaei, Centennial College
Jason Toole, Wilfrid Laurier University

UNIT 1 Media Literacy

Communications

KEY LEARNING OUTCOMES

- Creating an inquiry question
- Recognizing an author's purpose and thesis
- Annotating a text
- Writing a summary outline
- Choosing the right synonym
- Citing sources in APA or MLA format
- Paraphrasing
- Understanding clause structure
- Avoiding sentence fragments
- Writing a summary

EXPLORING IDEAS

Introduction

We live in a world full of complex media messages produced by specific people for specific purposes, all competing for our attention. We also live in a time when it is possible to create and transmit our own messages relatively easily. Media literacy—the ability to understand, judge, and create media messages—helps us to navigate this media-rich environment.

Activity A | Discuss the following questions with a partner or small group.

1. Which icons do you recognize in the image above? Do you use any of these apps regularly? If so, for what purposes?
2. What kinds of media messages do you most often interact with? In what ways do you interact with them? For example, you might *read* text messages or *write* articles for a student newspaper.
3. Think of an advertisement (ad) that you like. What product is being advertised? Where, when, and in what medium have you seen the ad? Why do you like it?
4. What do you think the difference is between *mainstream*[1] *media* and *alternative media*? Can you think of any examples of each?
5. Do you have any concerns about online media?

---

[1] widely accepted as normal

Activity B | With a partner or small group, categorize the following keywords related to media by grouping words that are similar in some way. You may also add your own keywords. Then give a title to each category. When you are finished, compare your categories with another group's. There may be more than one correct way to categorize these ideas.

ad	hyperlinks	Internet	sell
book	images	~~newspaper~~	story
bulletin board	inform	persuade	television
entertain	Instagram	political speech	Twitter
Facebook	interact	radio	words

Category Title:	Category Title:	Category Title:	Category Title:	Category Title:
newspaper				

Activity C | Writing Task: Short Paragraph | In your opinion, what is the most important purpose of modern media? Write a short paragraph explaining why it is the most important. When you are finished, exchange paragraphs with a partner and discuss. Did you and your partner agree on the main purpose of modern media?

Learning Strategy

Activating Prior Knowledge

Good learning strategies help you improve your English. Before you read a text on a new topic, it is helpful to activate your prior knowledge. In other words, take time to think about what you already know about that topic. Doing so helps you connect what you read to what you already know. This makes it easier to understand the texts you read. There are various ways you can activate prior knowledge:

- reflect on experiences from your life that are related to the topic;
- consider what interests you about this topic;
- reflect on why this topic is important in your life; and
- think about your opinion on issues related to that topic.

The activities in each unit's *Introduction* help you to activate your prior knowledge so that you will be well prepared to think and read about that unit's topic.

Source: Based on ideas in Oxford, R. L. (2011). *Teaching and researching language learning strategies*. Harlow, UK: Pearson.

Fostering Inquiry

Writing an Inquiry Question

An *inquiry question* is a question you ask yourself to help focus your investigation of a topic. It is a question about something that genuinely interests you. The most interesting inquiry questions are open-ended and begin with *who*, *what*, *where*, *when*, *how*, or *why*. Your inquiry question might change as you explore your chosen topic and will likely lead you to new questions. Try to choose an inquiry question that goes beyond what you are already familiar with. Challenge yourself to look at an issue from a new perspective or to explore a completely unknown subject. Your inquiry question provides an opportunity for you to learn and grow. To help you come up with an inquiry question, you could imagine asking a question to an expert on the topic to help you clarify your ideas.

Activity A | What do you want to know more about in relation to media literacy and the field of communications? For example, *How can I protect my privacy while using social media?* or *What strategies do advertisers use to sell products?*

1. Write down two or three questions you have about media literacy. Refer to the category table you filled out on page 3.
2. In a small group, share your questions.
3. Choose one question to be your guiding inquiry question for this unit. Your inquiry question can be different from the other group members' questions. The focus of your question may change as you work your way through this unit.
4. Write your inquiry question here and refer to it as you complete the activities in this unit.

   My Unit Inquiry Question:

   ____

   ____

   ____

   ____

Activity B | Writing Task: Freewriting | Write for at least five minutes on the topic of your Unit Inquiry Question. Do not stop writing during this time. After five minutes, read what you have written and circle two or three ideas that you would like to explore further in order to answer your Unit Inquiry Question.

Structure

Summary

Summarizing is the act of retelling the most important points of what somebody else has said or written, using your own words.

Summarizing is a crucial academic skill. It helps you understand and remember what you have read, which is necessary as you investigate research questions, synthesize information, and develop your ideas about a topic. In addition to serving as a useful tool for inquiry, summarizing also forms the basis of many types of academic writing (e.g., essay questions on exams, summary-and-response essays, and writing that integrates information from outside sources). Finally, summarizing effectively is a good way to avoid plagiarism—intentionally or unintentionally presenting another person's words or ideas as your own.

To summarize well, you need to be able to

- understand an author's purpose and the main idea of the text;
- distinguish between important supporting points and minor details; and
- paraphrase, or restate someone else's thoughts using different words or sentence structure.

Identifying Main Idea, Important Supporting Points, and Minor Details

The *main idea* of a text is the most important point, the one thing an author wants us to understand or believe. The title of a text is often a good clue for figuring out the main idea. In addition to the main idea, a text usually also contains both important supporting points and minor details. *Important supporting points* are necessary to fully convey the main idea. Without them, the reader will not be sufficiently persuaded or informed. *Minor details* provide additional interesting information. These make the text more enjoyable and may reinforce or illustrate the supporting points, but they are not essential for understanding the author's main idea.

Activity A | Read the text below to identify its main idea. Where do you think you would find a text like this? What would be a good title for this text? After you have finished reading, answer the questions that follow.

Persuasive narratives such as advertisements are designed primarily to influence audience attitudes and behaviours. The typical story formula for persuasive narratives is problem–solution, which is a very simple formula. It has to be very simple because audiences rarely pay attention to any one persuasive narrative. Persuasive narratives on TV are typically 15 seconds and appear in clusters of a dozen or more ads interrupting an entertainment program. Persuasive narratives in magazines, newspapers, and on websites are typically displayed on a small portion of a page or a screen.

Using this very simple problem–solution formula of storytelling, advertisers typically exaggerate our problems in order to increase our anxiety and fear. Then they exaggerate their product's effectiveness as the solution in order to motivate us to buy their product. This is an example of the *next-step reality* formula. The ads present real problems that we experience, but make those problems seem more urgent. At the same time, they portray their solutions as more dramatic than they are in reality.

When advertisers exaggerate their solutions, they must be careful not to present a factual falsehood that could be tested for its truth value. Therefore, their product claims are more likely to be *puffery*. Puffery is the practice of making claims for a product that sound very good on the surface but do not make any substantive claim that could be actually tested for its truth value. For example, have you ever seen an ad where any of the following claims were made: "the best in its class," "the most beautiful," or "the finest"? These slogans at first seem to be telling us something good about the advertised product. Upon closer examination, however, they are empty claims because they cannot actually be tested.

Source: Adapted from Potter, W. J. (2016). *Introduction to media literacy* (p. 118). Los Angeles, CA: SAGE.

1. Where do you think you would find a text like this?
2. Give the text a title.

____

3. Fill in the chart below by writing the main idea in the large circle, the important supporting points in the smaller circles, and the minor details on the lines beside the relevant supporting point. Note that there may be some lines left blank in the chart.

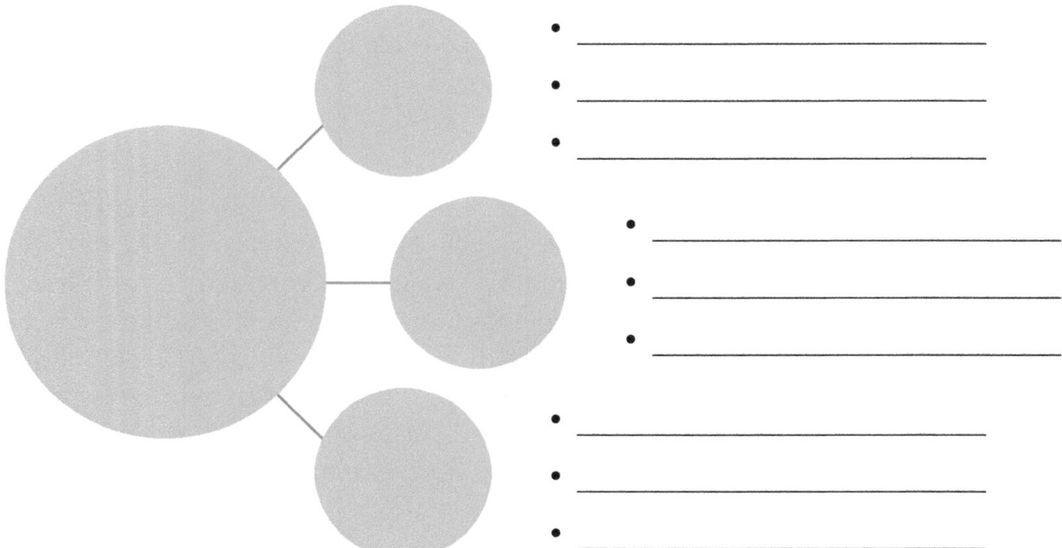

Preparing to Summarize: Annotating a Text

Reading is an active process of interpreting what is on the page and integrating the information with your background knowledge, opinions, and so on. One way to improve your understanding and ability to remember is to annotate as you read. *Annotate* means to make notes and symbols on the page or screen. It is an active reading strategy. If you know you are reading for a specific purpose, you may annotate in a particular way. For example, if you plan to write a summary of a text, you will want to annotate in a way that highlights the main idea and important supporting points. You may also want to cross out parts of the original that will not be included in your summary, like minor details or repetition.

Activity B | Reread the short text in Activity A on page 5 (the actual title of the passage is "Persuading") and follow these steps:

1. If you can find one sentence that expresses the main idea of the whole text, highlight it or make a star in the margin by that sentence. If you cannot find one sentence that does this, write in the margin what you think the main idea is.
2. Underline any sentences or phrases that contain important supporting points.
3. Cross out any sentences or phrases that simply repeat or recap information already stated.
4. Finally, cross out any minor details, which should not be included in your summary.

Activity C | Compare your annotated text with a partner's. Then compare your annotated text with the summary in Activity D on page 8.

Summary Structure

Summary

Introductory sentence
- Source information
- Main idea

Author's first important supporting point
Author's second important supporting point
...
Author's final important supporting point

A summary. . .

- begins with a sentence that provides the source information for the text being summarized as well as the main idea of the text.
- includes information or ideas from the original text only, without any commentary, inference, or opinion about those ideas.
- includes all and only the most important supporting points from the original.
- is much shorter than the text it summarizes, often a quarter of the length of the original.

- is typically not divided into paragraphs in the same way an essay is. However, if the original text is long and complex, the summary may be divided into sections.
- does not include a concluding paragraph in the same way that an essay does.

Activity D | With a partner or small group, read the following summary of "Persuading," the text you read on pages 5–6. Answer the questions that follow.

In a textbook excerpt entitled "Persuading," W. James Potter (2016) explains how advertisers use persuasive narratives to sway consumers. According to Potter, advertisers rely on stories that describe a problem and a solution. In order to sell products, they make the problem sound worse than it really is and suggest that their product is the best solution to the problem. Advertisers often use *puffery,* which are statements about a product that sound great but are impossible to confirm.

1. What information appears in the first sentence of the summary?
2. Which term or terms from the original text appear in exactly the same way in the summary? Why do you think the summary writer used the word(s) from the original?
3. Look back at the chart on page 6 where you filled in the main idea, important supporting points, and minor details of the original text. Does the summary include what you identified as the main idea and the important supporting points? Does it include any minor details?
4. Does the summary include any of the summary writer's opinion about the topic or about the original text?

Language Tip

Using Reporting Verbs

A summary restates what someone else has written or said. *Reporting verbs* indicate that you are conveying someone else's ideas and specify the original author's purpose for writing. They are often (but not always) followed by *that* and an independent clause, as in this example:

The authors argue that privacy no longer exists in the age of social media.

Here are some common reporting verbs.

argue	conclude	discuss	mention	state
claim	contend	explain	point out	stress
compare	describe	illustrate	report	write

Activity E | Revisit your Unit Inquiry Question on page 4. What new ideas have you thought of that will help you answer your question? Share your ideas with a partner or small group. At this point, you may consider revising your Unit Inquiry Question.

ACADEMIC READING

Vocabulary

Vocabulary Skill: Choosing the Right Synonym

Synonyms are words that have almost the same meaning (e.g., *big* and *large*). Having a strong vocabulary includes knowing synonyms for a given word. Using synonyms, rather than repeating the same word over and over, can help add variety to your writing. Using synonyms effectively is necessary when summarizing, because you must write the summary in different words than the original text.

A thesaurus, which lists synonyms for words, can be a very useful resource. However, it is important to understand that even though synonyms have nearly the same meaning, they are not always interchangeable.

For example, the online *Oxford Learner's Dictionary* lists four synonyms for the word *task*: *duties*, *mission*, *job*, and *chore*. Which synonym to use in a given context depends on a number of factors, such as

- the **precise meaning** that is intended. Synonyms share certain meanings, but not others. All the synonyms listed for *task* refer to something that somebody has to do, but each word has other meanings as well. For example, *duty* can also mean "something that you feel you have to do because it is your moral or legal responsibility."
- the **connotation** of the word. Some words convey a particular feeling or attitude. For example, a chore is usually unpleasant, while a mission is not.
- **collocation**. Certain words frequently appear together. For example, *household chores*, *routine tasks*, *a sense of duty*, or a *secret mission*.

Activity A | Choose the best word from the list to complete each sentence below. Use each word once. Use your dictionary to help you if necessary.

task	mission	chore	duty	job

1. Olivia took a ________________ as a waitress to make some extra money.
2. It is my ________________ as a citizen to vote in the upcoming election.
3. After setting a series of deadlines for the project, our next ________________ was to assign roles to all the team members.
4. The soldiers were given a dangerous fact-finding ________________ in the region.
5. Giving children regular household ________________, such as making their beds or taking out the garbage, can teach them a sense of responsibility.

Vocabulary Preview: The Academic Word List

The Academic Word List (AWL)[2] is a list of 570 word families that appear frequently in academic texts. Knowing the words on this list will help you understand the academic texts you encounter and will enrich your academic writing in English.

Activity B | Many words have more than one meaning. Read the sentences below, which have been taken or adapted from Readings 1 and 2 later in this unit. The bolded word in each sentence is from the AWL. Then choose the best definition of the AWL word.

1. Our **culture** is a grand supermarket of media messages.
   a. (n.) the customs and beliefs, art, way of life, and social organization of a particular country or group
   b. (n.) art, music, literature, etc., thought of as a group
2. We **encounter** a great many media messages without paying much attention to them.
   a. (v.) to experience something while you are trying to do something else
   b. (v.) to meet someone, especially suddenly or unexpectedly
3. Your spam filter may be blocking thousands of emails each day **automatically** so you don't have to be bothered by them.
   a. (adv.) as a necessary and inevitable result of a fixed rule or particular set of circumstances
   b. (adv.) by itself with little or no direct human control
4. Every once in a while, something in a message or in our environment **triggers** our awareness of a particular message and we pay attention to it, but most messages get filtered out unconsciously.
   a. (v.) to make something happen suddenly
   b. (v.) to cause a device to start functioning
5. The *automatic routine* is a **sequence** of behaviours that we learn from experience then apply again and again with little effort.
   a. (n.) a set of events, actions, numbers, etc. that have a particular order and that lead to a particular result
   b. (n.) the order that events, actions, etc. happen in or should happen in
6. Think of the **process** of learning to do something as the recording of instructions in our minds, much like how computer programmers write lines of code that tell the computer what to do.
   a. (n.) a method of doing or making something, especially one that is used in industry
   b. (n.) a series of things that happen, especially ones that result in natural changes

---

[2] See Coxhead, A. (2000). A new academic word list. *TESOL Quarterly, 34*(2), 213–238.

7. Once you have learned a sequence—such as tying your shoes, brushing your teeth, driving to school, or playing a song on the guitar—you can perform that **task** over and over again with very little effort compared to the effort it took you to learn it in the first place.
   a. (n.) an activity that is designed to help achieve a particular learning goal, especially in language teaching
   b. (n.) a piece of work that somebody has to do

8. To **illustrate** the concept of automatic processing, consider what you do when you go to the supermarket to buy food. Let's say you walk into the store with a list of 12 items you need to buy, and 15 minutes later you walk out of the store with your 12 items.
   a. (v.) to make the meaning of something clearer by using examples, pictures, stories, etc.
   b. (v.) to use pictures, photographs, diagrams, etc. in a book

9. The media create much of our filtering code for us, primarily by conditioning us for repeat **exposure** of the messages we like.
   a. (n.) contact with something
   b. (n.) the revelation of an identity or fact, especially one that is concealed or likely to arouse disapproval

10. There is also evidence that the **media** are trying to be even more proactive in determining our filtering codes. For example, Amazon focuses your attention on a handful of books based on what it knows about your history of book buying.
    a. (n.) the main ways that large numbers of people receive information and entertainment, that is, television, radio, newspapers, and the Internet
    b. (n.) methods or materials used in entertainment or art

Vocabulary Preview: Mid-frequency Vocabulary

Words can be categorized according to how frequently they are used. The 2000 word families that are most often used in English are called *high-frequency* words, and they make up about 80 percent of a typical academic text. Clearly, it is important to know these words, along with the words on the AWL. However, an academic text will also contain *low-frequency* and *mid-frequency* vocabulary—that is, words that do not appear as often in texts, but are necessary to convey a precise meaning.

Activity C | Fill in the blanks with the best mid-frequency word from the list below. Use the synonyms written in parentheses to help you choose the right word.

accomplish	aggressively	barely	chaos	filter
fraction	navigate	routine	~~saturated~~	temptation

Media these days are ___saturated___ with (flooded with; full of) advertising. It is impossible to watch TV, listen to the radio, or visit most websites without encountering some sort of marketing message. Sometimes, these messages are disguised as information and we may be ________________ (only just; almost not) aware that someone is trying to sell us something. Other times, companies ________________ (forcefully; with great determination) try to capture our attention with flashy and memorable advertising campaigns. Their goal is to create in us an irresistible ________________ (desire; longing) to buy their products. How can people ________________ (make their way safely through; make sense of) such a seemingly treacherous media landscape? Fortunately, research shows that consumers effectively ________________ out (screen; reject) many marketing messages without even being aware of doing it. We ________________ (achieve; succeed in doing) this task by using something called the *automatic* ________________ (habit; procedure), which is a series of behaviours that we learn through experience and then apply repetitively. This automation helps us make sense of the ________________ (confusion; disorder) created by many marketers simultaneously trying to win our business. In fact, it seems that consumers effectively ignore all but a small ________________ (part; portion) of the messages we encounter every day.

Reading 1

The reading "Our Media-Saturated Culture" is an excerpt from the textbook *Introduction to Media Literacy* by W. James Potter. This textbook is used in communications classes in Canadian post-secondary schools.

Activity A | How many media messages do you think you see or hear in a single day? Do you perceive this as a high number? Working with a partner, make a list of pros and cons of having access to a lot of media messages.

Activity B | Read "Our Media-Saturated Culture" once straight through. Then reread it and annotate it for the purpose of writing a summary. To annotate, follow these steps:

- Highlight or note the author's main idea.
- Underline the important supporting points.
- Cross out repeated information or minor details.

READING

Our Media-Saturated Culture

1 Our **culture** is **saturated** with a flood of information. Most of this information is delivered by **media** messages that **aggressively** compete for our attention. Hollywood releases more than 700 hours of feature films each year, which adds to its base of more than 100,000 hours of films they have already released in previous years. Commercial TV stations generate about 48 million hours of video messages every year worldwide, and radio stations send out 65.5 million hours of original programming each year. In addition, users of video platforms such as YouTube upload more than 100 hours of new video *every minute of every day* (YouTube, 2014). We now have more than 140 million book titles in existence, and another 1500 new book titles are published throughout the world each day. Then there is the world wide web—or Internet—which is so huge that no one knows how big it really is. Google started indexing web pages about a decade ago and has now catalogued more than 13.4 billion pages (de Kunder, 2013), which is a truly large number. However, Google has **barely** scratched the surface of the web, because these 13.4 billion pages have been estimated to be only one percent of all web pages (Sponder, 2012).

Automatic Routines

2 The powerful tool that the human mind uses to **navigate** through all this **chaos** is the automatic **routine**, which is a **sequence** of behaviours that we learn from experience, then apply again and again with little effort. Once you have learned a sequence—such as tying your shoes, brushing your teeth, driving to school, or playing a song on the guitar—you can perform that **task** over and over again with very little effort compared to the effort it took you to learn it in the first place. Think of the **process** of learning to do something as the recording of instructions in our minds, much like how computer programmers write lines of code that tell the computer what to do. Once that code is written, it can later be loaded into our minds and run **automatically** to guide us through that task with very little conscious thought or effort.

3 We have developed automatic routines to help us **filter** out almost all mass media messages and filter in only a tiny **fraction** of those messages. Thus, we **encounter** almost all media messages in a state of automaticity—that is, we put our minds on "automatic pilot" where our minds automatically filter out almost all message options. We cannot possibly consider every possible message and consciously decide whether to pay attention to it or not. There are too many messages to consider. So our minds have developed automatic routines that guide this filtering process very quickly and efficiently so we don't have to spend much, if any, mental effort.

4 To **illustrate** this automatic processing, consider what you do when you go to the supermarket to buy food. Let's say you walk into the store with a list of 12 items you need to buy, and 15 minutes later you walk out of the store with your 12 items. In this scenario, how many decisions have you made? The **temptation** is to say 12 decisions, because you needed to have made a decision to buy each of your 12 items. But what about all the items you decided *not to buy*? The average supermarket today has about 40,000 items on its shelves. So you actually made 40,000 decisions in the relatively short time you were in the supermarket—12 decisions to buy a product and 39,988 decisions not to buy a product. How did you

accomplish such an involved task in such a short period of time? You relied on automatic routines that reside in your unconscious mind and reveal themselves to you as your buying habits.

5 Our culture is a grand supermarket of media messages. Those messages are everywhere whether we realize it or not, except that there are far more messages in our culture than there are products in any supermarket. In our everyday lives—such as when we enter a supermarket—we load an automatic program into our mind that tells it what to look for and ignore the rest. Automatic processing guides most—but certainly not all—of our media **exposures**. With automatic processing, we encounter a great many media messages without paying much attention to them; thus, we have the feeling that we are filtering them out because we are not paying conscious attention to them. Every once in a while, something in a message or in our environment **triggers** our awareness of a particular message and we pay attention to it, but most messages get filtered out unconsciously.

References

de Kunder, M. (2013, February 2). *The size of the World Wide Web (The Internet).* Retrieved from www.worldwidewebsize.com

Sponder, M. (2012). *Social media analytics: Effective tools for building, interpreting, and using metrics.* New York, NY: McGraw-Hill.

YouTube. (2014). Statistics. Retrieved June 28, 2014 from www.youtube.com/yt/press/statistics.html

Source: Potter, W. J. (2016). *Introduction to media literacy* (pp. 1–4). Los Angeles, CA: SAGE.

Activity C | The following questions are based on the textbook excerpt you just read. Discuss with a partner or small group.

1. How many web pages had been indexed on the Internet as of 2013?

 ____

2. List three examples of automatic routines given in the text.
    - ____________________
    - ____________________
    - ____________________
3. List three examples of automatic routines that you follow every day (not from the text).
    - ____________________
    - ____________________
    - ____________________
4. How are media messages like items in a supermarket?
5. Do you think it is a good thing that we encounter most media messages "on automatic pilot"? Why or why not?

Activity D | Writing Task: Paragraph | Using your annotations on "Our Media-Saturated Culture", write a short paragraph explaining how automatic routines work to help us reduce the number of media messages we actively pay attention to. Try to include appropriate synonyms or alternate phrasing for five of the new vocabulary words introduced in this unit.

Critical Thinking

Bloom's Taxonomy—*Knowledge*

Thinking critically means examining an idea from multiple angles to understand it more deeply. One way of classifying critical thinking skills is via Bloom's (1956) taxonomy of learning objectives.[3] Bloom's taxonomy is represented by a triangle, with lower-order skills on the bottom and higher-order skills on the top.

Eval.
Synthesis
Analysis
Application
Comprehension
Knowledge

The triangle is meant to show that the basic (lower-order) skills provide a foundation for the more sophisticated (higher-order) skills. For example, before we can *apply* (Level 3) an idea to a new situation, we must first be able to *recall* the relevant information (Level 1) and *understand* it (Level 2). The Critical Thinking boxes in each unit of this textbook will suggest questions for thinking about a subject at each level of Bloom's taxonomy.

The first level of thinking in Bloom's taxonomy is *knowledge*. Having knowledge in this case means being able to recall facts and information that you have read. As you read, ask yourself the *wh-* questions that journalists use to report "just the facts." These include

Who . . . ?	Where . . . ?
What . . . ?	Why . . . ?
When . . . ?	How . . . ?

The answers to these questions can be found directly in the text. Keeping these questions in mind as you annotate a text can help you to better remember what you read.

Source: Bloom, B. S., Engelhart, M. D., Furst, E. J., Hill, W. H., & Krathwohl, D. R. (1956). *Taxonomy of educational objectives: The classification of educational goals. Handbook 1: Cognitive domain.* London, UK: Longman.

[3] Bloom's taxonomy was revised in 2001. Slightly different terminology was introduced, and the order of two skills was reversed. However, the learning objectives themselves are the same in both versions. In this book, we refer to the original (1956) version.

Activity E | Compare your paragraph to the sample paragraph "Automatic Routines" in Appendix 2. Did you use any of the same new vocabulary or synonyms for new vocabulary as the sample paragraph? When you are finished, exchange paragraphs with a partner or share your paragraphs in a small group. Did you and your partner(s) use any of the same new vocabulary or synonyms?

Reading 2

The reading "Filtering Decisions" is another excerpt from Potter's *Introduction to Media Literacy.*

Activity A | Read "Filtering Decisions" once straight through, then reread it and annotate it for the purpose of writing a summary. You will use these annotations to prepare a summary outline. To annotate, follow these steps:

- Highlight or note the author's main idea.
- Underline the important supporting points.
- Cross out repeated information and minor details.

READING

Filtering Decisions

1 As we go through each day, we are constantly flooded with information. In order to protect ourselves from being overwhelmed, we continually block out most of that flood of information by automatically ignoring most of it and paying attention to only a very small percentage of it. For example, think about when your cell phone, iPad, or computer signals that you have received a text. Sometimes you read it and answer it, but other times you ignore it, especially when you're receiving hundreds of texts a day. When you see the signal for a text and decide whether to respond or not, you are filtering consciously. But let's say you have a spam filter on your device where certain kinds of texts and emails are blocked and only a certain kind are allowed through. In this case, your spam filter may be blocking thousands of messages each day automatically so you don't have to be bothered by them.

2 Spam filters provide a great service—that is, until you think about who has programmed your spam filter. Maybe there are some messages that you do not want filtered out, but your spam filter has been programmed to block them. When someone important to you sends valuable messages that are blocked by your spam filter, this is a frustrating problem. To solve this problem, you need to get into your spam filter and reprogram its selection process to unblock those messages you want to get through. We all have a kind of spam filter running in the back of our minds every day to filter out almost all of the media messages available to us. We can see evidence of this spam filter working when we look at our *media*

exposure habits—that is, there are some media and certain types of messages that we completely avoid.

3 The media create much of our filtering code for us. They do this primarily by conditioning us for repeat exposure of the messages we like. This conditioning creates and reinforces exposure habits. When we follow our exposure habits, we leave no time to explore other media or other types of messages.

4 There is also evidence that the media are trying to be even more proactive in determining our filtering codes. For example, Amazon focuses your attention on a handful of books based on what it knows about your history of book buying. Also, Netflix offers 140,000 movies and TV shows, but you can't see a listing of them all. Instead, it personalizes what it shows you, thus focusing your choices on what you say you like most. Now, about 60 percent of all Netflix rentals come from personalized guesses of what Netflix thinks you would like.

5 Internet companies employ sophisticated algorithms[4] to churn through all the information they have about you to infer conclusions about what you like, then use those inferred conclusions to direct you to particular products and wall you off from other products in the name of efficient filtering. These algorithms are very sophisticated and very powerful in sorting through massive data files. The danger is that they have built-in assumptions that consumers are not aware of, and often, these algorithms can be harmful.

6 Imagine the following scenario. Let's say a company assembles a huge database about college students by pulling together information from Facebook pages, credit history, health history, parents' income level, etc. Then someone in that company develops an algorithm that churns through all that data and rank orders all the college students on potential for success and economic wealth. And let's say that the company's algorithm ranks you at the bottom as a probable loser but ranks your roommates at the top as probable winners. The company sells its ranking to other companies who then send your roommates all kinds of great offers for low interest credit cards, coupons for exciting trips, opportunities to network with successful professionals, and so on.

7 Meanwhile, you are ignored by these marketers because you are regarded as an undesirable target audience. But your roommates go on to live very successful and happy lives because of all the opportunities offered by marketers who bought data that told them that your roommates were highly desirable targets. Your roommates get higher paying jobs at graduation than you because employers looked at the rankings. Your roommates go on to get bigger raises and promotions, have better health care plans, travel more, meet more interesting people, etc. Marketers can set people off on different life paths by the opportunities they offer certain people and not others.

8 These marketers are not trying to be evil or trying to unfairly discriminate. Instead, marketers are simply trying to be efficient and get the most for their advertising dollars by targeting their advertising to those people who have the greatest potential of becoming valued customers. Thus, marketers depend on research companies to help them identify the right people to be the best targets for their expensive marketing campaigns.

[4] formulas or sets of rules that must be followed when solving particular problems, especially in computing

Source: Potter, W. J. (2016). *Introduction to media literacy* (pp. 94–96). Los Angeles, CA: SAGE.

Activity B | The following questions are based on the textbook excerpt you just read. Discuss with a partner or small group.

1. Fill in the following table with the pros and cons of a spam filter for media messages.

Advantages	Disadvantages

2. What are media exposure habits?
3. How do companies determine what media messages each of us will be exposed to?
4. Do you think it is a good thing that we are mostly exposed to media messages that we like? Why or why not?

PROCESS FUNDAMENTALS

Before You Write

Summary Outline

An outline is a plan for a piece of writing that contains notes about the ideas you want to include and lays out the structure for presenting those ideas. Outlines for different types of text will look different.

A summary outline includes notes about all the necessary parts of your summary: source information, main idea, and important supporting ideas from the original text. If you have annotated a text for the purpose of summarizing, writing a summary outline is very simple.

Activity A | Writing Task: Summary Outline | Look back at the annotations you made on Reading 1 or Reading 2 and fill in the summary outline below. Some information has been filled in for you.

Source Information

Title:
Author: W. James Potter
Year of publication: 2016
Type of text (if known): textbook excerpt (Introduction to Media Literacy)

Main Idea

Important Supporting Ideas

Integrating Information from an Outside Source

APA and MLA Citations

When you refer to information, ideas, or language from a text, or when you are writing a summary of that text, you must cite the source. Citing a source means giving information about a text's author(s), title, and date and place of publication. Two common formats for citing sources are the American Psychological Association (APA) style and the Modern Language Association (MLA) style. APA style is commonly used in social sciences, for example, psychology, sociology, or education. MLA style is common in the humanities, such as history or literature. If you are not sure which referencing style you should use in a course, ask your instructor.

Whether you use APA or MLA style, there are two components to proper citation. The first is an *in-text citation*, where you give partial information within your text about your source(s). The purpose of this citation is to help your reader find the relevant bibliographic information for that source in your References or Works Cited section (see below).

The second component is a list of the full bibliographic information for all sources you cite. This list is presented at the end of your written work, in a section called References (APA format) or Works Cited (MLA format). The purpose of this list is to allow a reader to access and read the exact source that you refer to.

1. APA Basics

In-text citations: Give the author's last name and the year of publication. If you are directly quoting the author (i.e., using the exact same words as in the original), provide the page number as well. Note that direct quotations must also be enclosed in quotation marks (see the examples below).

Potter (2016) explains that Amazon chooses which books to recommend based on a customer's previous shopping history.

Amazon chooses which books to recommend based on a customer's previous shopping history (Potter, 2016).

According to Potter (2016), "Amazon focuses your attention on a handful of books based on what it knows about your history of book buying" (p. 95).

"Amazon focuses your attention on a handful of books based on what it knows about your history of book buying" (Potter, 2016, p. 95).

Reference list: At the end of your paragraph or essay, list all sources cited in your References section.

1. For books, provide the following information:

Last Name, First Initial(s). (Year). *Title of book* [Capitalize only the first word, the word after a colon, and proper nouns]. City, Province or State or Country: Publisher.

References

Potter, W. J. (2016). *Introduction to media literacy.* Los Angeles, CA: SAGE.

2. For electronic sources, provide the following information:[5]

Author [if available]. (Date of publication [if available]). Title of article. *Website Name.* Retrieved from [URL]. Note the indents in the example below:

References

Statistics Canada. (2013, October 28). Individual Internet use and e-commerce, 2012. *The Daily.* Retrieved from http://www.statcan.gc.ca/daily-quotidien/131028/dq131028a-eng.htm

Stephenson, A. (2015, January 17). Researchers working to reduce methane emissions from cattle. *Calgary Herald.* Retrieved from http://calgaryherald.com/business/local-business/researchers-working-to-reduce-methane-emissions-from-cattle

[5] Note that there are many different types of online sources. The information presented here is intended to serve as a basic guide. For a complete list of all types and how to cite each type, please consult the relevant handbook (APA or MLA), an online referencing guide, or a reference librarian.

2. MLA Basics

In-text citations: Give the author's last name and the page number where the information is found in the original source.

> Potter explains that Amazon chooses which books to recommend based on a customer's previous shopping history (95).
>
> Amazon chooses which books to recommend based on a customer's previous shopping history (Potter 95).
>
> According to Potter, "Amazon focuses your attention on a handful of books based on what it knows about your history of book buying" (95).
>
> "Amazon focuses your attention on a handful of books based on what it knows about your history of book buying" (Potter 95).

Works Cited: At the end of your paragraph or essay, list all sources cited in your Works Cited section.

For books, provide the following information:

Last Name, First Name. *Title of Book* [capitalize all major words in the title]. Publisher, Year.

> **Works Cited**
>
> Potter, W. James. *Introduction to Media Literacy.* SAGE, 2016.

For online sources, provide the following information:[6]

Author [if available]. "Title of article." *Website Name.* Publisher name and date of publication [if available]. Date you accessed the online source.

Note the indent in the example below.

> **Works Cited**
>
> Statistics Canada. "Individual Internet Use and E-Commerce, 2012." *The Daily*, 28 October 2013, accessed 16 March 2015.

[6] Note that there are many different types of online sources. The information presented here is intended to serve as a basic guide. For a complete list of all types and how to cite each type, please consult the relevant handbook (APA or MLA), an online referencing guide, or a reference librarian.

Activity A | Look at the following passages and label each one according to its referencing style (APA or MLA).

1. Referencing style: ________________

> Potter contends that media messages in our culture are like items in a giant supermarket—there are an overwhelming number of choices, but we automatically ignore most of them and focus on only a few (4). He writes, "we encounter a great many media messages without paying much attention to them" (4).
>
> ***Work Cited***
> Potter, W. James. *Introduction to Media Literacy.* SAGE, 2016.

2. Referencing style: ________________

> Potter (2016) contends that media messages in our culture are like items in a giant supermarket—there are an overwhelming number of choices, but we automatically ignore most of them and focus on only a few. He writes, "we encounter a great many media messages without paying much attention to them" (p. 4).
>
> ***Reference***
> Potter, W. J. (2016). *Introduction to media literacy.* Los Angeles, CA: SAGE.

Activity B | What is the biggest difference between APA and MLA formatting? Why do you think the two styles differ in this way? Discuss your answer with a partner or small group.

Preventing Plagiarism

Acknowledging Sources

Is This Plagiarism?

Alpha is writing a summary of the first reading (pages 13–14) in this unit for a communications course. In her summary, Alpha writes the following, using information from paragraph 3 of the reading:

> *According to Potter (2016), we use "automatic routines" to help us block out most of what we are exposed to in the media. This is important because we cannot possibly consider every possible message and consciously decide whether to pay attention to it or not.*

Did Alpha commit plagiarism? Consider the details of the above scenario in the context of the definitions and rules regarding plagiarism established by your academic institution. Discuss your answer to this question with a partner or small group. You may use the following questions to guide your discussion:

1. How much of Alpha's language is original, and how much is taken directly from the source?
2. Has Alpha cited the source correctly? If not, what is missing or incorrect?
3. What would you do to prevent plagiarism in this scenario?

Note: For information on your institution's plagiarism policy, search the college or university's website for a statement on academic integrity and/or its academic code of conduct.

Thesis Skill

Recognizing an Author's Purpose and Thesis

As discussed, a summary begins with the main idea of the original text. To accurately state the main idea of the original text, it is necessary to understand both the author's purpose and thesis. In general, if you identify the author's reason for writing and his or her thesis, you can explain the main idea.

1. Author's Purpose

All texts are produced by an author or authors, to be read by an audience, for a particular purpose. Each of these factors (the author, the intended audience, and the purpose) affects the form of the text. For example, the following two texts look very different from each other.

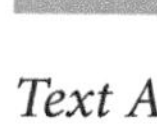

Text A

Text B

Activity A | Using the images on page 23, fill in the chart.

	Text A	Text B
What kind of text is this?		
Where would a text like this be found?		
Who wrote it?		
Who is the intended audience?		
What is the purpose? (i.e., what did the author hope to achieve?)		
What kind of language is used to achieve the purpose?		
What imagery is used to achieve the purpose?		
Is it effective? Why or why not?		

Activity B | To practise identifying an author's purpose for writing, draw a connecting line to match each text below with its purpose.

Text	Purpose
recipe	interact with a specific person
text message	inform the public
newspaper article about a recent event	persuade consumers to buy something
product advertisement	explain a process

Authors write academic texts to persuade, explain, narrate, or describe. Understanding the purpose behind a piece of writing is important for summarizing it accurately.

2. Author's Thesis

In most texts, the author has a thesis, a specific concept or idea that he or she wants the reader to believe or understand after having read the text. In a persuasive text, the author's thesis will relate to a position on a controversial issue. It is likely to be stated early in the text, usually in the introduction, and may be repeated throughout the text. Sometimes, however, the author's thesis is only implied (i.e., not stated explicitly), and the reader must figure out the thesis from the supporting points.

Activity C | Match each list of supporting points to the appropriate thesis.

Supporting Points	Thesis
A. ________ • Helpful aspects of social media: facilitate[7] communication, share ideas • However, social media is responsible for a lot of wasted time. • It is difficult to protect one's privacy on social media. • Most important, social media facilitate crimes such as cyberbullying.	1. Media literacy should be included in the elementary school curriculum.
B. ________ • Young people are growing up in an environment saturated with media. • Learning how to interact with media critically is an important skill for children. • Media literacy concepts can be tied into existing school subjects.	2. Marketers have become more aggressive with their media campaigns.
C. ________ • Advertising is often disguised as information. • Many ads target very young children. • Some ads try to create fear.	3. Social media are more harmful than helpful.

Not all academic texts have a clear or specific thesis. For example, a chapter in a textbook may present many related facts, describe a process, or explain various aspects of a phenomenon rather than taking a stance on an issue or focusing on one specific idea. When there is no clear thesis, your focus should be on determining the author's purpose for writing in order to figure out the main idea.

Introductions

Introducing a Summary

The first line of a summary establishes your purpose for writing (that is, to summarize another text), provides the source information of the original text, and states the main idea of the original text (author's purpose and thesis, if there is one).

The main idea of the original text appears first in the summary, even if it is not stated first in the original text. An author will not generally begin an academic text by stating the thesis in the first sentence. Instead, introductions to academic texts typically contain background information, a "hook" to grab the reader's attention, or another introductory device. When you summarize, however, it is important to present the main idea first.

[7] make (something) easier

Activity A | From the four sentences below, select the best introductory sentence for a summary of Reading 1 on pages 13–14. What is wrong with the others? Discuss your answers with a partner.

a. This text is about media literacy.
b. In "Our Media-Saturated Culture," Potter (2016) explains how people use automatic routines to reduce the number of media messages they must pay attention to.
c. We are living in a culture flooded with media messages, according to Potter (2016).
d. In his text "Our Media-Saturated Culture," author W. James Potter (2016) argues that modern media are dangerous for young people.

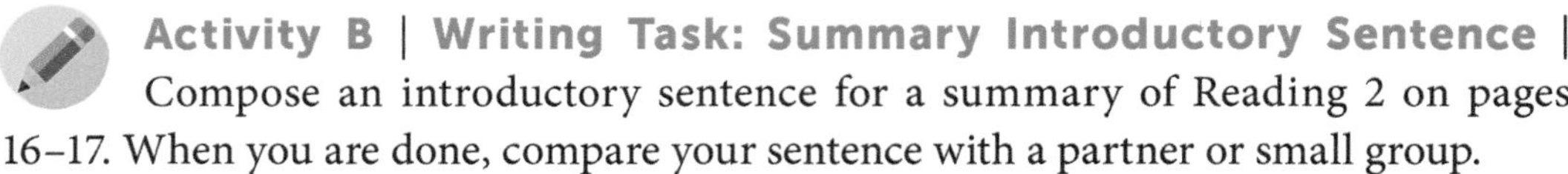

Activity B | Writing Task: Summary Introductory Sentence | Compose an introductory sentence for a summary of Reading 2 on pages 16–17. When you are done, compare your sentence with a partner or small group.

WRITING FUNDAMENTALS

Composition Skill

Paraphrasing

Paraphrasing is restating an idea in your own words. It is one of the necessary skills involved in writing a summary. Paraphrasing requires more than simply moving words around or substituting synonyms into an author's original text; it involves retelling the idea in a completely new way. There are three criteria for a good paraphrase:

1. The **meaning** is the same as that of the original text—all parts of the idea are included, and no new ideas or interpretations are added.
2. The **language** used to get the idea across is original, both in word and in structure.
3. The text makes clear that the idea came from another source by **attributing** it to the author (that is, by citing the source).

   Example

   Original text: *Puffery* is the practice of making claims for a product that sound very good on the surface but do not make any substantive claim that could be actually tested for its truth value. [Source: Potter, W. J. (2016). *Introduction to media literacy.* Los Angeles, CA: SAGE.]

   Paraphrase: Saying things about a product that sound great but are impossible to confirm is known as *puffery*, according to Potter (2016).

Tips

1. Remember that you are paraphrasing ideas, not sentences. Read the original text several times to make sure you understand it well. Then look away and try to retell the idea(s) to someone who has not read the original text. Do not be bound by the structure of the original text—create an entirely new text.
2. Sometimes it is necessary to use some keywords from the original text. In the example, the term *puffery* is repeated, because it is a key term referring to a specific phenomenon. The purpose of the original text is to define this term, so it would be confusing for your reader if you tried to avoid using the key term.

Activity A | Writing Task: Paraphrase | Read the original text below and the three paraphrases that follow it. Evaluate each paraphrase according to the three criteria outlined on page 26 (meaning, language, attribution) by circling either *good* or *needs revision* for each. Then write your own paraphrase. Compare your paraphrase with a partner's.

Original text: ...marketers are not trying to be evil or trying to unfairly discriminate. Instead, marketers are simply trying to be efficient and get the most for their advertising dollars by targeting their advertising to those people who have the greatest potential of becoming valued customers. [Source: Potter, W. J. (2016). *Introduction to media literacy.* Los Angeles, CA: SAGE.]

Paraphrase 1: Advertisers are not attempting to be cruel or aiming to unjustly differentiate. Rather, they are merely hoping to be labour-saving and maximize their marketing budget by aiming their commercials to the humans who show the highest chance of turning into important purchasers of the company's products, according to Potter (2016).

Meaning	good	needs revision
Language	good	needs revision
Attribution	good	needs revision

Paraphrase 2: Marketers may say they are only trying to be efficient, but the way they unfairly discriminate against people in the pursuit of profit is not right (Potter, 2016).

Meaning	good	needs revision
Language	good	needs revision
Attribution	good	needs revision

Paraphrase 3: Marketers target their advertising to consumers with the most potential to become long-term buyers or clients in order to be efficient and get the most from their advertising dollars. They are not evil or discriminatory.

Meaning	good	needs revision
Language	good	needs revision
Attribution	good	needs revision

Your paraphrase:

____

____

____

____

Sentence and Grammar Skill

Understanding Clauses and Avoiding Sentence Fragments

A clause is a group of words that contains a subject and a verb, as well as anything required by the verb (e.g., a direct object).

Example

Advertisers typically exaggerate our problems.
subject *verb* *direct object*

This group of words is a clause, because it contains a subject (*advertisers*) and a verb (*exaggerate*). In this case, the verb is followed by a direct object (*our problems*).

Clauses are different from phrases, which are groups of words that go together but do not contain both a subject and a verb.

Example

exaggerate our problems
verb *direct object*

This group of words is not a clause. Although the direct object (*our problems*) goes together with the verb (*exaggerate*), there is no subject.

Activity A | Which of the following groups of words from the readings in this unit are clauses? Circle all the clauses. Underline the subjects and double underline the verbs.

1. the next-step reality formula
2. puffery comes in many forms

3. because it is persuasive to audiences
4. these slogans at first seem to be telling us something good
5. such as tying your shoes, brushing your teeth, driving to school, or playing a song on the guitar

Clauses can be independent or dependent. An independent clause can function as a stand-alone sentence. It has a subject and a verb and makes a complete thought. It does not begin with a subordinating word:

Spam filters provide a great service.
subject *verb* *direct object*

A dependent clause cannot stand alone as a sentence. It contains a subject and a verb, but it begins with a subordinating word that makes its meaning incomplete:

When we look at our media exposure habits, . . .

Note that there is some information missing from the above. The reader is left wanting to know what happens when we look at our media exposure habits. This dependent clause must be attached to an independent clause in order to complete the thought.

Every sentence in English must have at least one independent clause. The independent clause contains the main or most important information in the sentence.

Activity B | Label each clause below IC (independent clause) or DC (dependent clause).

1. Google has barely scratched the surface of the web ________
2. because these 13.4 billion pages have been estimated to be only one percent of all web pages ________
3. once that code is written ________
4. it can later be loaded into our minds ________
5. there are too many messages to consider ________

Sentence fragments do not contain an independent clause; they are dependent clauses that are incorrectly punctuated as sentences. Generally, sentence fragments can be corrected by connecting them to an appropriate independent clause.

Compare these:

Incorrect: Google has barely scratched the surface of the web. Because these 13.4 billion pages have been estimated to be only one percent of all web pages.

Correct: Google has barely scratched the surface of the web, because these 13.4 billion pages have been estimated to be only one percent of all web pages.

Sometimes, all you need to do to correct a fragment is delete the subordinating word.

> **Incorrect:** Because these 13.4 billion pages have been estimated to be only one percent of all web pages.
>
> **Correct:** These 13.4 billion pages have been estimated to be only one percent of all web pages.

Activity C | Edit the following paragraph, making sure that every sentence includes at least one independent clause.

> When advertisers exaggerate their products' worth. They must be careful not to present a factual falsehood that could be tested for its truth value. Therefore, their product claims are often likely to be *puffery*. Puffery is the practice of making claims for a product that sound very good on the surface. But do not make any substantive claim that could be tested for its truth value. For example, have you ever seen an ad where any of the following claims were made: "the best in its class," "the most beautiful," or "the finest"? These slogans at first seem to be telling us something good about the advertised product. Upon closer examination, however, they are empty claims. Because they cannot actually be tested.
>
> Source: Adapted from Potter, W. J. (2016). *Introduction to media literacy* (p. 118). Los Angeles, CA: SAGE.

UNIT OUTCOME

Writing Assignment: Summary

Write a summary of 200 to 250 words of one of the two readings in this unit. (Your instructor may give you an alternative length.) Use either APA-style or MLA-style in-text citations and a References or Works Cited list.

Use the skills you have developed in this unit to complete the assignment. Follow the steps set out below to ensure that you practise each of your newly acquired skills to write a well-developed essay.

1. **Read carefully**: Reread the text to make sure you understand the purpose, main idea, and important supporting ideas.
2. **Annotate**: As you read, make notes in the text to prepare to write your summary outline.
   - Make a note about the main idea of the text.
   - Underline the important supporting ideas.
   - Cross out minor details and repeated ideas.

3. **Outline**: Fill in the outline below to plan your first draft.

Source Information

Title:
Author:
Year of publication:
Type of text (if known):

Main Idea

Important Supporting Ideas

---

4. **Write an introductory sentence**: Draft an introductory sentence that includes
    - the source information for the original text;
    - a reporting verb that conveys the purpose of the original text; and
    - the main idea of the original text.
5. **Prepare a first draft**: Use your outline to write the first draft of your summary. Use AWL and mid-frequency vocabulary from this unit where appropriate. In your first draft, you should
    - paraphrase effectively, ensuring that language in the summary is different from the original. Remember that you are paraphrasing ideas, not sentences. Review paraphrasing on pages 26–27 if necessary.
    - focus on getting your ideas down on paper without worrying too much about grammar.
6. **Ask for a peer review**: Exchange your first draft with a classmate. Use the Summary Rubric on page 32 to provide suggestions for improving your classmate's summary. Read your partner's feedback carefully. Ask questions if necessary.
7. **Revise**: Use your partner's feedback to write a second draft of your summary.

8. **Self-check**: Review your summary and compare it with the original text. Use the Summary Rubric to look for areas in which you could improve your writing.
    - Edit your summary for sentence structure. Make sure that every sentence in your summary contains at least one independent clause (i.e., that there are no sentence fragments).
    - Edit your essay for correct APA- or MLA-style citations. Make sure you include a References or Works Cited section.
    - Try reading your summary aloud to catch mistakes or awkward wording.
9. **Compose final draft**: Write a final draft of your summary, incorporating any changes you think will improve it.
    - When possible, leave some time between drafts.
10. **Proofread**: Check the final draft of your essay for any small errors that you may have missed. In particular, look for spelling errors, typos, and punctuation mistakes.

Evaluation: Summary Rubric

Use the following rubric to evaluate your essay. In which areas do you need to improve most?

E = **Emerging**: frequent difficulty using unit skills; needs a lot more work
D = **Developing**: some difficulty using unit skills; some improvement still required
S = **Satisfactory**: able to use unit skills most of the time; meets average expectations for this level
O = **Outstanding**: exceptional use of unit skills; exceeds expectations for this level

Skill	E	D	S	O
The introductory sentence mentions the source information and main idea of the original text.				
All the important supporting ideas from the original appear in the summary.				
The meaning of the original text is conveyed accurately.				
The language and sentence structure of the summary differs from that of the original.				
The summary is much shorter than the original text.				
There are no unnecessary details included in the summary.				
There are no personal opinions in the summary.				
Ideas are not repeated in the summary.				
Reporting verbs are used appropriately.				
Every sentence has at least one independent clause.				
AWL and mid-frequency vocabulary items from this unit are used when appropriate and with few mistakes.				
APA- or MLA-style in-text citations and a References or Works Cited list are formatted correctly.				

Unit Review

Activity A | What do you know about the topic of media literacy that you did not know before you started this unit? Discuss with a partner or small group.

Activity B | Look back at the Unit Inquiry Question you developed at the start of this unit and discuss it with a partner or small group. Then share your answers with the class. Use the following questions to guide you:

1. What ideas did you encounter during this unit that contributed to answering your question?
2. How would you answer your question now?

Activity C | Use the following checklist to review what you have learned in this unit. First decide which 10 skills you think are most important—circle the number beside each of these 10 skills. If you learned a skill in this unit that isn't listed below, write it in the blank row at the end of the checklist. Then put a check mark in the box beside those points you feel you have learned. Be prepared to discuss your choices with the class.

Self-Assessment Checklist	
☐	1. I can talk about media literacy.
☐	2. I can write an inquiry question.
☐	3. I can distinguish between important supporting points and minor details.
☐	4. I can annotate a text to prepare to summarize it.
☐	5. I can use reporting verbs.
☐	6. I can choose the right synonym for variety or paraphrasing.
☐	7. I can use the AWL and mid-frequency vocabulary from this unit.
☐	8. I can write a summary outline.
☐	9. I can cite my sources using APA or MLA style.
☐	10. I can avoid plagiarism by acknowledging my sources when using someone else's words or ideas in my writing.
☐	11. I can identify the purpose of a text.
☐	12. I can identify an author's thesis.
☐	13. I can write an introductory sentence for a summary.
☐	14. I can paraphrase effectively.

☐	15. I can identify independent and dependent clauses.
☐	16. I can avoid or correct sentence fragments.
☐	17. I can write an effective summary.
☐	18.

Activity D | Put a check mark in the box beside the vocabulary items from this unit that you feel you can now use with confidence in your writing.

Vocabulary Checklist	
☐ accomplish (v.) 6000	☐ illustrate (v.) AWL
☐ aggressively (adv.) 3000	☐ media (n.) AWL
☐ automatically (adv.) AWL	☐ navigate (v.) 6000
☐ barely (adv.) 3000	☐ process (n.) AWL
☐ chaos (n.) 4000	☐ routine (n.) 3000
☐ culture (n.) AWL	☐ saturated (adj.) 5000
☐ encounter (v.) AWL	☐ sequence (n.) AWL
☐ exposure (n.) AWL	☐ task (n.) AWL
☐ filter (v.) 3000	☐ temptation (n.) 3000
☐ fraction (n.) 4000	☐ trigger (v.) AWL

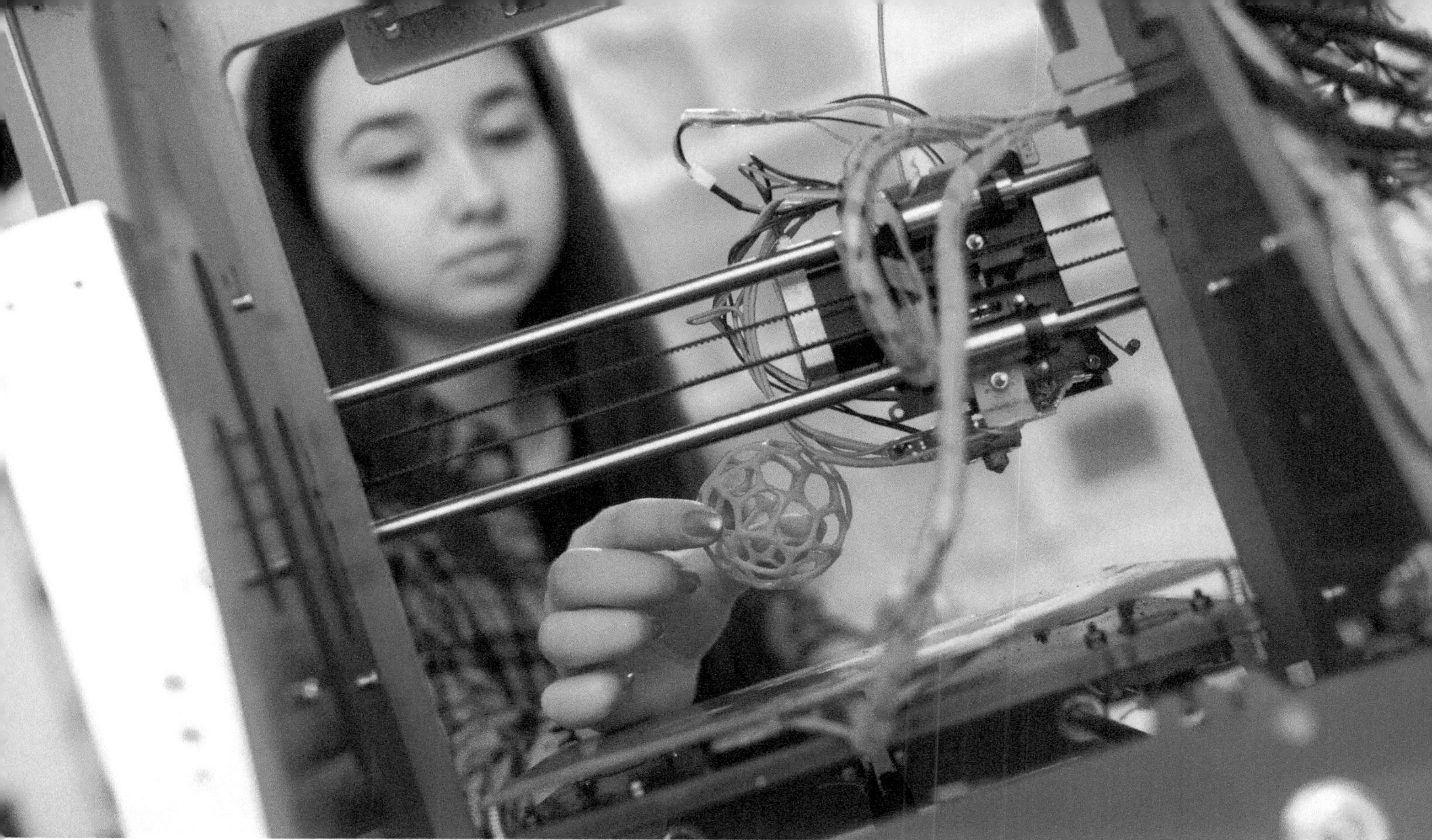

UNIT 2

Technological Innovation in Society

Sociology

KEY LEARNING OUTCOMES

- Creating an inquiry question for investigating an idea
- Understanding your dictionary
- Brainstorming through freewriting and listing
- Selecting information from sources
- Avoiding plagiarism by acknowledging ideas
- Using the passive voice
- Writing an anecdote or scenario introduction
- Concluding an essay by looking to the future
- Writing well-developed paragraphs
- Writing an expository essay

EXPLORING IDEAS

Introduction

Activity A | Discuss the following questions with a partner or small group.

1. Does the social situation represented in the photograph above reflect your own experience? Does the photograph represent a positive or a negative experience for you?
2. What technological changes have you experienced in your lifetime?
3. Do you see these technological changes as positive or negative? How might older generations view these changes?
4. Why might people react negatively to technological change?
5. Are you an early adopter[1] of new technology? Why or why not?

---

[1] An early adopter is a person who starts using a new technology enthusiastically before most people have started using it or even know about it.

Activity B | Reflect on the effects of technological change on a society using the question words to guide your thinking.

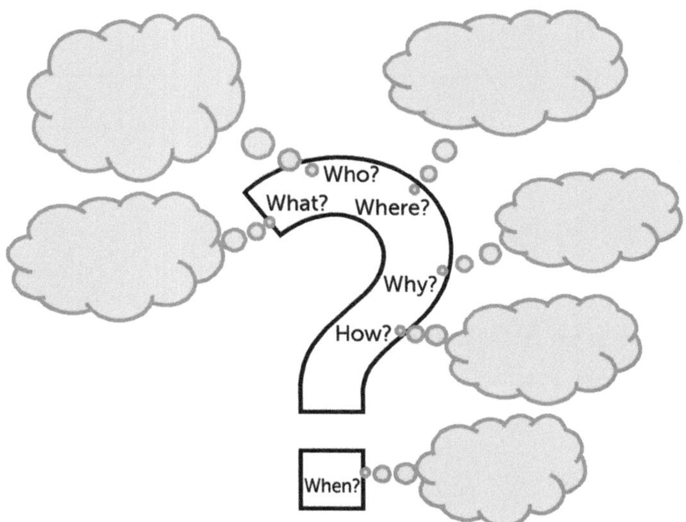

Activity C | Writing Task: Short Paragraph | Write a short paragraph about the effects of technological change on a society. Are these changes positive or negative?

Fostering Inquiry

Investigating an Issue

Investigating issues and presenting evidence in support of an answer are important academic skills that form the foundation of much of the writing done in university.

An inquiry question is a question you ask yourself to help focus your investigation of a topic. It is a question about something that genuinely interests you. The most interesting inquiry questions are open-ended and begin with *who*, *what*, *where*, *when*, *how*, or *why*. Your inquiry question might change as you explore your chosen topic and will likely lead you to new questions. Try to choose an inquiry question that goes beyond what you are already familiar with. Challenge yourself to look at an issue from a new perspective or to explore a completely unknown subject. Your inquiry question provides an opportunity for you to learn and grow.

Activity A | What do you want to know more about in relation to technological innovation and the field of sociology? For example, *How can technology be used to solve social problems?* or *Why does technology change?*

1. Write down two or three questions you have about technological innovation in society. Refer to the question graphic you filled out above.
2. In a small group, share your questions.
3. Choose one question to be your guiding inquiry question for this unit. Your inquiry question can be different from the other group members' questions. The focus of your question may change as you work your way through this unit.

4. Write your inquiry question here and refer to it as you complete the activities in this unit.

   My Unit Inquiry Question:

   ____

   ____

   ____

   ____

Activity B | Writing Task: Freewriting | Write for at least five minutes on the topic of your Unit Inquiry Question. Do not stop writing during this time. After five minutes, read what you have written and circle two or three ideas that you would like to explore further in order to answer your Unit Inquiry Question.

Structure

Expository Essay

The purpose of an expository essay is to explain an issue or phenomenon by presenting evidence in the form of facts, details, examples, or other relevant information. A North American academic audience will more readily accept your explanation if it contains references to information from reliable outside sources. This is a key characteristic of academic writing.

Activity A | With a partner or small group, consider this example of a student paragraph on the topic of Internet use in Canada. Answer the questions that follow.

Internet use has become increasingly widespread in Canada in the last few years. According to a 2012 survey from Statistics Canada, 83 percent of Canadians have Internet access in their homes (Statistics Canada, 2012). This is three percent higher than in 2000. The report states that Canadians use the Internet to communicate via social networking sites like Facebook or Twitter and to buy products and services. Furthermore, Internet use is increasing not only among young people, but among elderly people as well; 48 percent of people over age 65 used the Internet in 2012 (Statistics Canada, 2012). Finally, more people are accessing the Internet from their cellphones or other mobile devices. In 2012, a majority of Internet users used a mobile device to connect to the Internet. Thus, more Canadians are accessing the Internet from more places and for more activities than ever before.

Reference

Statistics Canada (2013, October 28). Individual Internet use and e-commerce, 2012. *The Daily*. Retrieved from http://www.statcan.gc.ca/daily-quotidien/131028/dq131028a-eng.htm

1. What is the main idea of this paragraph?
2. What kind of evidence does the writer use to illustrate the main idea?
3. Where does the evidence come from?

Expository Essay Structure

An expository essay follows standard essay structure with an introduction, two or more body paragraphs, and a conclusion. The introduction contains a thesis statement that outlines the key points to be explained further in the essay. Each body paragraph has a single controlling idea—the aspect of the topic on which your paragraph focuses—that is directly related to the thesis statement. The connection between the body paragraphs and the thesis statement ensures that the essay stays on topic and answers the appropriate question.

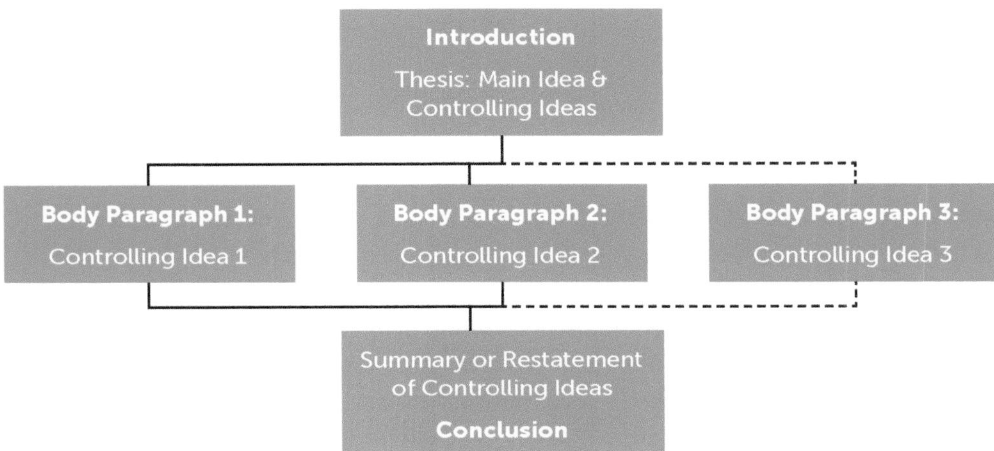

FIGURE 2.1 Expository essay structure

Activity B | The following essay illustrates the tight connection between the body paragraphs and the thesis statement as set out in Figure 2.1. Read the essay closely, noting the function of each paragraph, and answer the questions that follow.

Technology in Our Everyday Life

A typical university student in Canada today might wake up in the morning and heat up her breakfast in the microwave. While riding the bus to school, she might use her phone to play a game, read a book, or connect to the Internet. When she arrives at school, she might text a friend to set up a meeting time for lunch. A hundred years ago, this morning routine would have looked very different, even though students at that time had the same fundamental needs. Indeed, technology often brings about new ways to fulfill basic human needs, and some of the most dramatic changes have occurred in the ways in which we find information and communicate with others.

First of all, computer technology has revolutionized the way we find information. Information used to be passed from person to person by word of mouth. Later, it was written down and published in books. Books were stored in libraries and were located using a card catalogue that contained an index card for each book in the library ("History," n.d.). Digital technology allowed the card catalogue to be computerized, so that it could be searched more quickly and in this way, books could be found more efficiently. The rise of the Internet allowed content to be published directly on the world wide web, which can be searched from almost anywhere with the click of a mouse. Indeed, it is said that we are now living in the information age (Dewar, 1998). Of course we still have many questions, but the way we look for answers to our questions has changed due to technology.

Technology has not only revolutionized information-seeking, but has also given us new ways to communicate with others. In the past, communication mostly occurred face to face, that is, by talking to someone. Later, developments in transportation allowed for messages to be sent over long distances via post, and the invention of the telephone in 1876 allowed people to talk to each other over long distances (Costain, 1960). More recently, computer technology has enabled people to send emails and even talk face to face from distant locations via video conferencing. Cellphones are used to send short text messages and social media helps us keep in touch with friends by sharing pictures, videos, and other content. Communication is not new, but we have more ways of interacting with others now than ever before.

It is clear that technological innovation has brought us many new ways to meet our basic human needs for information and communication. There is no doubt that we will continue to see our options increase in the future. In some places people are now travelling via driverless cars. Will we one day be able to teleport,[2] as imagined in science fiction movies? Only time will tell.

---

[2] to move instantaneously from one place to another place (intransitive) or to move somebody or something in this fashion (transitive)

References

Costain, T. B. (1960). *The chord of steel: The story of the invention of the telephone*. Garden City, NY: Doubleday.

Dewar, J. (1998). *The information age and the printing press: Looking backward to see ahead*. Santa Monica, CA: RAND.

History of the Card Catalog. (n.d.). Retrieved March 16, 2015, from LISWiki: http://liswiki.org/wiki/History_of_the_card_catalog

1. What is the main idea of this essay?
2. What is the controlling idea of the first body paragraph?
3. What evidence or support does the author give for the first controlling idea?
4. Where does the evidence come from?
5. What is the controlling idea of the second body paragraph?

6. What evidence or support does the author give for the second controlling idea?
7. Where does the evidence come from?
8. Which sentence in the conclusion provides a reminder of the main idea?

Activity C | Writing Task: Expository Paragraph | Think of a basic human need. How has technology changed the way people fulfill this need? Write a short paragraph on this topic using your own ideas.

Activity D | Exchange your paragraph with a partner. Read your partner's paragraph and use the following questions to provide feedback.

1. What is the main idea of this paragraph?
2. Is there a clear topic sentence? If so, underline it.
3. What supporting ideas does your partner provide?
4. Are all the supporting ideas directly related to the main idea in the topic sentence? Make a note of any off-topic ideas.
5. Can you think of any additional information or ideas that would improve this paragraph?
6. Does the paragraph contain a concluding sentence? If not, do you think it needs one?
7. What do you like best about this paragraph?
8. How would you improve this paragraph?

Activity E | Revisit your Unit Inquiry Question on page 38. What new ideas have you thought of that will help you answer your question? Share your ideas with a partner or small group. At this point, you may consider revising your Unit Inquiry Question.

Language Tip

Showing Relationships among Ideas

Each idea in an essay is related to the others in a specific way. Connectors show your reader how the ideas are related. Here are some common transitional expressions used in expository essays.

First of all . . .	In addition . . .	Therefore . . .
Furthermore . . .	In fact . . .	Thus . . .
For example . . .	Moreover . . .	Finally . . .

This list includes some common examples, but note that these are not the only connectors used in English.

ACADEMIC READING

Vocabulary

Vocabulary Skill: Understanding Your Dictionary

A dictionary is an excellent resource to use when you want to get help, an excellent learning strategy for improving your English. A dictionary contains useful information about unfamiliar words that you may encounter in texts. In addition to providing the meanings of words, the dictionary also offers other important information such as pronunciation, grammar, and related words. If you do not have a good dictionary, ask your instructor to recommend one.

Activity A | Examine the dictionary entry[3] for *access*, one of the vocabulary words in this unit, and answer the questions below.

> **ac·cess** 🔑 AW /ˈækses/ *noun, verb*
> ■ ***noun*** [U] **1** 🔑 a way of entering or reaching a place: *The police **gained access** through a broken window.* ◇ **~ to sth** *The only access to the farmhouse is across the fields.* ◇ *Disabled visitors are welcome; there is good wheelchair access to most facilities.* ➲ compare EGRESS **2** 🔑 **~ (to sth)** the opportunity or right to use sth or to see sb/sth: *Students must **have access** to good resources.* ◇ *You need a password to **get access** to the computer system.* ◇ *access to confidential information* ◇ *Journalists were **denied access** to the President.* ◇ *Many divorced fathers only have access to their children at weekends* (= they are allowed by law to see them only at weekends). ➲ compare VISITATION
> ■ ***verb* 1 ~ sth** (*computing*) to open a computer file in order to get or add information **2 ~ sth** (*formal*) to reach, enter or use sth: *The loft can be accessed by a ladder.*

1. As what parts of speech can the word *access* be used? ________________
2. How many meanings does each part of speech have? ________________
3. Read the sample paragraph in Activity C on page 44. As which part of speech is *access* used? ________________ What does *access* mean in that paragraph? Write the number of the correct meaning. ________________
4. What information in the text helped you choose the correct meaning?

   ____

   ____

   ____

To save space, a dictionary uses various abbreviations, labels, and codes to communicate information. If you want to use your dictionary efficiently and effectively, you must be familiar with the common codes.

[3] information about a word that is included in a dictionary

Activity B | Use the sample codes and abbreviations from the *Oxford Advanced Learner's Dictionary* in Figure 2.2 to answer the questions about the dictionary entry for *access*.

Short Form					
adj. ***adv.*** ***n.***	adjective adverb noun	***phr. v.*** ***prep.*** ***pron.***	phrasal verb preposition pronoun	***sb*** ***sth*** ***v.***	somebody something verb
Labels					
FORMAL expressions are usually only used in serious or official language and would not be appropriate in normal everyday conversation. **INFORMAL** expressions are used between friends or in a relaxed or unofficial situation. They are not appropriate for formal situations.			**SPECIALIST** language is used by people who specialize in particular subject areas. **OLD-FASHIONED** expressions are passing out of current use. **BrE** British English **CanE** Canadian English		
Grammar Codes					
C countable noun **U** uncountable noun			**I** intransitive verb **T** transitive verb		

FIGURE 2.2 Legend of dictionary codes and abbreviations

1. Is *access* a countable or non-countable noun? ______________________
2. Which types of words commonly follow *access*?

   ____
3. What other grammatical information can you obtain from the dictionary entry?

   ____

Learning Strategy

Getting Help

Good learning strategies help you improve your English. When you do not know the meaning of a word you read or you are not sure whether you are using a new word correctly, getting help is an excellent strategy to use. There are various ways in which you can get help:

1. Look up the new word in your dictionary to check the meaning and the appropriate use of the word.
2. Ask someone who speaks English very well, like your English instructor.
3. Ask a friend or classmate who is also learning English. He or she may know what the word means or how to use it.

The dictionary activities above will help you to make better use of this excellent resource when you need to get help.

Source: Based on ideas in Oxford, R. L. (2011). *Teaching and researching language learning strategies*. Harlow, UK: Pearson.

Vocabulary Preview: The Academic Word List

Activity C | Read the paragraphs below, paying particular attention to the bolded words. These words are from the AWL. After reading the text, match each word with the right definition below by writing the word in the appropriate blank.

With each technological step forward, it is inevitable that society will make **adjustments** to accommodate the change. Companies make adjustments when they **implement** new **technology** to **generate** new business opportunities and to **promote** the growth of their business. Individuals also adopt new technologies and integrate them into their lives. As technology develops, more and more people around the globe have **access** to these technologies, and some have come to rely on instant and frequent access to these technologies. Many academics, including social scientists, philosophers, and scientists, wonder if we are currently placing too much **emphasis** on technological advancement and not enough emphasis on the changes brought about by these innovations.

Sociologists, anthropologists, and psychologists are still trying to **assess** the impact of technology on humanity. This involves understanding the role technology plays in our daily lives. However, strong **theories** just beginning to take shape indicate that technological development is having, and always has had, a profound effect on the way we live our lives. It is for this reason that we will focus our attention on the effects of technology on the **individual**, the family, and societies.

1. ________________ (n.) a change in the way a person behaves or thinks
2. ________________ (n.) a formal set of ideas that explains why something happens or exists
3. ________________ (n.) a person considered separately rather than as part of a group
4. ________________ (n.) machinery or equipment designed using the latest scientific knowledge
5. ________________ (n.) the opportunity/right to use something or to see somebody/something
6. ________________ (n.) special importance that is given to something
7. ________________ (v.) to make something that has been officially decided start to happen or be used
8. ________________ (v.) to produce or create something
9. ________________ (v.) to help something to happen or develop
10. ________________ (v.) to make a judgment about the nature or quality of somebody/something

Vocabulary Preview: Mid-frequency Vocabulary

Activity D | Read the following sentences. Of the words that follow, select the two that best match the meaning of the bolded mid-frequency vocabulary word in each sentence.

1. For some people, the promises made in the promotion of new devices make them **irresistible**.
   a. fascinating b. repulsive c. tempting
2. For this reason, they **obey** their impulse to go the store and purchase a new device as soon as it becomes available to the public.
   a. follow b. ignore c. respond to
3. They do so even though the original **impetus** to purchase the device was deliberately generated by the company that sells it.
   a. impulse b. discouragement c. motivation
4. These people may show **impatience** when forced to wait months before a new device is released to the public.
   a. peacefulness b. eagerness c. irritation
5. This impatience comes from the belief that the new technological device was made just for them and was **destined** for their hands.
   a. designed b. intended c. remote
6. Opposing reactions to the arrival of new technology can create **discord** in a society by separating early adopters and those lagging behind into different camps.
   a. agreement b. disagreement c. disharmony
7. When people decide not to adopt new technology, it may lead to a sense of **disorientation**; that is, they may feel out of touch with friends and colleagues.
   a. confusion b. expectation c. uncertainty
8. The excitement that accompanies the arrival of a new device is sometimes **premature** as the effects of any new technology cannot be known until much later.
   a. delayed b. hasty c. untimely
9. People can develop a level of **dependency** on a particular technology if they use it excessively.
   a. addiction b. autonomy c. need
10. People often lack the necessary break from the technology that would allow them to **recharge** before using the technology again.
    a. energize b. restore c. weaken

Reading 1

The reading "Technology and Societal Change" is an excerpt from the textbook *Transitions in Society: The Challenge of Change* by Colin Bain, Jill Colyer, Dennis DesRivieres, and Sean Dolan. This textbook is used in social studies classes in Canadian high schools.

Activity A | How does technology affect your life? Working with a partner or small group, make a list of technologies or devices that you use daily. Then choose one of the technologies or devices on your list that is very important for your lifestyle. How would your life be different if this technology had never been invented?

Activity B | The textbook excerpt "Technology and Societal Change" contains several images and subtitles. Read the subtitles and look at the pictures. What do you think this textbook excerpt will be about? Exchange your ideas with a partner.

Activity C | As you read the excerpt below, underline examples of the impact of new technologies on society. When you are finished, compare your annotations with a partner and use your annotations to answer the questions that follow the text.

READING

Technology and Societal Change

1 The introduction of any new **technology** into a society brings with it some degree of change. In fact, technology itself is an instrument of change. A classic example of technology causing social change can be seen with the invention of the printing press in Europe in 1450. Johannes Gutenberg's technology took the process of reading from a handful of monks and academics and extended it to the masses. Over time, every person trained in the skill of reading would have the opportunity to read a variety of mass-produced books. In other words, technology brought with it change and opportunity. The eventual result was the replacement of limited learning (because previously there were so few manuscripts to read) with mass learning.

2 The invention of the printing press also resulted in a number of what some people may regard as negative consequences. The skill of memorization and oral recitation would rapidly begin to lose favour. The Roman Catholic Church would lose its hold on some of its congregation as the Bible became mass produced and **individuals** could analyze and **assess** the text for themselves. During the 1500s, a Roman Catholic priest named Martin Luther used his knowledge of the printed word to challenge the authority of the Church and **generate** the **impetus** for a rift between Christian denominations that lasts to this day. The technology of the printing press initiated change—for better or worse—with new institutions surfacing while others either died out or were forced to make **adjustments.**

Technological Change

3 Technology is the creation of tools or objects that both extend our natural abilities and alter our social environment. It has also been noted that periods of intense technological change can cause a revolution or dramatic change in the structure of society. The outstanding question is, how do the individual and

Abb. 38. Abbildung einer Buchdruckerpresse von 1520. Aus der Sammlung des Börsenvereins der deutschen Buchhändler zu Leipzig.

society cope with technological change? Members of one school of thought accept technology and become active in working to **implement** it. Members of another school vehemently oppose the new technology and do everything they can to halt its progress. Members of the latter group are often referred to as *Luddites*.

4 According to some sources, the term *Luddite* is derived from the secret society whose goal it was to destroy the new textile machines introduced into England in the 1810s during the early years of the Industrial Revolution. The society's name came from Ned Ludd, who organized the machine-smashing raids[4] in Nottingham in a desperate attempt to preserve the skilled weavers' way of life. Today, *Luddite* refers to a person who opposes technological advancement. While most people are not Luddites, there is often a suspicion and concern over new technology based on the fact that it brings with it corresponding change and a demand for adaptation.

Coping with Technological Change

5 The question of how individuals and societies cope with technological change is still relevant today, with many social scientists studying the effects of the dramatic new information technologies of the twenty-first century. In a sense, the jury is still out[5] on the psychological impact of the technologies of the information age. Research takes time and money, and the technologies are evolving so quickly that social scientists have difficulty keeping up. In the meantime, what we do have are some expert opinions on stresses brought on by new technology.

6 Like many people around the world, Canadians have been eager to embrace new technologies. From the cellphone and the pager to the computer and the Internet, Canadians have demonstrated a strong desire to get connected and stay connected. This eagerness has been accompanied by an almost nonchalant[6] attitude to the introduction of new technologies. Canadians often embrace new technologies without really

understanding the consequences of the technology itself. For example, while the Internet allowed many people instant **access** to enormous amounts of information, it also allowed young children access to pornographic sites, hate propaganda, and detailed instructions on how to make pipe bombs.

7 A second source of stress is the rate of change that people are forced to endure as a result of current technological changes. Author and futurist Alvin Toffler (1971) warned of the implications of rapid change being driven by technology in his classic book *Future Shock*. Toffler described the term *future shock* as the "dizzying **disorientation** brought on by the **premature** arrival of the future." He went on to say that until people learned to control the rate of change in their own lives, as well as in society in general, they are **destined** for a "massive adaptational breakdown."

8 Stephen Bertman of the University of Windsor expands on this theme in his 1998 book *Hyperculture: The Human Cost of Speed*. Bertman claims that societal change is occurring at such a staggering[7] rate—largely driven by new technologies—that the fundamental values of society are being blurred. Bertman claims that technology has brought with it acceleration. Take the Internet as an example; we have only to type in a few keywords and the information arrives almost immediately. This rapidity often comes at the expense of our patience. This **impatience** is then transferred

[4] an attack on a building, etc., in order to commit a crime

[5] The expression *the jury is (still) out* means that something is still not certain.

[6] feeling or appearing casually calm and relaxed

[7] so great, shocking, or surprising that it is difficult to believe

into our basic value structure. Bertman states, ". . . we quickly lose patience with those we might otherwise love if they do not respond swiftly, or **obey** as readily as the machines we know" (Bertman, 1998, p. 5). He goes on to say living in a society of "hyperculture" results in the deterioration of the family where "the virtues of sacrifice and long-term commitment, so essential to effective parenthood, become rare" (Bertman, 1998, p. 5).

9 A third source of stress is caused by our dependence on technology. According to American social scientists Larry Rosen and Michelle M. Weil (1997), authors of *Technostress*, we tend to rely so heavily on our machines that when they don't do what we want them to do, we experience tremendous anxiety. The term that Weil and Rosen use to describe an overblown **dependency** or attachment to technology is *technosis*. People demonstrate technosis when they feel "out of touch" if they don't check their email messages, or when they don't have their cellphone or pager on at all times. Rosen and Weil are concerned with the psychological implications of dependency on technology to the extent that it can cause both phobias[8] and addiction.

[8] a strong unreasonable fear of something

Psychologist Kimberly Young and her colleagues at the University of Pittsburgh argue that "addictive use of the Internet directly leads to social isolation, increased depression, familial **discord**, divorce, academic failure, financial debt and job loss" (Young et al., 1999, p. 475).

Managing Our Relationship with Technology

10 In his book *Hyperculture*, Stephen Bertman (1998) calls on people to resist the powerful pull of technology by intelligently evaluating the impact of technology on their lives. People can do this by focusing on their own sense of mental health. Bertman encourages people to step back from technology—taking what he calls a weekly sabbatical[9]—so that they can **recharge** and see the role it plays in their lives. He also encourages people to actively preserve their sense of history. Whether we are referring to family, national, or world history, the danger of the information age is the possibility that real history will become lost in a mass of information that results in the creation of a virtual history. Bertman claims that things like family traditions need to be **promoted**, especially among the young, in order to preserve a sense of cultural and personal identity.

11 Similarly, Rosen and Weil (1997) conclude that, while the pull of technology is almost **irresistible**, the key is to avoid becoming slaves to the machines. Instead, people must step back thoughtfully every once in a while and introspectively assess their thoughts and feelings. Humans need rest and separation from things like work and technology. Those boundaries have to be built by each individual. Without boundaries, people lose their sense of security, their peace of mind, and the opportunity for downtime.

References

Bertman, S. (1998). *Hyperculture: The human cost of speed.* Westport, CT: Praeger.

Rosen, L., & Weil, M. (1997). *Technostress: Coping with technology @Work @Home @Play.* New York, NY: Wiley.

Toffler, A. (1971). *Future shock.* New York, NY: Bantam Books.

Young, K., Pistner, M., O'Mara, J., & Buchanan, J. (1999). Cyber disorders: The mental health concern for the new millennium. *CyberPsychology & Behavior, 2*(5), 475–479.

Source: Bain, C. M., Colyer, J. S., DesRivieres, D., & Dolan, S. (2002). *Transitions in society: The challenge of change* (pp. 104, 110). Don Mills, ON: Oxford University Press.

[9] a break

Activity D | The following questions are based on the textbook excerpt you just read. Discuss with a partner or small group.

1. What is *technology*?

 ____

 ____

2. Identify three examples of technological innovations from different periods in history that the authors mentioned in the text. Make a list of positive and negative changes that each of them brought to society.
 a. Fifteenth-century technological innovation:

 ____

Positive Changes	Negative Changes

 b. Nineteenth-century technological innovation:

 ____

Positive Changes	Negative Changes

 c. Twentieth- and twenty-first–century technological innovation:

 ____

Positive Changes	Negative Changes

3. What are three sources of stress arising from the spread of twenty-first-century information technologies?

   a. ______________________________

   b. ______________________________

   c. ______________________________

4. What are two ways in which people can reduce the stress caused by technology?

   a. ______________________________

   b. ______________________________

5. Do you think that you suffer from *technosis*? Why or why not?

   ____

   ____

Activity E | Writing Task: Expository Paragraph | Write a short paragraph describing society's reaction to the introduction of new technologies. Use examples from the textbook excerpt to support your ideas. Remember to include references to the source of the information whenever you use information from the textbook excerpt.

Activity F | Compare your paragraph to the sample paragraph "Society's Reaction to New Technologies" in Appendix 2. The sample paragraph uses two variations on the unit vocabulary word *technology*. Which vocabulary words did you incorporate into your paragraph? Answer the following questions about the sample paragraph.

1. What is the main idea of the paragraph?
2. What examples are used to illustrate the main idea?
3. A well-developed paragraph does not leave any unanswered questions for the reader. After reading the sample paragraph, do you have any questions about its main idea?

Critical Thinking

Bloom's Taxonomy—*Comprehension*

The second level of thinking in Bloom's taxonomy is *comprehension*. At this level, you not only recall what somebody wrote, but you understand what he or she means. This is crucial for selecting information from sources to integrate into your own writing.

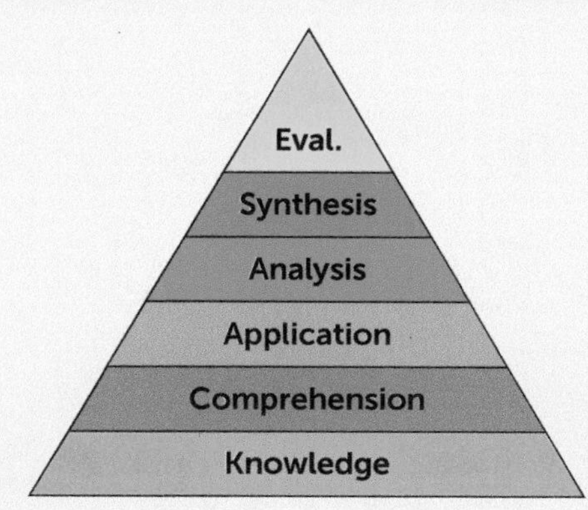

As you read about a topic, ask yourself questions like

- What is the most important thing the author wants me to understand or believe after reading this text?
- Can I explain the information that appears in the text?
- Can I say the same thing using different words and sentences?
- Can I write an outline of this text?

Source: Bloom, B. S., Engelhart, M. D., Furst, E. J., Hill, W. H., & Krathwohl, D. R. (1956). *Taxonomy of educational objectives: The classification of educational goals. Handbook 1: Cognitive domain*. London, UK: Longman.

Reading 2

The reading "Technology and Jobs: More of One and Less of the Other?" is an excerpt from the textbook *Society and Technological Change* by Rudi Volti. This textbook is used in social studies classes in Canadian high schools.

Activity A | Read the following textbook excerpt and underline examples of the relationship between employment and technology. When you are finished, compare your annotations with a partner. You will use your annotations to answer the questions that follow and prepare an outline of the information in this text, which will help you in preparing for your final unit writing assignment.

READING

Technology and Jobs: More of One and Less of the Other?

1 Mention technological change to some workers, and a cold chill is likely to go down their backs. Lurking behind many an innovation is the threat of a job lost. This is not an irrational fear. Throughout history, and especially in the modern era, many production technologies have been explicitly motivated by the desire to increase productivity. Since productivity is usually measured in terms of output per worker, the consequences of productivity increases seem clear: the reduction or elimination of labour. For example, if worker productivity increases at a rate of two percent a year—less than the post–World War II average in the United States—the size of an economy will double in about 35 years. Or to put it somewhat differently, at the end of this period, producing the same amount of goods and services will require only half the number of workers that had been employed 35 years earlier.

2 While productivity gains have made our material lives much richer, they caused concerns about mass unemployment. If relatively few workers can perform all the necessary labour, large numbers of people will end up with no jobs and no work to do. At least that is the fear. Fortunately, the situation is more complicated. Technology's effects on employment are substantial, but they also can be contradictory. We will trace the complex connections between technological change and unemployment by looking at the historical record, and by considering where the productivity improvements wrought by technological change seem to be leading us.

The Threat of Machine-Made Unemployment

3 A cursory examination of technological change reveals many examples of jobs lost because of

technological advance. In 1920, the American railroads employed 113,000 locomotive engineers and 91,000 firemen. In 2002, these railroads carried a much greater volume of freight but needed only 40,000 engineers and no firemen to do so. During the early 1980s, studio musicians saw recording jobs erode by more than a third as a result of the growing use of musical synthesizers. From 1972 to 1977, 21 percent more telephone calls were made throughout the Bell System, yet the number of operators fell by 32 percent. Over a five-year period beginning in 2002, steel production increased by almost five percent, yet employment fell 10 percent. During the same period, corn production went up by 30 percent while farm payrolls dropped by about the same percentage.

The Technological Threat in Historical Perspective

4 Striking as these developments have been, they are not unique to our times. Beginning in the late eighteenth century, the power loom forced many handloom weavers out of their traditional craft, while those who stayed on did so only because they were willing to accept miserably low wages. Many similar examples could be extracted from the history of the Industrial Revolution. The introduction of machinery threatened the livelihood of many workers and produced a considerable amount of social unrest. Attempts to introduce the spinning jenny[10] into the English woolen trade during the late eighteenth century resulted in numerous riots. By the early nineteenth century, worker resistance to new machinery was widespread in several regions of England, culminating in the machine-smashing Luddite outbreaks.

5 Opposition to new technologies because of their consequences for employment has not been confined to the workers whose jobs were threatened. The fear of the effects of new technology on employment has on occasion moved public officials to take drastic actions. In 1638, the British government banned the use of "engines for working of tape, lace, ribbon, and such, wherein one man doth more amongst them than seven English men can do." A more extreme example comes from the Polish city of Danzig, where in 1661 the municipal authorities destroyed a mechanical ribbon loom and drowned its inventor, for fear that the new device would put hand weavers out of work. Consignment to a watery oblivion was also advocated for a mechanical cotton picker by the Jackson, Mississippi *Daily News* in the late 1930s: "It should be driven right out of the cotton fields and sunk into the Mississippi River, together with its plans and specifications. Nothing could be more devastating to labour conditions in the South than a cotton-picking machine."

A Case for Optimism

6 Examples, however numerous, do not conclusively prove that technological advance is incompatible with high levels of employment. Although there can be no dispute that particular technological changes have resulted in job losses and attendant personal tragedies, this does not tell the whole story. The effects of technological change are complex, and it is easy to fix upon one particular result and ignore others. Rather than dwell exclusively on the fate of particular industries and occupations, it is essential to consider the larger picture.

7 When considering the effects of technological change on the overall level of employment, one thing must always be kept in mind: even if all available technologies were used to their utmost, there would still be plenty of work to do. In many parts of the world today, including many "developed" countries, there are still large numbers of people who lack the basic necessities and amenities of life. More and better food needs to be produced and distributed, more houses built, more clothing manufactured. People need to be educated, healed, and entertained. Even with high levels of affluence, needs and wants do not decrease. When it comes to the consumption of goods and services, it is likely that high levels of consumption do not diminish the desire for still higher levels of consumption; appetite may grow with eating. Although it may not be a particularly noble trait, the desire to acquire more and more is present in most human beings. As a result,

---

[10] A frame with multiple spindles that allowed eight spools of yarn to be spun simultaneously, the spinning jenny is considered one of the machines that launched the Industrial Revolution.

progressively higher levels of economic development may generate the need for continued high (or perhaps higher) levels of production.

8 It is also important to bear in mind that the level of demand is affected by the price of a particular product or service. If productivity increases bring down the cost, more people can afford it, thereby increasing the level of demand. This in turn may motivate an employer to take on more workers so that the increased demand is met. Much of the history of mass production conforms to this pattern, as exemplified by the automobile industry and the interrelated increases in productivity, employment, production, and purchases that began when Henry Ford began to produce large numbers of Model T cars during the second decade of the twentieth century.

9 As a final point, it is also important to remember that technological change often generates problems, which require that a great deal of work be done. Animal and plant habitats need to be restored, bodies of water require purification, and victims of accidents and pollution need medical care. Many nuclear power plants are nearing the end of their useful lives, and safely decommissioning them will entail years of labour by thousands of workers. In general, the cost of environmental cleanups is hardly trivial; recall that the United States spends well over a billion dollars each year just to deal with hazardous wastes and old refuse dumps. The funds spent on environmental cleanup and protection can be the basis of many jobs.

Source: Volti, R. (2008). *Society and technological change* (6th ed., pp. 171–174). New York, NY: Worth Publishers.

Activity B | The following questions are based on the textbook excerpt you just read. Discuss with a partner or small group.

1. Why do people fear that technology will lead to higher rates of unemployment?

____

____

2. What examples are given in the text to illustrate that technology can lead to an increase in the rate of unemployment?

Period	Examples
1920–2002	
1972–1977	
2002–2007	
late-18th–early-19th century	
1638	
1661	
1930s	

3. Despite the growing use of technology, why is there still a great amount of work to be done? List several sectors of the economy that will continue to require workers.

____

____

4. How are the negative effects of technology linked to an increase in employment?

____

____

Activity C | Use your annotations on the text to complete this outline of important information.

Author's Purpose

Main Supporting Ideas	Supporting Details
Machine-made unemployment	
Technological threats in the past	
Positive effects	

PROCESS FUNDAMENTALS

Before You Write

Brainstorming

Brainstorming is the process of opening your mind to generate a lot of ideas. You can brainstorm by yourself or with other people. The most important part of brainstorming is that you allow yourself to think of anything and everything that might be relevant to your topic. You will make judgments about these ideas later and eventually choose the best ones. *Listing* and *freewriting* are two brainstorming strategies. In Activities A and B below, you will practise these techniques. When you have finished, think about which one was more helpful to you in generating ideas.

1. Listing When listing, you make a list of keywords or phrases relevant to your topic.

Activity A | Look back at your Unit Inquiry Question. Thinking about your own experiences, what you have heard from others, and what you have read, brainstorm ideas relevant to this question. Make a list of keywords and phrases below.

____

____

____

____

____

____

Now organize your list.

1. Do any keywords or phrases connect to others? Cross out any ideas that are repetitive and draw lines to connect ideas that belong together.
2. Are there any ideas that do not seem relevant to or useful for answering your inquiry question? Cross them out.
3. From the remaining keywords, choose those that seem most interesting or worthwhile. Consider including these ideas in the first draft of your writing assignment. Note that you may have to do more research before you can write about them.

2. Freewriting When freewriting, you begin writing about your topic and do not stop writing for a set amount of time or until you have produced a certain amount of text.

Activity B | Choose one of the following topics related to technology (or think of your own) and write about it for five minutes. Write down anything that comes into your head; do not try to write a coherent text that focuses on only one idea. Do not stop writing during the five minutes. If you cannot think of anything to write, simply write "I don't have anything to write" or "blah, blah, blah, blah" as many times as necessary until an idea comes into your head. Do not worry about spelling or grammar.

Sample topics:
smartphones; careers in technology; social media

Activity C | Read what you wrote in Activity B. Did you take a certain direction or keep returning to one or more ideas? If so, it might be that you are most interested in writing about that particular aspect of the topic. Underline words or sentences that you want to research more and consider including these ideas in the first draft of your writing assignment.

Activity D | Look back at your notes from Activities A to C. Create a rough outline for an essay based on these ideas.

Integrating Information from an Outside Source

Selecting Information from Sources

In Unit 1 (pages 5–8, 18–19, and 26–28), you practised summarizing and paraphrasing. These skills are essential for integrating information from outside sources into your own writing. There are many kinds of information writers use to enhance their own texts. Among them are

- *facts* or *statistics* relevant to the writer's topic;
- expert *opinions* that support the writer's claims;
- interesting *stories*;
- *examples* to illustrate the writer's point; and
- *ideas* or *claims* that the writer wants to respond to in some way.

In addition to paraphrasing and summarizing, writers can also *directly quote* an outside source, that is, use the exact same words that the original author used. A direct quotation is enclosed in quotation marks ("...") and the page number where it appears in the original is indicated. **All information and ideas from outside sources must be cited, even when you paraphrase it in your own words.** If the citation is missing, it is not clear that you are using the words or ideas of someone else, which is an example of plagiarism. See Unit 1 (pages 19–21) for citation formats.

It is generally preferable to paraphrase information from outside sources. However, there are instances when you might choose to quote directly instead:

- The author's words include a well-known and respected quotation.
- The author's words are especially beautiful or well suited to express the idea.
- The author's words include technical terms or comprise a list.

Look back at paragraph 9 from the text "Technology and Societal Change," on pages 46–48. In this paragraph, the authors refer to two outside sources:

- First, they *summarize* the main idea of a book by scientists Weil and Rosen.
- Then they *paraphrase* additional relevant information from this source, including the definition of a technical term (*technosis*).
- Finally, in the last sentence, the authors use a *direct quotation* from psychologist Kimberly Young. The quotation expands on the idea that comes directly before it—the idea that dependence on technology can cause addiction. It is relevant because it lists some negative consequences of addiction to the Internet. Notice the use of quotation marks and the page number.

Activity A | Consider how information from an outside source is used in the following paragraph. With a partner or small group, answer the questions that follow.

One reason that people sometimes resist innovation is simply the fear of change. Change brings with it possibilities of unknown or unintended consequences, which can cause anxiety. For example, many people worry these days that the ever-growing presence of handheld digital gadgets is changing fundamental social values and behaviours—and not for the better. While it remains to be seen how society will adapt to this development, fears that technological innovation can disrupt accepted societal norms are not new and are not unfounded. Bain, Colyer, DesRivieres, and Dolan (2002) note that introducing the printing press resulted in radical change to—and even the end of—some ways of life at the same time that it created opportunities for new ways of life to emerge. It is impossible now to imagine a world in which the printing press had never been invented. Nevertheless, the changes it caused in people's lives at the time were real, and it is easy to see why some feared and resisted it.

1. What is the main idea of this paragraph?
2. Is the outside information paraphrased or quoted directly?
3. How does the outside information relate to the writer's own ideas?
4. Underline the sentence that connects the outside information to the writer's own ideas.

Activity B

Step 1: To practise selecting information from an outside source, first look back at the list of brainstormed ideas you generated in Activity A in *Before You Write* on page 55.

Step 2: Then reread the text "Technology and Jobs: More of One and Less of the Other?" on pages 51–53. As you read, underline or highlight parts of the text that relate to the ideas on your brainstormed list. If you do not find any relevant information in this text, you will need to consult a different reading or do some independent research.

Step 3: Write two or three pieces of information from the text(s) you read that you might use in the first draft of your writing assignment. Consider whether you will summarize, paraphrase, or directly quote the information.

____

____

____

____

____

Preventing Plagiarism

Acknowledging Ideas

Is This Plagiarism?

Alpha is working on his final paper for a course. Alpha includes the following passage about technology, which contains information from paragraph 9 of the reading "Technology and Societal Change" in this unit:

> *Technology can cause stress. For example, because many of us are used to employing machines for many tasks, it actually causes panic when these machines do not respond in the way we expect. Therefore, we need to learn to change our relationship to technology.*

Did Alpha commit plagiarism? Consider the details of the above scenario in the context of the definitions and rules regarding plagiarism established by your academic institution. Discuss your answer to this question with a partner or small group. You may use the following questions to guide your discussion:

1. How much **information** in Alpha's passage is original, and how much is taken from the source?
2. How much of Alpha's **language** is original, and how much is taken directly from the source?
3. Has Alpha cited the source correctly? If not, what is missing or incorrect?
4. What would you do to prevent plagiarism in this scenario?

Note: For information on your institution's plagiarism policy, search the college or university's website for a statement on academic integrity and/or its academic code of conduct.

Activity C | Look back at the paragraph you wrote in Activity E after Reading 1 (page 50). Did you use any outside sources to support your main idea? Is that information summarized, paraphrased, or quoted appropriately? Is it cited correctly? Check Unit 1 (pages 19–21) for citation formats and revise if necessary.

Thesis Skill

Writing a Thesis Statement That Answers a Question

The thesis statement of an expository essay provides the answer to a question, such as the inquiry question you developed at the beginning of this unit. Often, the thesis statement will also include the controlling ideas that you plan to develop in the body paragraphs of the essay. Having a specific, focused thesis statement helps you to stay on the assigned topic.

Activity A | For each of the following thesis statements, write a question that the statement answers. The first one has been done for you.

1. Some of the most dramatic technological changes have occurred in the ways we find information and communicate with others.

   In what areas of our lives have dramatic technological changes occurred?

   ____

2. Technological innovation is both creative and destructive. A new tool will accelerate some existing practice or process and, at the same time, make another tool obsolete.

   ____

   ____

3. Reactions to technological change range from eagerness to adopt the innovation to outright rejection.

   ____

   ____

4. The three main sources of stress associated with new technologies are unforeseen consequences, a rapid rate of change, and extreme dependency.

   ____

   ____

Some common thesis problems to avoid are

- using a question, rather than an answer, as your thesis;
- announcing the general topic of the essay, rather than giving a specific answer to a question;
- answering a question other than what was required in the assignment; and
- writing a thesis statement that is too vague or too broad to be answered in a short essay.

Activity B | Which of the following is a good thesis statement that answers the given question? What is wrong with the others?
Question: What are some ways in which technology generates jobs?

1. Although some people believe that technology creates many new jobs, in fact, it is the enemy of paid labour since it replaces human workers with machines.
2. Technology stimulates employment by creating consumer demand for new products and by establishing the need for skilled workers to maintain, repair, and troubleshoot new machines and devices.

3. Social, cultural, and economic factors have influenced the worldwide creation of jobs by technology throughout history.
4. In this essay, I will explore the ways that technology enhances employment.
5. The question is: does technology really create jobs?

Activity C | Writing Task: Thesis Statement | Look back at your Unit Inquiry Question on page 38 and the notes you have taken while brainstorming and reading throughout this unit. Create the first draft of a working thesis statement that directly answers your Unit Inquiry Question. You may also revise your inquiry question, if you wish. When you are done, exchange your thesis statement with a partner and discuss.

Introductions

Anecdote or Scenario

An anecdote is a brief story about something that has actually happened, used to illustrate a particular point. An anecdote may be a personal—a story about something that happened to you or someone you know—but it doesn't have to be. A scenario is like an anecdote, except that it is hypothetical—the situation has not actually occurred, but one can imagine it happening. The best anecdotes or scenarios to use in an introduction should

- be amusing or interesting, drawing your reader in and encouraging her to keep reading;
- give a concrete, easy-to-understand example of the specific point you are making in your essay;
- depict a situation familiar in some way to your reader, establishing common ground so he feels a connection to your topic; or
- depict a situation completely foreign to your reader, creating a desire to learn more about your topic.

When using an anecdote or scenario to introduce your thesis, be sure to make an explicit link between the story and the thesis. Do not leave it to your reader's imagination to make the connection. Consider the following example of an anecdote introduction. For an example of a scenario introduction, see the sample essay on pages 39–40.

Yesterday while I was cleaning up the basement with my 10-year-old son, we came across an old portable cassette player that I had used in high school. "What's this?" he asked with the curiosity of a scientist who has just discovered a fossil. "That's what I used to listen to music with," I told him. "Oh, you mean like an MP3 player? But it's so big! How many songs does it hold?" he asked excitedly. When I explained to him that it didn't "hold" any songs, that the music was stored on cassettes that had to be rewound, flipped over at the end of one side, and stored in endless shoeboxes, he looked at me in disbelief. "Seems like a lot of hassle," he concluded, as he popped in his earbuds and scrolled through his library of thousands of songs, which fits on a device roughly the size of a credit card. As I looked nostalgically through an old box of cassette tapes, I marvelled at how much faster, smaller, and more powerful our gadgets have become. Indeed, my old cassette player reminded me that technological innovation is both creative and destructive. A new tool will accelerate some existing practice or process and, at the same time, make another tool obsolete.

Activity A | Think of a funny or otherwise interesting personal story related to using technology. What does your story exemplify about technology? In other words, in what ways might the point of your story be relevant in a more general context? Share your story with a partner and discuss how you might be able to use it in the introduction to an essay about technology.

Activity B | For each thesis statement below, come up with a relevant anecdote or scenario to introduce it. Share your anecdotes or scenarios with a partner.

1. Reactions to technological change range from eagerness to adopt the innovation to outright rejection.
2. The three main sources of stress associated with new technologies are unforeseen consequences, a rapid rate of change, and extreme dependency.
3. The relationship between technology and employment is not as simple as it seems; while machines increase productivity and thus reduce demand for workers, technological innovations create new categories of work that did not exist before.

Activity C | Writing Task: Anecdote or Scenario Introduction | Look back at the thesis statement you wrote for your Unit Inquiry Question (Activity C on page 60). Write an anecdote or scenario introduction that includes this thesis statement. Make an explicit link between your anecdote or scenario and the thesis statement. Share your introduction with a partner to see if you were successful in making that link.

Conclusions

Look to the Future

A conclusion leads the reader from your thesis back to the real world. One strategy for doing this is to end with a comment or question related to what the future holds. Once you have thoroughly explained an issue in your essay, you summarize your controlling ideas and then conclude with this comment or question. As with any conclusion, you are not introducing a new idea, but rather commenting thoughtfully on what the information you have just presented means. Look-to-the-future conclusions are especially appropriate for essays that explain issues that are rapidly changing or develop over time.

Consider the following example of a look-to-the-future conclusion.

> Clearly, we cannot stop the march of progress, which brings us untold benefits even as it makes some of our cherished ways of life outdated. The same progress that gave us the ability to travel great distances via motorized vehicles put many wagon-makers out of business. It is important not to get too attached to any one particular form of technology, since the rate of innovation is faster than it has ever been. Just as vinyl records, cassette tapes, and CDs were destined to be replaced by better and smaller formats, we are destined to have to adapt, once again, to changes brought about by new technological innovation.

Activity A | For each concluding statement below, write a relevant prediction or question about the future that could be included in a look-to-the-future conclusion. Look back at the anecdotes or scenarios you brainstormed for introductions in Activity B on page 61 for inspiration.

1. Thus, acceptance of new technologies is not a one-size-fits-all phenomenon.
2. To summarize, people often experience stress with the introduction of new technological tools or processes.
3. In short, technology is not necessarily a job-killer.

Activity B | Writing Task: Look-to-the-Future Conclusion | Look back at the anecdote or scenario introduction you wrote for your Unit Inquiry Question in Activity C on page 61. Write a look-to-the-future conclusion that makes a prediction or comment about the future relevant to your thesis statement.

WRITING FUNDAMENTALS

Composition Skill

Developing Body Paragraphs with the Question Technique

The topic sentence of a body paragraph contains a controlling idea directly connected to your thesis statement. In the rest of your paragraph, you develop this controlling idea.

One strategy for developing an idea is to put yourself in your reader's shoes and ask a number of questions about the idea in the topic sentence. The answers to these questions will develop the idea. Some typical important questions include

- What do you mean by [*term*]?
- How?
- Why?
- Can you give an example of this?
- So what? (In other words, why is this important to understanding the thesis of this essay?)

Keep in mind that you can use information from outside sources to help answer these questions.

Activity A | For each topic sentence below, write a series of questions for the writer to answer when developing the idea in the sentence.

1. Human reaction to new technologies can be extreme.
2. Technological innovation has brought about many improvements in our lives.
3. In addition to the many clear benefits, technology also comes with drawbacks.

Activity B | Writing Task: Well-Developed Expository Paragraph | Choose one of the topic sentences above and write a well-developed paragraph based on the questions you wrote. Integrate information you learned in Readings 1 and 2 from this unit.

Activity C | Exchange your paragraph with a partner. Use the following questions to provide feedback on the development of your partner's paragraph.

1. Does the paragraph fully develop the idea in the topic sentence? If not, write some questions you have about the topic that could help your partner to further develop his or her paragraph.
2. Are there any off-topic ideas in the paragraph?
3. Are there any unclear ideas in the paragraph?
4. Does the paragraph include relevant information from an outside source?
5. Is the outside information cited appropriately using APA or MLA format? (For APA and MLA style, see Unit 1, pages 19–21.)

Sentence and Grammar Skill

Using the Passive Voice

The passive voice allows writers to change the grammatical subject of a sentence. In an active voice sentence, the grammatical subject is the agent or doer of the action; it performs the action of the verb. If the receiver of the action is mentioned in an active voice sentence, it is the grammatical object.

The passive voice, on the other hand, makes the receiver of the action the grammatical subject of the sentence. What was the object is moved to the beginning of the sentence to become the subject. You can only transform an active voice sentence into a passive voice sentence if it has a transitive verb (i.e., a verb that has a direct object).

Active: In contemporary Canadian society, we **see** technology as essential.
subj. *obj.*

Passive: In contemporary Canadian society, technology **is seen** as essential.
subj.

Active: Canadians **use** a variety of technological devices on a daily basis.
subj. *obj.*

Passive: A variety of technological devices **are used** by Canadians on a daily basis.
subj.

There are three reasons why the passive voice is used in academic writing:

1. The passive voice is necessary when the agent or doer of the action is not mentioned because (1) the agent is redundant or readily assumed, (2) the agent is unknown, or (3) the writer does not want to mention the agent.

   Examples
   Many of our technological devices are produced in factories outside of Canada.

   If a new technological device does not work, it may be returned to the manufacturer.

   Information was given to the media about the release of a new smartphone.

2. The passive voice is used to create a smoother flow of the information in the text. If the receiver of the action is more closely related to the theme or topic of the text than the agent of the action, then the passive is used.

   Example
   In the twenty-first century, Canadians rely on smartphones for many daily tasks as well as entertainment, but they would not have had access to this technology for these activities in the past. Smartphones are used for everything from communicating with others by email, text, or phone call to reviewing work documents, reading books, playing games, and even watching TV shows or movies.

3. In academic writing in particular, the focus is not always on the person who performs the action, such as a researcher, but on the results of the research or the topics discussed in the text.

   Example
   A survey was recently conducted about Canadians' attitudes toward smartphones. It was discovered that many Canadians would rather get rid of their television than spend a day without their smartphone.

The Agent

Sometimes, the agent is included in a passive voice sentence, but most of the time it is not mentioned. There are three cases in which it should be included in written texts: (1) when mentioning the agent provides new and relevant information for the reader, (2) when the agent is non-human (such as a device) since we expect agents to be human, and (3) when the agent is a well-known person whose name should be mentioned.

Examples
Modern communication devices are used by children as young as two years old.

The communication habits of young Canadians have been greatly influenced by cellphones in general and smartphones in particular.

Apple's most successful technological devices were all developed by Steve Jobs.

Activity A | Read the following paragraph from the sample essay on pages 39–40. Underline all the verbs. Are they in the passive or active voice?

Technology has not only revolutionized information-seeking, but has also given us new ways to communicate with others. In the past, communication mostly occurred face to face, that is, by talking to someone. Later, developments in transportation allowed for messages to be sent over long distances via post, and the invention of the telephone in 1876 allowed people to talk to each other over long distances (Costain, 1960). More recently, computer technology has enabled people to send emails and even talk face to face from distant locations via video conferencing. Cellphones are used to send short text messages and social media helps us keep in touch with friends by sharing pictures, videos, and other content. Communication is not new, but we have more ways of interacting with others now than ever before.

Activity B | Read the following paragraph on the topic of smartphone use by students. Edit the use of passive and active use in this paragraph by asking yourself these questions:

- Which verbs are in the passive voice and which are in the active voice?
- Is each choice appropriate?

Make any necessary changes. When you are finished, compare your corrections with a partner's. Did you and your partner make the same changes?

Students use their smartphones on a regular basis for a variety of purposes. One of the primary purposes that they use smartphones for is to communicate with their friends. Facebook, Twitter, and various other apps are used by students for this communication. Phones can of course also be used for voice calls, but written communication via apps or text is preferred by today's youth. These devices are also used by students for their entertainment. If students have a little free time, they like to use their smartphones to pass the time. Movies or TV shows are liked by students because the opportunity is offered by smartphones to watch these shows wherever there is an Internet connection or a data network. When this is not possible, games are often played by students. The advantage of many downloadable games is the fact that the smartphone does not have to be connected to a network for the game to work. In brief, young people rely on smartphones both for communication with others and for their own entertainment.

Activity C | Choose one of the paragraphs you have written for this unit. Underline all the verbs.

- Are they in the passive or active voice?
- Is each choice appropriate?
- Edit your paragraph for appropriate passive or active voice usage.

UNIT OUTCOME

Writing Assignment: Expository Essay

Write an expository essay of 350 to 450 words on a topic related to technology and social change. (Your instructor may give you an alternative length.) Use either APA- or MLA-style in-text citations and a References or Works Cited list.

You may write an essay that answers your Unit Inquiry Question. If you choose to do so, look back at the work you have done in this unit:

- the latest version of your Unit Inquiry Question on page 38;
- the thesis statement you wrote in Activity C on page 60;
- the introduction you wrote in Activity C on page 61;
- the ideas you brainstormed on pages 55–56;
- the information you selected in Activity B on pages 57–58;
- the conclusion you wrote in Activity B on page 62.

Decide whether you want to include drafts of any of the above in your essay. You may have to revise your writing to integrate these elements into your essay.

If you do not want to write about your Unit Inquiry Question, you may develop a new question or write an essay that answers one of the following questions instead:

- What are the drawbacks of becoming dependent on technology?
- What are the most important technological innovations of the twentieth and twenty-first centuries?
- Why do some people resist technological innovations?

Use the skills you have developed in this unit to complete the assignment. Follow the steps set out below to ensure that you practise each of your newly acquired skills to write a well-developed expository essay.

1. **Brainstorm**: Use the listing or freewriting technique to generate ideas related to the question you will answer.
2. **Find outside sources of information**: Select appropriate information from Readings 1 and 2 to support your argument.
    - Make a note of page numbers if you are using any direct quotations.
3. **Write a thesis statement**: Develop a focused thesis statement that provides a specific answer to your question.
4. **Outline**: Fill in the outline on page 67 to plan your first draft.
    - Develop your body paragraphs using the question technique. Remember to focus on one controlling idea in each paragraph.
    - Include information from Readings 1 and 2 in each body paragraph, if appropriate.

Introduction	Anecdote that illustrates a point relevant to your chosen topic: A clear link between your anecdote and your thesis statement: Thesis statement:
Main Body Paragraphs	Topic sentence 1: Questions about the topic sentence that a reader might want answers to: Information from outside source with page #, if necessary: Concluding sentence 1 (optional):
	Topic sentence 2: Questions about the topic sentence that a reader might want answers to: Information from outside source with page #, if necessary: Concluding sentence 2 (optional):
Conclusion	Concluding statement (summary or restatement of controlling ideas): Prediction or question about the future:

5. **Prepare a first draft:** Use your outline to write the first draft of your essay. Use AWL and mid-frequency vocabulary from this unit where appropriate. In your first draft, you should
   - focus on getting your ideas down on paper without worrying too much about grammar.
   - skip a section if you get stuck and come back to it later. For example, consider writing the body paragraphs before writing the introduction and conclusion.

6. **Ask for a peer review**: Exchange your first draft with a classmate. Use the Expository Essay Rubric below to provide suggestions for improving your classmate's essay. Read your partner's feedback carefully. Ask questions if necessary.
7. **Revise**: Use your partner's feedback to write a second draft of your essay.
8. **Self-check**: Review your essay and use the Expository Essay Rubric to look for areas in which you could improve your writing.
   - Edit your essay for use of passive voice. Make sure you have used the passive voice when appropriate, and that your use of the passive is grammatically correct.
   - Edit your essay for correct APA- or MLA-style citations. Make sure you include a References or Works Cited section. Include page numbers for direct quotations.
   - Use spelling and grammar checking features on your word-processing software to catch mistakes.
   - Try reading your essay aloud to catch mistakes or awkward wording.
9. **Compose final draft**: Write a final draft of your essay, incorporating any changes you think will improve it.
   - When possible, leave some time between drafts.
10. **Proofread**: Check the final draft of your essay for any small errors you may have missed. In particular, look for spelling errors, typos, and punctuation mistakes.

Evaluation: Expository Essay Rubric

Use the following rubric to evaluate your essay. In which areas do you need to improve most?

E = **Emerging**: frequent difficulty using unit skills; needs a lot more work
D = **Developing**: some difficulty using unit skills; some improvement still required
S = **Satisfactory**: able to use unit skills most of the time; meets average expectations for this level
O = **Outstanding**: exceptional use of unit skills; exceeds expectations for this level

Skill	E	D	S	O
The thesis statement answers a specific question.				
The introduction includes a relevant anecdote or scenario and a link to the thesis.				
Each body paragraph develops one controlling idea.				
All body paragraphs are well developed.				
Transitional expressions show how each idea is related to others.				
Relevant information from readings in this unit has been used to support the main idea.				

Sources are acknowledged when referring to the ideas of others to avoid plagiarism.				
The conclusion makes an appropriate prediction for the future.				
AWL and mid-frequency vocabulary items from this unit are used when appropriate and with few mistakes.				
Passive voice is used where appropriate and is grammatically correct.				
APA- or MLA-style in-text citations and a References or Works Cited list are formatted correctly.				

Unit Review

Activity A | What do you know about the topic of technology and change that you did not know before you started this unit? Discuss with a partner or small group. Be prepared to report what you have learned to the class.

Activity B | Look back at the Unit Inquiry Question you developed at the start of this unit and discuss it with a partner or small group. Then share your answers with the class. Use the following questions to guide you:

1. What ideas did you encounter during this unit that contributed to answering your question?
2. How would you answer your question now?

Activity C | Use the following checklist to review what you have learned in this unit. First decide which 10 skills you think are most important—circle the number beside each of these 10 skills. If you learned a skill in this unit that isn't listed below, write it in the blank row at the end of the checklist. Then put a check mark in the box beside those points you feel you have learned. Be prepared to discuss your choices with the class.

Self-Assessment Checklist	
☐	1. I can talk about technology and change in society.
☐	2. I can develop an inquiry question to explore new information on a topic.
☐	3. I can evaluate a peer's writing and give feedback for improvement.
☐	4. I can use peer feedback to improve first drafts.
☐	5. I can use transitional expressions to connect the ideas in my writing.
☐	6. I can use my dictionary to find information about new words.
☐	7. I can use the AWL and mid-frequency vocabulary from this unit.
☐	8. I can brainstorm ideas using listing and freewriting techniques.

Self-Assessment Checklist	
☐	9. I can prepare an essay outline using the ideas generated through brainstorming.
☐	10. I can identify information from readings in this unit to support my ideas.
☐	11. I can integrate information from outside sources into my own writing.
☐	12. I can avoid plagiarism by acknowledging the source when referring to the ideas of others in my writing.
☐	13. I can cite my sources using APA or MLA style.
☐	14. I can write a thesis statement that answers a question.
☐	15. I can write an effective introduction using an anecdote or scenario.
☐	16. I can write an effective look-to-the-future conclusion.
☐	17. I can use the question technique to develop my body paragraphs effectively.
☐	18. I can use the passive voice effectively.
☐	19. I can write an expository essay of four or more paragraphs.
☐	20.

Activity D | Put a check mark in the box beside the vocabulary items from this unit that you feel you can now use with confidence in your writing.

Vocabulary Checklist	
☐ access (n.) AWL	☐ impetus (n.) 6000
☐ adjustment (n.) AWL	☐ implement (v.) AWL
☐ assess (v.) AWL	☐ individual (n.) AWL
☐ dependency (n.) 5000	☐ irresistible (adj.) 6000
☐ destined (adj.) 4000	☐ obey (v.) 4000
☐ discord (n.) 8000	☐ premature (adj.) 4000
☐ disorientation (n.) 7000	☐ promote (v.) AWL
☐ emphasis (n.) AWL	☐ recharge (v.) 8000
☐ generate (v.) AWL	☐ technology (n.) AWL
☐ impatience (n.) 4000	☐ theory (n.) AWL

UNIT 3 Travel

Tourism and Hospitality Management

KEY LEARNING OUTCOMES

- Creating an inquiry question for making comparisons
- Learning to use new words using a dictionary
- Brainstorming using a Venn diagram
- Using reporting verbs to integrate information from outside sources
- Using sentence patterns to integrate information from outside sources
- Achieving sentence variety and avoiding run-on sentences and comma splices
- Introducing an essay topic with a thought-provoking question
- Concluding an essay by synthesizing ideas
- Achieving essay unity
- Writing a compare-and-contrast essay

EXPLORING IDEAS

Introduction

For many people, a dream vacation involves a change from their usual daily routine and often includes some form of travel. There are many different ways of travelling and types of holiday destinations. One person's dream vacation could be another person's worst holiday ever.

Visiting the Great Wall of China

Spending time on the beach

Hiking in the mountains

Visiting a big, modern city

Visiting ancient ruins

Taking a cruise

Activity A | Discuss the following questions with a partner or small group.

1. Do you enjoy travelling? Why or why not?
2. Which of the vacations shown in the photos would be your favourite? Why?
3. If you have had the chance to travel in the past, what was your best experience? What was your worst experience?
4. What are the positive and negative impacts of tourism on local communities?
5. Are some ways of travelling better than others? What makes them better or worse?

Activity B | Choose two of the types of vacations shown in the photos on the previous page. Fill out the T-chart below with similarities and differences between these two types of vacations. Discuss your ideas with a partner or small group.

Vacation 1: ______________________________

Vacation 2: ______________________________

Similarities between Vacations 1 and 2	Differences between Vacations 1 and 2

Activity C | Writing Task: Short Paragraph | Write a short paragraph about the similarities and differences between Vacation 1 and Vacation 2.

Fostering Inquiry

Comparing and Contrasting Characteristics

Comparing and contrasting the characteristics of two ideas, theories, or objects is an important academic skill because doing so helps you analyze these characteristics and thereby more fully understand them. Developing an inquiry question with a focus on comparing and contrasting characteristics will help you better understand the topic. Such a question often begins with *what* or *how.*

Activity A | What do you want to know more about in relation to travel and tourism? For example, *What are some important differences between [two different travel destinations]?* or *What are the differences in using different modes of transportation when travelling?*

1. Write down two or three questions you have about travel and tourism. Refer back to the T-chart and your ideas on the discussion questions on page 73.
2. In a small group, share your questions.
3. Choose one question to be your guiding inquiry question for this unit. Your inquiry question can be different from the other group members' questions. The focus of your question may change as you work your way through this unit.
4. Write your inquiry question here and refer to it as you complete the activities in this unit.

   My Unit Inquiry Question:

   ____

   ____

   ____

   ____

   ____

Activity B | Writing Task: Freewriting | Write for at least five minutes on the topic of your Unit Inquiry Question. Do not stop writing during this time. After five minutes, read what you have written and circle two or three ideas that you would like to explore further in order to answer your Unit Inquiry Question.

Structure

Compare-and-Contrast Essay

The purpose of a compare-and-contrast essay is to discuss the similarities and differences between (usually) two objects, processes, theories, people, animals, materials, concepts, or phenomena. The reasons for comparing and contrasting can vary: it may be that you simply want to better understand the two items or that you want to help your reader make a choice between the two.

Activity A | With a partner or small group, consider this example of a student paragraph that contrasts three modes of transportation. Answer the questions that follow.

Productive time and carbon dioxide emission are two important differences between travelling by train and travelling by car or plane. For some people, it may be important that they get something accomplished while travelling. A businessperson, for example, may want to use travel time to prepare for or review notes from a meeting. A student, on the other hand, may want to do course reading or work on an assignment. Travelling by train and travelling by car or plane allow different amounts of time to do that. For example, when taking the train between Toronto and Montreal, a passenger can work for the whole five-and-a-half hours of the trip. In contrast, a person driving a car has no opportunity to work, and an airline passenger can use only the one hour of the flight because the rest of the travel time is taken up by checking in and going through security at the airport (VIA Rail, n.d.). Furthermore, these three modes of transportation result in different amounts of air pollution, in particular carbon dioxide. For a trip from Montreal to Toronto, the train emits about 15 kilograms of carbon dioxide per seat, whereas the car releases about 34 kilograms per seat. The plane emits more than five times as much per seat, that is 83 kilograms, than the train (VIA Rail, n.d.). In other words, one's choice of transportation has a significant impact on the environment. When choosing a means of transportation, it is worthwhile considering the environmental effects as well as the best use of one's time.

Reference

VIA Rail. (n.d.). *Compare the train with the car and the plane.* Retrieved from http://www.viarail.ca/en/plan-your-trip/book-travel/compare-train-and-car

1. What is the main idea of this paragraph?
2. What kind of information is used to illustrate the author's point?
3. How is the information organized?

Compare-and-Contrast Essay Structure

A compare-and-contrast essay follows the standard essay structure described in Unit 2 (pages 38–41) with an introduction, two or more body paragraphs, and a conclusion. The introduction contains a thesis statement that outlines the key points on which the essay focuses. Each body paragraph contains a single controlling idea that is directly related to the thesis statement. Because a compare-and-contrast essay often discusses both similarities and differences between, for example, two different modes of transportation, the organization of ideas can be challenging. Two different patterns are commonly used to structure the body paragraphs of such an essay.

The block pattern focuses, one at a time, on each item to be compared (e.g., bikes and cars) and discusses the relevant points of comparison (e.g., pollution) for each item. The point-by-point pattern focuses, one at a time, on each point of comparison (e.g., pollution) that is addressed and includes information about both items (e.g., bikes and cars) in each paragraph. You should choose the pattern that leads to the least repetition of information in your text.

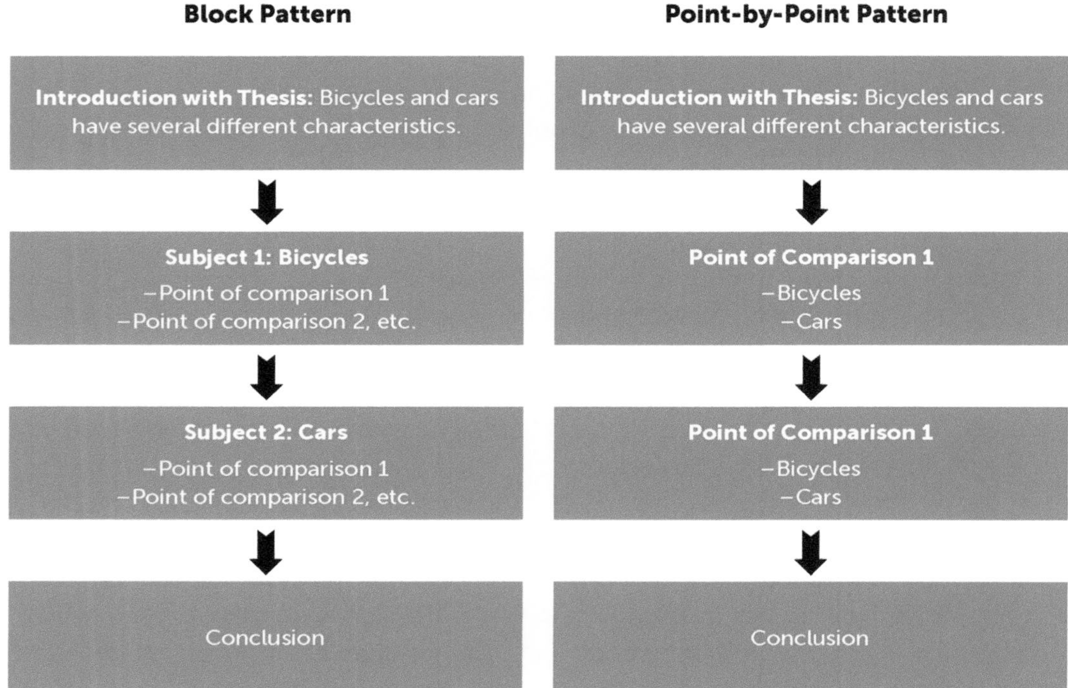

FIGURE 3.1 Compare-and-contrast essay structure

Activity B | The following essay illustrates one of the organizational patterns shown in Figure 3.1 above. Read the essay closely, paying attention to the organizational pattern, and answer the questions that follow.

The Car and the Bicycle—Two Very Different Modes of Transportation

How do you get to work or school in the morning? Do you simply get into your car without thinking about it? Or do you prefer to bike to work, no matter the weather? People decide to commute by car or by bike for different reasons. Some people have no choice but to drive because they live too far from their workplace or school. Others enjoy the commute by car. Some organizations are trying to convince commuters to switch from the car to other modes of transportation. Environmental factors and commuter satisfaction are two important aspects to consider when making your choice.

The car and the bicycle have very different impacts on the environment in which they are used. First of all, a car takes up a lot of more space on the roads than a bike. In visual campaigns to convince commuters to make the switch, cycling advocates have taken photographs to illustrate that people in cars take up about twice the amount of space on the road than people with bikes (Cycling Promotion Fund, 2014). In addition, parking a car requires a lot more space than parking a bike. A parking space designed for one car can accommodate between 10 to 15 parked bikes (CityMetric, 2014). Another important difference is the energy necessary to commute by car or bike. It takes more than 20 times the amount of energy to travel by car than it does to ride a bike: 0.56 kWh per kilometre by car versus only 0.025 kWh per kilometre by bicycle (Berger-Schauer, 2015). Finally, driving a car obviously causes more air pollution than riding a bicycle. According to the Union of Concerned Scientists (2014), there are several different types of major pollutants that cars emit when driven. The pollutants include greenhouse gases, of which carbon dioxide is the most commonly known; however, other greenhouse gases, such as hydrocarbons (HC), nitrogen oxides (NO_x), and sulphur dioxide (SO_2), are also emitted and can cause health problems for humans (Union of Concerned Scientists, 2014). In contrast, riding a bike does not cause any pollution. It is clear, therefore, that riding a bicycle is much better for the environment.

Another issue to consider is how happy people are when they commute by bicycle or by car. Research has found that, in general, cyclists are happier commuters than car users. In fact, 81.85 percent of cyclists are satisfied with their commute, whereas only 77.42 percent of car drivers feel the same about their commute (St-Louis, Manaugh, van Lierop, & El-Geneidy, 2014). The researchers believe this difference is due to how active commuters are during their trip to work or school. Cyclists, in general, not only get to their destination but also enjoy the trip itself. Drivers, on the other hand, do not experience the same level of joy during their commute. The weather, however, has an important impact on the level of satisfaction. For car commuters, who are not exposed to the weather, the level of satisfaction is not affected by whether is it sunny and warm or cold and snowy. Cyclists, in contrast, experience the weather first-hand. As a result, their level of satisfaction decreases by 6.5 percent on cold and snowy days (St-Louis et al., 2014). Finally, travel time is a significant factor that influences commuter satisfaction. Drivers' satisfaction level is significantly affected by how long their commute takes. According to St-Louis and her colleagues (2014), this is because they are directly affected by the road network and the level of congestion. Cyclists, on the other hand, are generally not affected by either of these things; consequently, their daily commute time, unaffected by external factors, is generally the same each day. In brief, those who cycle to work are happier than those who drive.

In terms of their environmental impact and their users' satisfaction, the car and the bicycle are very different. The car requires more space and energy and produces more pollution than the bicycle. In addition, cyclists are generally more satisfied with their commute than drivers—at least when the weather is nice. Will you consider switching from commuting by car to riding your bicycle to work or school on the next sunny day?

References

Berger-Schauer, C. (2015, October 12). *Efficiency master: A comparison of different modes of transportation.* Retrieved from http://www.bikecitizens.net/efficiency-master-for-modes-of-transportation/

CityMetric. (2014, November 14). *In pictures: Do cars take up too much space on city streets?* Retrieved from http://www.citymetric.com/transport/pictures-do-cars-take-too-much-space-city-streets-483

Cycling Promotion Fund. (2014). *About us*. Retrieved from http://www.bikeoz.com.au/index.php/about-us

St-Louis, E., Manaugh, K., van Lierop, D., & El-Geneidy, A. (2014). The happy commuter: A comparison of commuter satisfaction across modes. *Transportation Research Part F: Traffic Psychology and Behaviour, 26*, 160–170.

Union of Concerned Scientists. (2014, December 5). *Cars, trucks, and air pollution.* Retrieved from http://www.ucsusa.org/clean-vehicles/vehicles-air-pollution-and-human-health/cars-trucks-air-pollution#

1. What is the main idea of the essay?
2. How is the topic introduced?
3. Does the essay discuss both similarities and differences or only one of the two?
4. Which organizational pattern does the essay use: the block pattern or the point-by-point pattern?
5. What evidence is used to support similarities and/or differences between these two modes of transportation in the body paragraphs?
6. What connectors does the writer use to link information on similarities and/or differences?
7. Which sentences in the conclusion summarize the main points of the essay?

Language Tip

Using Compare-and-Contrast Connectors

Connectors play an important role in helping your reader understand the relationships between ideas in your text. In a compare-and-contrast essay, appropriate connectors communicate to the reader whether you are focusing on a similarity or difference in a particular part of your text.

The list of connectors to the right shows their use. Some link similar ideas; others link contrasting ideas. These are some common examples, but note that these are not the only compare-and-contrast connectors in English.

Similar Ideas	**Contrasting Ideas**
in the same way	but
similarly	whereas
likewise	in contrast
like (+ noun)	on the other hand
as (+ noun)	unlike (+ noun)
similar to (+ noun)	in contrast to (+ noun)

Activity C | Writing Task: Compare-and-Contrast Paragraph | Think of two other modes of transportation and write a short paragraph in which you compare and contrast the two.

Activity D | Exchange your paragraph with a partner. Read your partner's paragraph and use the following questions to provide feedback.

1. What is the main idea of this paragraph?
2. Does it focus on both similarities and differences or only one of the two?
3. Which organizational pattern does it appear to be using?
4. Does the paragraph contain good details to illustrate the similarities and/or differences?
5. What do you like best about this paragraph?
6. How would you improve this paragraph?

Activity E | Revisit your Unit Inquiry Question on page 74. What new ideas have you thought of that will help you answer your question? Share your ideas with a partner or small group. At this point, you may consider revising your Unit Inquiry Question.

ACADEMIC READING

Vocabulary

Vocabulary Skill: Learning to Use New Words Using a Dictionary

When you encounter a new word while reading a text or want to use a word that is relatively new to you, a good dictionary is a useful tool. You can obtain information about the precise meaning of the word. Moreover, you can use the dictionary to find out information that is essential for using the word well in your own writing.

Consider the dictionary entry below for *impact*, one of the vocabulary words in this unit. You can see that this word can be used as both a noun and a verb. Both the noun and the verb have several different meanings (see numbers in the dictionary entries). For each meaning, the dictionary gives an explanation in simple words followed by at least one example sentence to illustrate the proper usage of the word and its meaning. The dictionary entry also provides important grammatical information. For both the noun and the verb, the entry tells you with which prepositions the word is used. It also tells you that *impact* can be used as a transitive verb (with a direct object—something/someone **impacts** something) and as an intransitive verb (without a direct object but with a preposition—something/someone **impacts** on/upon/with something).

im·pact 0-ㅠ AW *noun, verb*
■ ***noun*** /ˈɪmpækt/ [C, usually sing., U] **1** 0-ㅠ **~ (of sth) (on sb/sth)** the powerful effect that sth has on sb/sth: *the environmental impact of tourism* ◇ *The report assesses the impact of AIDS on the gay community.* ◇ *Her speech made a profound impact on everyone.* ◇ *Businesses are beginning to feel the full impact of the recession.* **2** 0-ㅠ the act of one object hitting another; the force with which this happens: *craters made by meteorite impacts* ◇ *The impact of the blow knocked Jack off balance.* ◇ *The bomb explodes* ***on impact*** (= when it hits something). ◇ *The car is fitted with* ***side impact*** *bars* (= to protect it from a blow from the side).
■ ***verb*** /ɪmˈpækt/ **1** [I, T] to have an effect on sth SYN **affect**: **~ on/upon sth** *Her father's death impacted greatly on her childhood years.* ◇ **~ sth** (*business*) *The company's performance was impacted by the high value of the pound.* **2** [I, T] **~ (on/upon/with) sth** (*formal*) to hit sth with great force

Once you have obtained useful information from the dictionary, it is important to apply your new knowledge so that you can use the new word in your own writing.

Activity A | Consider the two meanings of the verb and of the noun given in the dictionary entry for *impact*. Write one sentence for each of these meanings of the word. When you have finished, compare your sentences with a partner or small group.

verb

1. ______________________________

2. ______________________________

noun

3. ____

____

4. ____

____

Activity B | Use your dictionary to look up all the unfamiliar words in the *Vocabulary Preview* on pages 81–83. Answer the following questions about each of the words you look up.

- How many different meanings does each word have?
- What is each meaning?
- How many parts of speech (i.e., noun, verb, adjective, and adverb) can this word take?
- What grammatical information does the dictionary provide about this word?

Make notes about each word you look up in a notebook or in a file on your computer. You can add information about new entries whenever you encounter a new word. Include your own example sentences with each new word. Check your example sentences with a partner, in a small group, or with your instructor.

Learning Strategy

Organizing Ideas

Good learning strategies help you improve your English. When you are working with new vocabulary or are collecting information from sources before you write a text, organizing ideas is an excellent strategy to use. There are various ways in which you can organize your ideas, and the best way depends on your preferences and the task you are working on.

- When you are collecting information about new vocabulary words in your notebook or on your computer, organize them alphabetically, by unit, or by topic.
- When you are selecting information from sources to prepare for a writing assignment, organize your information by the main ideas you want to cover.
- When you are reviewing notes for a course, organize your notes in a way that makes sense according to the material. There may be different ways to achieve that.

The activities in the vocabulary skill section in this unit provide a good opportunity to try out the organizing ideas strategy.

Source: Based on ideas in Oxford, R. L. (2011). *Teaching and researching language learning strategies*. Harlow, UK: Pearson.

Vocabulary Preview: The Academic Word List

Activity C | Read the following sentences, paying close attention to the bolded AWL words for this unit. Decide if each word has been used correctly in terms of meaning and grammar. If necessary, consult your dictionary, your own notes, a partner, or your instructor. Rewrite any sentences in which the AWL word has been used incorrectly. Hint: in some sentences, you will have to change the word(s) around the bolded word; in other sentences, you may have to replace the bolded word with a different word altogether.

1. Tourism plays a significant role in many countries' **economic** policies.
2. All tourists have an **impact** in the countries and cities that they visit.
3. Until the beginning of the twentieth century, only a small **portion** in society had the time or money to travel.
4. The tourism **revolution** is a relatively recent phenomenon.
5. All forms of tourism have some negative effects on the natural **environment**.
6. With an increase in visitors, communities and hotels must **dispose** of additional waste.
7. To reduce their effects on local communities, tourists should respect the people and the culture of that **area**.
8. The goal of **sustainable** tourism is to minimize the impact of tourists' activities on the environment.
9. The **migrants** decided to take a city bus tour on the first day of their four-day visit.
10. The guide **defined** the features of the historic building for the visitors.

Vocabulary Preview: Mid-frequency Vocabulary

Activity D | Complete the following sentences using the words from the box that best match the synonyms or paraphrase given in parentheses.

cater	hiking	overnight	vacations	destination
classification	likewise	receipts	rafting	necessities

1. The ____________________ (putting something/someone into groups) of travellers is done based on their reasons or purpose for travelling.
2. If you travelled to a nearby town for a hockey tournament, you would not be considered a tourist. ____________________ (similarly, in the same way), if you decided to spend a year in a foreign country to study, you would not be a tourist.
3. Tourists are people who stay at least 24 hours or ____________________ (spend the night) but less than a year in one location.
4. In some countries, people now view ____________________ (holiday, break) as ____________________ (requirements) rather than luxuries.
5. In 2014, worldwide tourist ____________________ (money a business receives) totalled more than $1.133 billion.
6. Whole resort towns, theme parks, and tourism business districts have been developed to ____________________ (provide what is needed) to huge numbers of tourists.

7. Banff, Alberta, is one example of a town that grew up around a tourist __________________ (place where someone is going), the Banff Springs Hotel.
8. Sustainable tourism can include __________________ (travelling on a river on a flat structure) down the Ottawa River or __________________ (taking a long walk in the countryside) in a national park.

Reading 1

The reading "Tourism" is an excerpt from the textbook *Travel Quest: Travel & Tourism in the 21st Century* by Fraser Cartwright, Gerry Pierce, and Randy Wilkie. This textbook is used in geography classes in Canadian high schools.

Activity A | What is tourism? Work with a partner or small group to try to define the term and come up with some examples of trips that would be considered tourism and some that would not. What is the difference between tourism and other kinds of trips?

Activity B | Take a look at the figure accompanying the text. Is your definition of *tourism* correct? If necessary, make corrections to your definition.

Activity C | Read the textbook excerpt straight through. Then read it again and highlight important information in each of the three sections of the text. Use that information to answer the questions that follow the text.

READING

Tourism

Introduction

1 What is it that drives people to travel, to go on trips to faraway places? Most of us travel to get a break from our daily routines. We want to have new experiences and see what life is like in different countries. [...] Your definition of tourism probably includes travel away from home and some aspect of fun. Travel away from a home **environment** seems an obvious part of tourism, but does tourism always have to be for pleasure? And is distance of travel or length of stay a factor? Is a person who visits a place for only a few hours or another who stays for several years still considered a tourist? [...]

2 According to the World Tourism Organization, tourists are people who visit one location for at least 24 hours (**overnight**) but less than a year. Some types of travellers are not considered tourists. These include **migrants** (people who move their residence permanently or semi-permanently) and same-day visitors (travellers who stay in a location for fewer than 24 hours). If you travelled to a nearby town for a hockey tournament and returned the same day, you would not be considered a tourist. **Likewise**, if you decided to spend a year in a foreign country to work, study, or visit relatives, you would be a migrant and not a tourist. When you examine statistics on the number of tourists visiting a particular region, the data will not include same-day

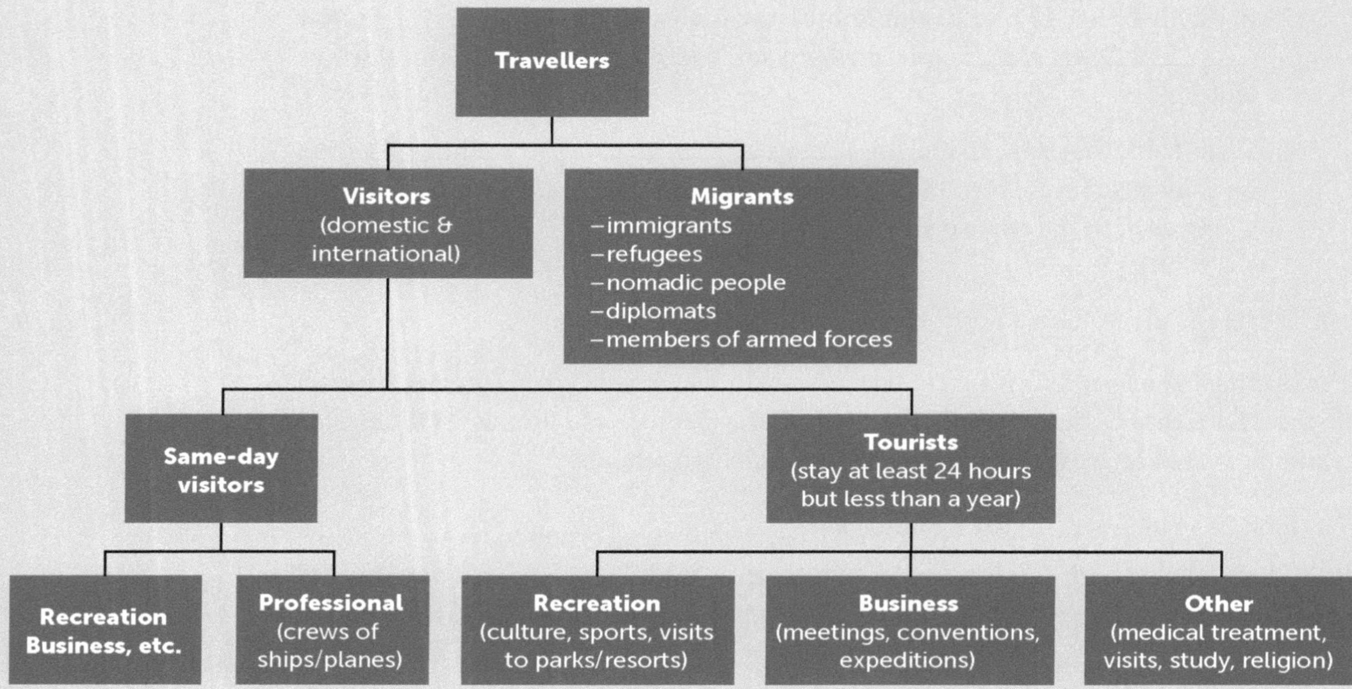

FIGURE 3.2

visitors or migrants. Figure 3.2 shows **classification** of travellers. [...]

The Tourism Revolution

3 Each day in the year 2000, an estimated million people worldwide travelled out of their home country. On average, these people spent about $1000 per trip on accommodations, meals, entertainment, and shopping. Worldwide tourism **receipts** totalled more than $700 billion. At the same time, the number of domestic travel (people travelling within their own country) continued to be 10 times higher than the number of international travellers (people travelling between countries).

4 The tourism **revolution** is a relatively recent phenomenon, however. Until the beginning of the twentieth century, only a small **portion** of society had the time or money to travel. It took dramatic **economic**, social, and technological changes to make tourism an activity available to a much larger portion of the population. New labour laws that guaranteed paid **vacation** time gave more middle-class people the time and money to travel. Today, approximately 80 percent of the industrialized world's population receive at least three weeks off from work with pay. In these countries, people now view vacations as **necessities** rather than luxuries.

[...]

5 One consequence of people travelling in large numbers, especially for pleasure, is what industry analysts call *mass tourism*. Mass tourism can be **defined** as the movement of large numbers of people to specialized tourist locations. Whole resort towns, theme parks, and tourism business districts have been developed to **cater** to huge numbers of tourists. In Canada, Banff, Alberta, is one example of a town that grew up around a tourist **destination**, the Banff Springs Hotel.

[...]

Something New: Sustainable Tourism

6 It is difficult to imagine any form of tourism that does not have some sort of negative effect on the natural environment. Tourist **areas** must build airports to accommodate travellers, build and maintain roads, cope with the pollution from the cars tourists drive, and **dispose** of the additional human waste. All tourists leave an **impact** on the areas they

visit. Mass tourism usually has the greatest impact. The thousands of tourists who cram into the high-rise, beachfront condominiums[1] of St. Petersburg, Florida, for example, have an effect on the local environment so severe it may be permanent.

7 The fastest-growing sector in the tourism industry today is not in mass tourism, however. It is actually with a branch of alternative tourism known as **sustainable** tourism. This is the kind of tourism that provides travellers with large-scale and small-scale forms. On a large scale, sustainable tourism can include **rafting** down the Ottawa River, fishing in Great Slave Lake, bicycle touring in New England, scuba diving[2] in Key Largo, or whale watching on the St. Lawrence River. On a small but no less important scale, it can involve camping on a local river, **hiking** along the Niagara Escarpment,[3] or taking a bird-watching trip into the rain forests of Costa Rica.

8 Whatever form it takes, sustainable tourism should satisfy four fundamental requirements:

a) It should protect the existing and future use of an environment.
b) It should respect the people and the culture of the local area.
c) It should allow for the long-term use of the area.
d) It should provide long-term economic benefits to the people living in the tourist area. [...]

9 Sustainable tourism known as *ecotourism* is one of the fastest-growing types of tourism in the world today. Even though people have always travelled to places to enjoy scenic natural environments, ecotourism didn't grow into a major industry until the late 1980s. The Filipino writer Héctor Ceballos-Lascuráin first defined the term as "travelling to undisturbed areas and enjoying the scenery and its wild plants and animals." Today ecotourism has become so popular that it generates about $34 billion, mostly in the developing countries of the world.

Source: Excerpted from Cartwright, F., Pierce, G., & Wilkie, R. (2001). *Travel quest: Travel & tourism in the 21st century* (pp. 4, 6, 8, 9, 21–23). Don Mills, ON: Oxford University Press.

[1] an apartment building or group of houses in which each flat/apartment/house is owned by the person living in it but the shared areas are owned by everyone together

[2] the sport or activity of swimming underwater using special breathing equipment consisting of a container of air which you carry on your back and a tube through which you breathe the air

[3] a steep slope that separates an area of high ground from an area of lower ground

Activity D | The following questions are based on the textbook excerpt you just read. Discuss your answers with a partner or small group.

1. In the chart below, categorize the examples of travelling mentioned in the text into two groups: tourism and other travel.

Tourism	Other Travel

2. Find the following statistics about worldwide tourism in the year 2000.

   a. Number of international travellers per day: ______________

   b. Average amount spent per trip on accommodations, meals, entertainment, and shopping: ______________

   c. Ratio of domestic to international travellers: ______________

3. What impact does tourism have on local communities? In addition to the examples mentioned in the text, can you think of other impacts of tourism?

   ____

   ____

4. What examples of sustainable tourism are mentioned in the text? What makes these activities sustainable? Consider the four requirements for sustainable tourism mentioned in the text.

   ____

   ____

5. According to Héctor Ceballos-Lascuráin, sustainable tourism means "travelling to undisturbed areas and enjoying the scenery and its wild plants and animals." Think of the area where you live now and/or the area where you are from. What types of activities are done in those areas that Ceballos-Lascuráin would consider sustainable tourism? If necessary, do some research into sustainable tourism activities in those areas.

Critical Thinking

Bloom's Taxonomy—*Application*

The third level of thinking in Bloom's taxonomy is *application*. In this level, you apply facts, rules, and principles to new situations and problems. This process forms the basis of comparing or contrasting. For example, question 5 above asks you to think about a concept from the reading (sustainable tourism) and apply it in another context.

As you do this, you are comparing and contrasting the two contexts in terms of sustainable tourism. Doing so also helps you understand the original concept of sustainable tourism more deeply.

As you consider what you read, ask yourself questions like

- Is this an example of some larger phenomenon? What phenomenon? How does it illustrate that phenomenon?
- Is this related to other facts, events, etc. that I know about? Which ones? How is it related?
- Is this important? Why?
- Is this applicable to situations in different times or places?

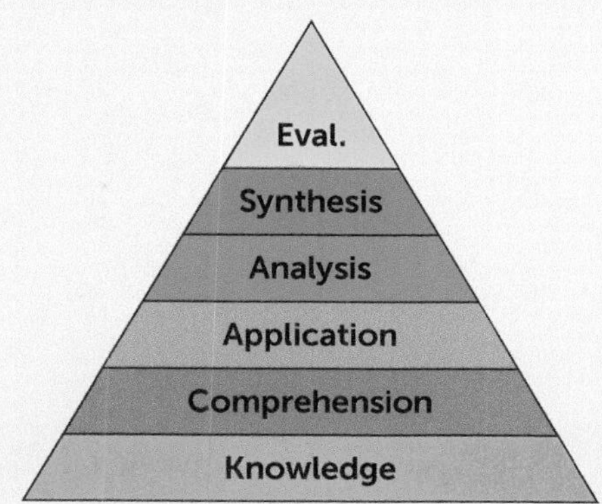

Source: Bloom, B. S., Engelhart, M. D., Furst, E. J., Hill, W. H., & Krathwohl, D. R. (1956). *Taxonomy of educational objectives: The classification of educational goals. Handbook 1: Cognitive domain*. London, UK: Longman.

Activity E | Writing Task: Compare-and-Contrast Paragraph | Write a short paragraph in which you describe a sustainable tourism activity that travellers can do in a region that you are familiar with. How does it compare or contrast with what travellers usually do in that region? You may want to do some research to find information to support your ideas.

Activity F | Compare your paragraph to the sample paragraph "Sustainable Tourism" in Appendix 2. Then answer the following questions about the sample paragraph.

1. What is the main idea of the paragraph?
2. Does it focus on both similarities and differences or on only one of the two?
3. What details does it include to illustrate the similarities and/or differences between the two types of activities?
4. Which organizational pattern is used in the paragraph?
5. Note how unit vocabulary was used in the sample paragraph. Discuss with a partner if and where any of the unit vocabulary could be used in your own compare-and-contrast paragraph.

Reading 2

The reading "Weed Your Way around the World" comes from the Canadian newsmagazine *Maclean's*. This magazine is published every week and contains articles on a wide range of topics.

Activity A | Read the magazine article and highlight all the relevant details about WWOOFing as a travel experience. Use that information to answer the questions that follow.

READING

Weed Your Way around the World

1 The routine was brutal. He got up at 4:30 am and started weeding at five. Two hours later they passed around the bread for breakfast. On his hands and knees, loaned out to a neighbour's farm, he thrust his gloved hands into mud and yanked out potatoes. The woman next to him grabbed what she thought was the stem of a potato plant and pulled up a rat instead. After lunch, they packaged the vegetables harvested that morning for market, slaving until nine at night. Then James Bejar fell into the men's quarters, a mouldy, dank place, and slept. He was not an indentured servant; Bejar was on holiday.

2 "It was just back-breaking work," says the 31-year-old Toronto public servant, whose vacation à la Dickens dates back to a two-week stint WWOOFing—volunteering on an organic farm in exchange for room and board—in Nagano, Japan. His story might suggest his was a one-time experiment; yet Bejar has returned again and again to what he sees as a cheap method of travel offering a glimpse of "part of a society and of a people you don't get by travelling from hotel to hotel."

3 WWOOFing organizations—the acronym stands for World Wide Opportunities on Organic Farms—now exist in over 100 countries, connecting volunteers with farmers. In exchange for weeding, feeding, and shovelling manure—normally for no more than six hours a day (Bejar's Nagano jaunt was an anomaly)—the volunteers receive food and accommodation, usually living as part of the family.

4 Begun in England in 1971, WWOOFing isn't new. But growing interest in local food and organics, along

with a recession that's preventing many new graduates from entering the workforce, is helping turn it into a growth industry. Five years ago, WWOOF Canada boasted 1000 volunteers and 500 participating farms; there are now well over 2000 WWOOFers signed up and close to 900 hosts, though the organization does no advertising. "With this so-called economic downturn, we haven't experienced anything—our numbers are up," says WWOOF Canada founder John Vanden Heuvel. "We're easily doing 10 percent growth every year. But I don't want to be equated with a business. We are a program providing interesting experiences."

5 Indeed, WWOOFing may soon replace the old roughing-it standbys of hostelling and kibbutzing. "Why would anyone want to do the backpacking and hostelling experience when they could do WWOOFing—there is the work, but in exchange you get so much more," says 25-year-old Mark Wade, who graduated from McMaster University with a poli-sci degree last spring and set out for BC. His resources thinning, Wade reached out to a farmer in Duncan: "Farmer John was his name," Wade recalls. "He says, 'Yes, come tomorrow and we will feed you.'" WWOOFing introduced the Toronto boy to a world of new vegetables—Swiss chard and garlic scapes (his enthusiasm has persuaded his mum to shop at the farmers' market)—and to square dancing in Cape Breton. "I'd never done that before," he says.

6 There are now perhaps as many as 20,000 WWOOFers around the world, Vanden Heuvel says, most in their 20s. WWOOF love affairs are not uncommon (65 percent of WWOOFers in Canada are women). The majority have never even gardened before. "I'd never chopped wood—I almost took off my leg the first time I did it," says Alan Wong, a 38-year-old Montreal Ph.D. student. "Some people think, 'Oh, it's just a way of getting cheap labour,'" says Tony McQuail, who receives WWOOFers on his farm north of London, Ont. "It's not really, because you have to invest a fair bit of time and training and instruction." Many WWOOFers seek adventure, others a gardening primer (Anne Duchesne, a 44-year-old Quebec City IT consultant, planted a garden at home after she and her husband learned the ropes on a farm in the mountains of Tuscany). The farmers, meanwhile, unable to leave their fields for travel, see the world come to them.

7 Not all billets—or WWOOFers—are equal. "You've got two strangers meeting at the front door and then all of a sudden you're living together," says Vanden Heuvel. The occasional WWOOFer is lazy; some farmers are too demanding or mean with lunches and dinners. But the best pitfall of all is the familiarity that breeds contempt. "We never had any bad WWOOFers," says 23-year-old Nora Kidston, who grew up with WWOOFers on her parents' farm in the Annapolis Valley. "They kind of become part of the family. And as all family members do, they get annoying."

Source: Köhler, N. (2009, September 17). Weed your way around the world: WWOOF connects volunteers with organic farmers. *Maclean's*. Retrieved from http://www.macleans.ca/society/life/weed-your-way-around-the-world/

Activity B | The following questions are based on the magazine article you just read. Discuss your answers with a partner or small group.

1. What is WWOOFing?

____

____

____

2. Complete the following information about WWOOFing:

   a. Typical number of working hours per day: ____________________

   b. Year the movement started: ____________________

   c. Evidence for growth of movement: ____________________

   ____

3. Why are people interested in WWOOFing?

   - ____________________
   - ____________________
   - ____________________

4. Why are farmers interested in having WWOOFers on their farms?

   ____

   ____

   ____

5. What do you see as the negative aspects of WWOOFing? Would you consider WWOOFing for your next trip? Why or why not?

   ____

   ____

   ____

PROCESS FUNDAMENTALS

Before You Write

Venn Diagram

In Unit 2 (pages 55–56), you learned about two general brainstorming techniques: listing and freewriting. Depending on the topic you want to write about, it can be useful to use the listing technique in a format that helps guide your thinking about a particular type of question.

A Venn diagram (see page 91) is particularly useful if you want to list the similarities and differences between two things in an organized way. In each circle, write down characteristics of whatever it is you are comparing and contrasting. In each lightly shaded area, write the characteristics that apply only to one of the items you are comparing. In other words, the lightly shaded sections will contain the differences. In the darker space where the two circles overlap, note the similarities between the two. Remember, you still need to evaluate and choose the ideas most relevant to your topic after completing the Venn diagram.

Activity A | Look at the Venn diagram on page 91. Thinking about your own experiences, what you have heard from others, and what you have read, brainstorm more similarities and differences on these two different ways of travelling. Add your ideas to the diagram. Then share your ideas with a partner or small group.

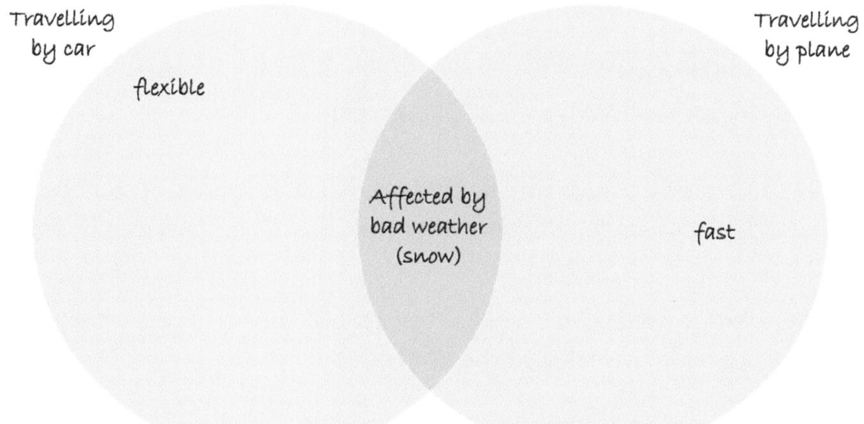

Activity B | Look back at your Unit Inquiry Question. Thinking about your own experiences, what you have heard from others, and what you have read, brainstorm similarities and differences on your topic using the Venn diagram below.

Activity C | Look back at the Venn diagram you created for your Unit Inquiry Question in Activity B. Create a rough outline for an essay based on this Venn diagram. As you learn more about your topic, use your outline to add more ideas and details to support your topic. This rough outline will help you identify gaps in your knowledge. If you end up writing an essay on your Unit Inquiry Question, this rough outline may be helpful in guiding your planning.

Integrating Information from an Outside Source

Sentence Patterns for Integrating Source Material, Part 1

In Unit 1, you learned about reporting verbs, such as *state*, *explain*, and *argue* (see page 8 for a list of common reporting verbs). These help a writer to indicate to the reader that what follows is someone else's information or idea. When you include someone else's ideas or information in your own text, you must always indicate where the ideas or information come from. The most common pattern for using these reporting verbs to indicate your sources is the following:

Name(s) + reporting verb + *that* + idea/information from the source.

Cartwright, Pierce, and Wilkie (2001) state that . . .

Activity A | In the essay comparing bicycles and cars as modes of transportation, the writer includes the following statement near the end of the paragraph on commuter satisfaction:

According to St-Louis and her colleagues (2014), this is because they are directly affected by the road network and the level of congestion.

Which of the reporting words below can be used to rewrite this sentence to fit the common pattern shown above? Choose the most appropriate word and rewrite the sentence using that reporting verb.

compare	conclude	describe	explain	illustrate

____

____

____

Activity B | Writing Task: Paraphrasing with Reporting Verbs | The following statements have been taken from Reading 1 (Source: Cartwright, F., Pierce, G., & Wilkie, R. (2001). *Travel quest: Travel and tourism in the 21st century* (pp. 4, 6, 8, 9, 21–23). Don Mills, ON: Oxford University Press). Rewrite each using one of the reporting verbs from the list in Unit 1 (page 8) or another suitable reporting verb. Remember, the following statements are taken word for word from the text. You will have to paraphrase them to include the information in your own sentence.

1. "Until the beginning of the twentieth century, only a small portion of society had the time or money to travel."

____

____

____

2. "It is difficult to imagine any form of tourism that does not have some sort of negative effect on the natural environment."

____

____

____

3. "Even though people have always travelled to places to enjoy scenic natural environments, ecotourism didn't grow into a major industry until the late 1980s."

____

____

____

Preventing Plagiarism

Taking Ownership

Is This Plagiarism?

Alpha is taking English 301 this semester and asked a friend, Beta, who took the course last semester, for his final course paper since Beta got an A on the paper. Alpha explained to Beta that she would like to see what a well-written paper looked like so she could learn from Beta and also produce a well-written paper. However, Alpha was busy at the end of the semester and did not have time to analyze Beta's paper properly, so she decided to just submit Beta's paper to the professor.

Did Alpha commit plagiarism? Consider the details of the above scenario in the context of the definitions and rules regarding plagiarism established by your academic institution. Discuss your answer to this question with a partner or small group. You may use the following questions to guide your discussion:

1. How much of the **information** in Alpha's essay (the one she submitted) is original?
2. How much of the **language** in Alpha's essay (the one she submitted) is original?
3. Did Beta do anything wrong? Explain your reasoning.
4. What do you think the consequences might be if it is discovered that Alpha submitted Beta's paper?
5. What would you do to prevent plagiarism in this scenario?

Note: For information on your institution's plagiarism policy, search the college or university's website for a statement on academic integrity and/or its academic code of conduct.

Topic Skill

Writing Topic Sentences

A good topic sentence lets the reader know what to expect from a paragraph. It states the broad topic of the paragraph and specifies the controlling idea (the focus of the topic or the main idea that is discussed in the paragraph).

Activity A | In the following topic sentences from the essay on cars and bicycles in this unit, identify the topic and the controlling idea.

1. The car and the bicycle have very different impacts on the environment in which they are used.
2. Another issue to consider is how happy people are when they commute by bicycle or by car.

Common problems with topic sentences include the following:

- The topic sentence does not go with the thesis of the essay.
- The topic sentence is not directly related to the paragraph that it introduces.
- The topic sentence is too broad to be discussed in a single paragraph.
- The topic sentence includes specific details that should be mentioned later in the paragraph.
- The controlling idea is not specific enough.

Activity B | Choose the best topic sentence from each set and decide what is wrong with the other options, referring to the list of problems with topic sentences above. Discuss your answers with a partner or small group.

Set A

1. All humans have transportation needs.
2. On short trips within cities, you can save up to five minutes by taking a bicycle instead of a car to your destination.
3. The car is better than the bicycle.
4. In big cities, commuting by bicycle is more practical than commuting by car.

Set B

1. A 600-kilometre trip between two big cities generally takes less time by plane than by car.
2. Both planes and cars emit significant pollutants into the atmosphere.
3. Air pollution is a big problem.
4. Both planes and cars cause pollution.

Set C

1. Taking a cruise and hiking in the mountains are two very different types of vacations.
2. Taking a cruise and hiking in the mountains allow travellers to admire the landscape and nature of a particular region in two different ways.
3. An average cruise ship travels at about 20 knots (about 40 kilometres per hour), whereas the average hiker travels at five kilometres per hour when the terrain is flat.
4. There are many different options for travelling and vacationing.

Activity C | Writing Task: Topic Sentences | Look back at your Unit Inquiry Question and the notes you took while brainstorming using the Venn diagram. Based on your ideas about your Unit Inquiry Question, write two or three working topic sentences that could be used to introduce a paragraph in a compare-and-contrast essay on that topic.

1. ____

   ____

2. ____

   ____

3. ____

   ____

Introductions

Thought-Provoking Question

Take another look at the essay on cars and bicycles on pages 76–78. How was the topic in that essay introduced? What is the writer's purpose in asking the reader "How do you get to work or school in the morning? Do you simply get into your car without thinking about it? Or do you prefer to bike to work, no matter the weather?" By starting the introduction of an essay with a question, the writer wants to engage the reader in the topic, make the reader curious about what is to come, and encourage the reader to reflect on his or her own opinions. The questions can be concrete and personal (e.g., *What is your dream vacation?*) or abstract and philosophical (e.g., *What is the purpose of working?*) The best questions to introduce the topic of an essay

- require readers to think about their own lives, experiences, and views;
- encourage readers to reflect on a question that is central to the topic of the essay; and
- allow the writer to transition smoothly from the question to the thesis statement in a few sentences.

Consider the following example of such an introduction.

> What is the most important aspect to consider when choosing a holiday destination? If you are in the middle of a long, cold Canadian winter, the weather may be the most important consideration. What the destination has to offer to its visitors is also important, of course. Some people would like to see and learn new things, whereas others want to enjoy beautiful surroundings. Few people, however, think about how their presence in a certain destination affects the local community and the environment. Popular tourist destinations differ greatly in terms of their sustainability.

Activity A | For each thesis statement below, think of a good question that could be used to introduce it. In order to write the question, you may have to think about what ideas you would want to include in your essay. Share your questions with a partner or small group.

1. Visiting a modern city is quite similar in many ways to visiting ancient ruins.
2. A hiking holiday and a beach vacation have both similar and different characteristics.
3. Although the world's most visited cities are in different continents, they are surprisingly similar in certain aspects.

Activity B | Writing Task: Thought-Provoking Introduction | Look back at your Unit Inquiry Question. Write a working thesis statement for a compare-and-contrast essay on that question. Then write an introduction that begins with a thought-provoking question and includes that working thesis statement. Make a clear connection between the thought-provoking question and the thesis statement.

Conclusions

Synthesizing Main Ideas

A common technique for concluding an essay is to summarize and synthesize the main ideas discussed in the essay. Synthesizing is more interesting for the reader than simply summarizing the main ideas because a synthesis allows the writer to clearly illustrate the connections between the ideas mentioned in the essay. In other words, a good conclusion does not simply repeat the ideas discussed in the essay, but rather explains how they are linked to each other.

Consider the following example of such a conclusion.

> In brief, not all destinations are as sustainable as tourists and local communities would like them to be. In order to be considered sustainable, tourist activities and infrastructure have to respect the local environment and the ecology of the ecosystem. In addition to the environment, members of the local community have to be respected in terms of their needs and their cultural identity; they should not be exploited to provide entertainment for tourists. Only then can there be a positive outlook for the future of a touristic destination.

Common problems in conclusions include

- repeating the thesis statement without paraphrasing;
- mentioning new ideas that require detailed discussion or support; and
- ending the conclusion with a statement that is too general or unconnected to the ideas in the essay.

Activity A | Read the three topic sentences below and think about the link between these ideas. Then try to write a conclusion that not only summarizes but also shows the connection between these ideas.

1. Young people can combine work and travel to reduce the cost of their next vacation.
2. Finding cheap or free accommodation is incredibly useful.
3. Carpooling and using budget airlines are both good options for young travellers.

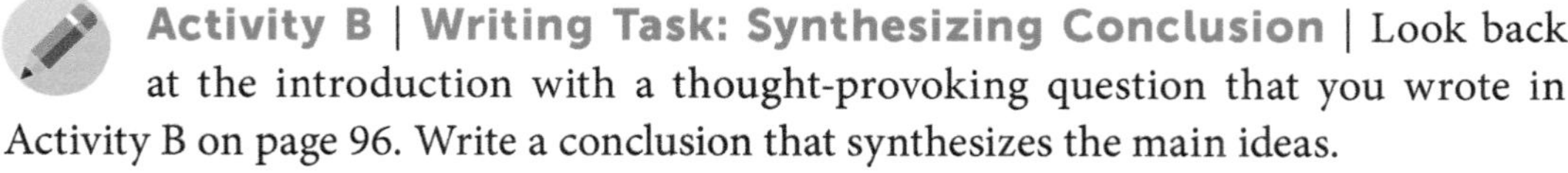

Activity B | Writing Task: Synthesizing Conclusion | Look back at the introduction with a thought-provoking question that you wrote in Activity B on page 96. Write a conclusion that synthesizes the main ideas.

WRITING FUNDAMENTALS

Composition Skill

Achieving Essay Unity

As you learned in Unit 2 (pages 62–63), you have to provide enough information to answer any question that the reader may have about the information in your text. It is also important to ensure that you have essay and paragraph unity—that all the information you provide is directly related to the focus of the essay and/or the focus of each paragraph. To achieve essay unity, all the topic sentences must be directly related to the thesis. To achieve paragraph unity, every sentence in a paragraph must be directly related to the topic sentence and its controlling idea.

Activity A | Some of the following topic sentences are not related to the thesis statement. Select the topic sentences that are not related to the thesis statement and explain the reasons for your choice. Discuss your choices with a partner or small group.

Thesis Statement: Although the world's most visited cities are in different continents, they are surprisingly similar in certain aspects.

Topic Sentences:

1. Many of these cities are important cultural centres in their countries.
2. Only some of these cities are important religious centres.
3. Some of these cities are modern, but others have ancient city centres.
4. These cities have played an important role in their country's history.

Activity B | Read the following paragraph and cross out any sentences that do not relate directly to the topic sentence and the controlling idea.

Modern cities are quite similar in some ways to ancient ruins. Both a modern city and a site of ancient ruins tell us a lot about the societies that built them. Architecture and building design are driven by social needs and cultural traditions, and all humans have the need to gather and celebrate meaningful festivals. Therefore, both modern cities and ancient ruins have squares or other public areas where people can assemble to do that. However, these places look nicer in modern cities and are not as big in ancient ruins. Second, both a modern city and a site of ancient ruins will reflect their respective climates. In hot countries, for example, both new and ancient homes will feature a lot of open outdoor space, such as courtyards so that people can spend time outdoors. Canadian houses do not have this feature because of our climate. Indeed, modern cities and ancient ruins share certain characteristics.

Sentence and Grammar Skill

Increasing Sentence Variety and Avoiding Run-ons and Comma Splices

Increasing Sentence Variety

A text can be interesting to read, or it can be painfully boring. Much depends on whether or not you are interested in the topic. However, writing style is often equally important in determining whether a reader finds a text interesting. One important part of writing style relates to the types of sentences used and how each sentence is structured.

A simple sentence starts with the subject and verb.

> Bicycles are different from cars.
> *subject verb complement*

However, you can also start a sentence with the following:

- an adverb (e.g., *however, moreover, recently, today*);
- a prepositional phrase (e.g., *in the past, according to experts, from experience*); or
- a dependent clause (e.g., *because we need to commute to work, when cars break down*—see also Unit 1, pages 28–30).

Starting certain sentences with something other than the subject and verb increases variety.

Another way to increase sentence variety is to change the number of clauses each sentence has. The most basic sentence consists of only one independent clause.

> Bicycles are different from cars.

However, a sentence can have more than one clause. You could, for example, add a dependent clause to your sentence.

> Bicycles are different from cars in that cars require the burning of fuel to move.

There can also be more than one independent clause in a sentence.

> Bicycles are different from cars, but each one has its own advantages.

There could even be three or four clauses in one sentence.

> Bicycles are different from cars in that cars require the burning of fuel to move, but each one has its own advantages.

Having a different number of clauses and different types of clauses in your sentences also makes them more interesting.

Activity A | Look back at one of the paragraphs you wrote earlier in this unit.

- Do your sentences all start with the subject and verb, or do you have some sentences that start in a different way?
- How many clauses and what kinds of clauses do your sentences contain?

If many of your sentences start with the subject and verb or have only one independent clause, rewrite some of the sentences to increase your variety by starting them in different ways and using different combinations of clauses.

Avoiding Run-On Sentences and Comma Splices

When your sentences have more than one independent clause, you need to connect those two clauses appropriately. When two independent clauses are used together without proper punctuation, the result is a run-on sentence. A run-on sentence is a grammatical error.

Bicycles require human energy to move car engines burn fossil fuels.

When two independent clauses are joined by a comma without the right connector, the result is a comma splice. A comma splice is a grammatical error.

Bicycles require human energy to move, car engines burn fossil fuels.

You can correct a run-on sentence or a comma splice in the following ways:

1. Add a period: Bicycles require human energy to move**. Car** engines burn fossil fuels.
2. Add a semicolon: Bicycles require human energy to move**;** car engines burn fossil fuels.
3. Add a coordinator: Bicycles require human energy to move**, but** car engines burn fossil fuels.
4. Add a subordinator: Bicycles require human energy to move **whereas** car engines burn fossil fuels.

English has seven coordinators, known as the FANBOYS

FOR
AND
NOR
BUT
OR
YET
SO

Activity B | Identify each of the following as a grammatically correct sentence (✓), as a run-on sentence (RO), or as a comma splice (CS). Correct each run-on sentence or comma splice using one of the suggested methods.

1. _____ Planes travel faster than cars planes use more energy and create more pollution.
2. _____ Some people are afraid of flying because they are worried about air traffic accidents.
3. _____ Passengers in airplanes can enjoy the in-flight entertainment, drivers need to concentrate on driving.
4. _____ Airplane passengers have to be at the airport long before the departure of their plane that is not necessary for people who travel by car.
5. _____ Car drivers can stop to take a break at any time, but airplane passengers are stuck in the plane for the whole flight.

Activity C | To practise paragraph editing, look back at the paragraph you revised in Activity A under *Increasing Sentence Variety* on page 99. Does it contain any run-on sentences or comma splices? If necessary, correct those run-on sentences using one of the suggested methods.

Activity D | Look back at a paragraph that you wrote earlier in this unit. Does it contain any run-on sentences or comma splices? Once you have completed your editing, exchange it with a partner and check your partner's paragraph for run-on sentences and comma splices. Help each other to correct any problem sentences you find.

UNIT OUTCOME

Writing Assignment: Compare-and-Contrast Essay

Write a compare-and-contrast essay of 350 to 450 words on a topic related to tourism. (Your instructor may give you an alternative length.). Use either APA- or MLA-style in-text citations and a References or Works Cited list.

You may write an essay that answers your Unit Inquiry Question. If you choose to do so, look back at the work you have done in this unit:

- the latest version of your Unit Inquiry Question on page 74;
- the working thesis and introduction you wrote in Activity B on page 96;
- the topic sentences you wrote in Activity C on page 95;
- the ideas you brainstormed on pages 90–91; and
- the conclusion you wrote in Activity B on page 97.

Decide whether you want to include drafts of any of the above in your essay. You may have to revise your writing to integrate these elements into your essay.

If you do not want to write about your Unit Inquiry Question, you may develop a new question or write an essay using one of the following topics instead:

- Compare and contrast travel habits or preferences in Canada with those in another country you are familiar with.
- Compare and contrast the town or city you currently live in with a destination you have visited as a tourist.
- Compare and contrast irresponsible and sustainable tourism practices in a region that you are familiar with.

Use the skills you have developed in this unit to complete the assignment. Follow the steps set out below to ensure that you practise each of your newly acquired skills to write a well-developed compare-and-contrast essay.

1. **Brainstorm**: Use a Venn diagram to generate ideas related to the topic you will write about.
2. **Find outside sources of information**: Select appropriate information from Readings 1 and 2 to support your argument as you learned in Unit 2 (pages 56–58).
3. **Write a thesis statement**: Develop a focused thesis statement that provides a specific answer to your question.

4. **Outline**: Fill in the outline below to plan your first draft.
   - Develop your body paragraphs using the question technique you learned in Unit 2 (pages 62–63).
   - Include information from Readings 1 and 2 in each body paragraph, if appropriate.

Introduction	Question that engages reader: A clear link between your question and your thesis statement: Thesis statement:
Main Body Paragraphs	Topic sentence 1: Information to be included: Concluding sentence 1 (optional):
	Topic sentence 2: Information to be included: Concluding sentence 2 (optional):
Conclusion	Summary and synthesis of main ideas:

5. **Prepare a first draft**: Use your outline to write the first draft of your essay.

   Use AWL and mid-frequency vocabulary from this unit where appropriate. In your first draft, you should

   - focus on getting your ideas down on paper without worrying too much about grammar.
   - skip a section if you get stuck and come back to it later. For example, consider writing the body paragraphs before writing the introduction and conclusion.

6. **Ask for a peer review**: Exchange your first draft with a classmate. Use the Compare-and-Contrast Essay Rubric on page 104 to provide suggestions for improving your classmate's essay. Read your partner's feedback carefully. Ask questions if necessary.
7. **Revise**: Use your partner's feedback to write a second draft of your essay.
8. **Self-check**: Review your essay and use the Compare-and-Contrast Essay Rubric to look for areas in which you could improve your writing.
   - Edit your essay for sentence variety and errors with run-on sentences and comma splices. Make sure that your text is interesting for your reader and the sentence structure is accurate.
   - Check that you have used reporting verbs when integrating other people's ideas into your writing.
   - Edit your essay for correct APA- or MLA-style citations. Make sure you include a References or Works Cited section. Include page numbers for direct quotations.
   - Use spelling and grammar checking features on your word-processing software to catch mistakes.
   - Try reading your essay aloud to catch mistakes or awkward wording.
9. **Compose final draft**: Write a final draft of your essay, incorporating any changes you think will improve it.
   - When possible, leave some time between drafts.
10. **Proofread**: Check the final draft of your essay for any small errors that you may have missed. In particular, look for spelling errors, typos, and punctuation mistakes.

Evaluation: Compare-and-Contrast Essay Rubric

Use the following rubric to evaluate your essay. In which areas do you need to improve most?

E = **Emerging**: frequent difficulty using unit skills; needs a lot more work
D = **Developing**: some difficulty using unit skills; some improvement still required
S = **Satisfactory**: able to use unit skills most of the time; meets average expectations for this level
O = **Outstanding**: exceptional use of unit skills; exceeds expectations for this level

Skill	E	D	S	O
The introduction starts with a thought-provoking question and includes a link to the thesis statement (see Unit 2, pages 60–61).				
The thesis statement is clear (see Unit 2, pages 58–60).				
Each body paragraph starts with a clear topic sentence.				
The essay and all its paragraphs have unity.				
Each body paragraph develops one controlling idea.				
The ideas are organized according to the block or point-by-point pattern.				
Compare-and-contrast connectors have been used to show similarities and differences.				
Information from readings in this unit has been integrated appropriately using reporting verbs.				
AWL and mid-frequency vocabulary items from this unit are used when appropriate and with few mistakes.				
Varied sentences are used to make the text interesting.				
There are few mistakes in terms of run-on sentences and comma splices.				
APA- or MLA-style in-text citations and a References or Works Cited list are formatted correctly.				

Unit Review

Activity A | What do you know about the topic of travel and tourism that you did not know before you started this unit? Discuss with a partner or small group. Be prepared to report what you have learned to the class.

Activity B | Look back at the Unit Inquiry Question you developed at the start of this unit and discuss it with a partner or small group. Then share your answers with the class. Use the following questions to guide you:

1. What ideas did you encounter during this unit that contributed to answering your question?
2. How would you answer your question now?

Activity C | Use the following checklist to review what you have learned in this unit. First decide which 10 skills you think are most important—circle the number beside each of these 10 skills. If you learned a skill in this unit that isn't listed below, write it in the blank row at the end of the checklist. Then put a check mark in the box beside those points you feel you have learned. Be prepared to discuss your choices with the class.

Self-Assessment Checklist	
☐	1. I can talk about travel and tourism.
☐	2. I can write a compare-and-contrast inquiry question.
☐	3. I can use a block or point-by-point pattern to organize similarities and/or differences.
☐	4. I can use compare-and-contrast connectors to show similarities and/or differences.
☐	5. I can evaluate a peer's writing and give feedback for improvement.
☐	6. I can use peer feedback to improve first drafts.
☐	7. I can use my dictionary to learn how to use new words.
☐	8. I can use AWL and mid-frequency vocabulary from this unit.
☐	9. I can use a Venn diagram to find similarities and differences.
☐	10. I can prepare an essay outline using the ideas generated through brainstorming (see Unit 2, pages 55–56).
☐	11. I can use reporting verbs to integrate source information into my own writing.
☐	12. I can avoid plagiarism by submitting only my own work.
☐	13. I can cite my sources using APA or MLA style.
☐	14. I can write topic sentences that clearly state the topic and the controlling idea.

☐	15. I can write an effective introduction that starts with a thought-provoking question.
☐	16. I can write an effective conclusion that synthesizes the main ideas.
☐	17. I can achieve essay and paragraph unity.
☐	18. I can write varied sentences.
☐	19. I can identify and correct run-on sentences and comma splices.
☐	20. I can write a compare-and-contrast essay of four or more paragraphs.
☐	21.

Activity D | Put a check mark in the box beside the vocabulary items from this unit that you feel you can now use with confidence in your writing.

Vocabulary Checklist	
☐ area (n.) AWL	☐ likewise (adv.) 4000
☐ cater (v.) 4000	☐ migrant (n.) AWL
☐ classification (n.) 4000	☐ necessity (n.) 4000
☐ define (v.) AWL	☐ portion (n.) AWL
☐ dispose (v.) AWL	☐ overnight (adv.) 4000
☐ destination (n.) 4000	☐ rafting (n.) 6000
☐ economic (adj.) AWL	☐ receipt (n.) 4000
☐ environment (n.) AWL	☐ revolution (n.) AWL
☐ hiking (n.) 5000	☐ sustainable (adj.) AWL
☐ impact (n.) AWL	☐ vacation (n.) 5000

UNIT 4

Immunity

Biology

KEY LEARNING OUTCOMES

- Creating an inquiry question for examining cause and effect
- Using vocabulary learning strategies
- Brainstorming using a flow chart
- Using phrases to integrate information from outside sources
- Avoiding plagiarism by using sentence patterns to integrate source material
- Using adverbials
- Using strategies to write a cause-and-effect introduction
- Concluding an essay with a thought-provoking comment
- Revising an essay
- Writing a cause-and-effect essay

EXPLORING IDEAS

Introduction

When we get sick, a lot of the symptoms we experience, such as a fever or a cough, are actually signs that our bodies are fighting bacteria or a virus that entered our bodies. We may not feel good, but our bodies are doing exactly what they need to be doing to help us feel better. But how can we avoid getting sick in the first place?

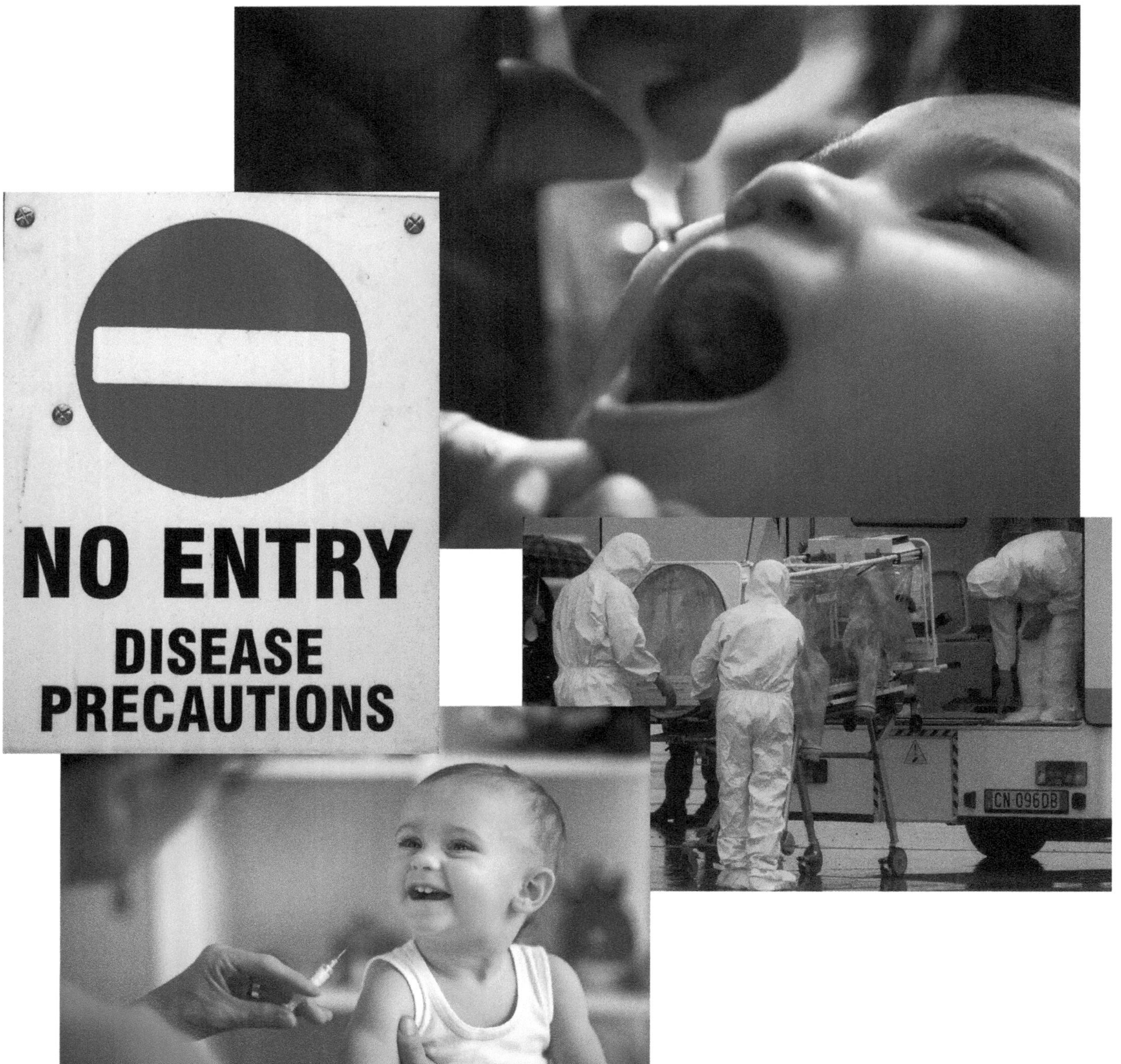

Activity A | Read the dictionary entries below for *immunity* and *epidemic* and then discuss the questions that follow with a partner or small group.

> **im·mun·ity** /ɪ'mjuːnəti/ *noun* [U, C] (*pl.* -ies) **1** the body's ability to avoid or not be affected by infection and disease: **~ (to sth)** *immunity to infection* ◇ **~ (against sth)** *The vaccine provides longer immunity against flu.* ➲ COLLOCATIONS at ILL **2 ~ (from sth)** the state of being protected from sth: *The spies were all granted immunity from prosecution.* ◇ ***parliamentary/congressional immunity*** (= protection against particular laws that is given to politicians) ◇ *Officials of all member states receive certain privileges and immunities.* ➲ see also DIPLOMATIC IMMUNITY

> **epi·dem·ic** /ˌepɪ'demɪk/ *noun* **1** a large number of cases of a particular disease happening at the same time in a particular community: *the outbreak of a flu epidemic* ◇ *an epidemic of measles* **2** a sudden rapid increase in how often sth bad happens: *an epidemic of crime in the inner cities* ▸ **epi·dem·ic** *adj.*: *Car theft is now reaching* ***epidemic proportions.*** ➲ compare PANDEMIC

1. What do you know about the body's immune system?
2. What causes diseases?
3. Which diseases do you consider serious? What makes them serious?
4. How do diseases spread?
5. What causes epidemics?
6. Which of the photographs on the previous page show examples of how we can avoid the spread of disease? Explain the reasons for your choices.

Activity B | Think about the causes and the effects of an epidemic. Then fill in the graphic organizer below. Discuss your ideas with a partner or small group.

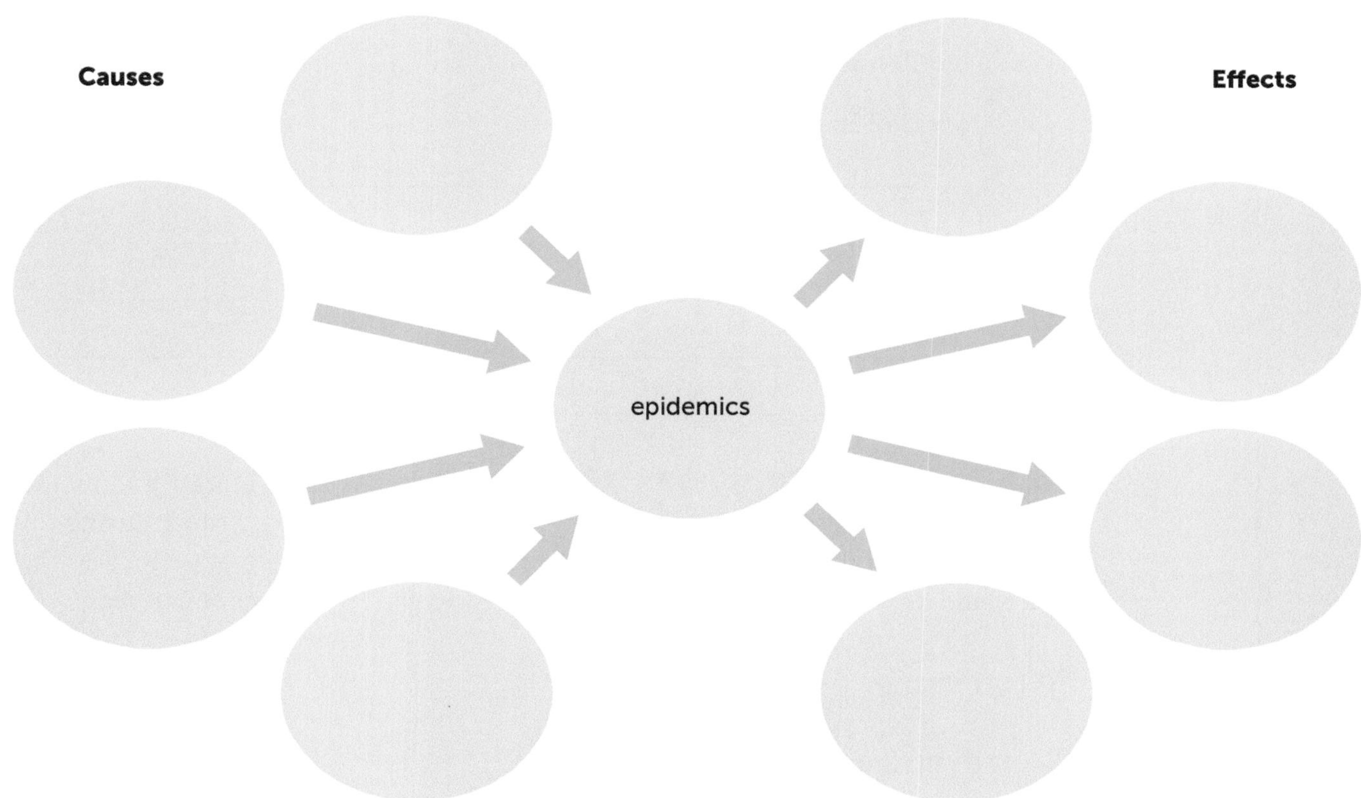

Activity C | Writing Task: Paragraph Exploring Causes or Effects | Write a short paragraph about the causes or the effects of an epidemic.

Fostering Inquiry

Analyzing Causes and Effects

Analyzing the reasons why an event takes place, why people behave in particular ways, or why a certain phenomenon occurs helps us to understand the relationship between different aspects of an issue or situation. Similarly, studying the effects of actions or events helps us to understand how actions or events are related to each other. Good inquiry questions that focus on the reasons or causes for something start with *why*, whereas good effect inquiry questions start with *what*.

Activity A | What do you want to know more about in relation to the body's response to disease and the field of biology? For example, *What happens when diseases spread quickly?* or *Why do diseases spread so quickly?*

1. Write down two or three questions you have about immunity.
2. In a small group, share your questions.
3. Choose one question to be your guiding inquiry question for this unit. Your inquiry question can be different from the other group members' questions. The focus of your question may change as you work your way through this unit.
4. Write your inquiry question here and refer to it as you complete the activities in this unit.

   My Unit Inquiry Question:

   ____

   ____

   ____

   ____

   ____

Activity B | Writing Task: Freewriting | Write for at least five minutes on the topic of your Unit Inquiry Question. Do not stop writing during this time. After five minutes, read what you have written and circle two or three ideas that you would like to explore further in order to answer your Unit Inquiry Question.

Structure

Cause-and-Effect Essay

The purpose of a cause-and-effect essay is to discuss the causal relationships between events or phenomena. A cause-and-effect essay usually focuses on either the causes or the consequences of an event or phenomenon, but not both. It is important to understand that causal relationships are two-way relationships. For example, on the one hand, we can consider the effects of an epidemic (e.g., many deaths). On the other hand, we can look at the cause of a patient's death (e.g., an epidemic).

Activity A | With a partner or small group, read the example of a student paragraph that analyzes the causes of human fear of a major flu epidemic. Answer the questions that follow.

Some people believe that the Canadian government intentionally overreacted during the swine flu outbreak in 2009 to encourage all Canadians to get the swine flu vaccine. However, considering the effects of the Spanish flu pandemic of 1918, the government's reaction seems reasonable. The 1918 flu was extremely deadly. Between 50 and 100 million people died during the 1918–1919 pandemic ("1918 flu pandemic," 2016). That means three to five percent of the world's population died during that outbreak. In other words, more people died from that virus than died fighting in World War I or from the bubonic plague (the Black Death) between 1347 and 1351. As a result, there was great fear that the 2009 swine flu pandemic could have a similar effect. This fear was based on the fact that both viruses were new viruses at the time, so humans had not yet developed any immunity. Moreover, the Spanish flu had had a serious effect on the economy since most people who got sick were between 15 and 44 years old (Brainerd & Siegler, 2002). Most viruses affect mainly the very young or the elderly. However, during the Spanish flu pandemic, 99 percent of the people who died were under 65; 50 percent of the victims were between 20 and 40 years old ("1918 Flu Pandemic," 2016). In the United States, for instance, over one percent of the male population between 25 and 34 died because of that pandemic. As a result, businesses not related to health care lost a significant number of workers as well as a significant portion of their revenue (Brainerd & Siegler, 2002; Garrett, 2007). If we understand the effects of the 1918 flu pandemic, we can understand the Canadian government's reaction to the swine flu in 2009.

References

1918 flu pandemic. (n.d.). Retrieved May 12, 2016, from Wikipedia: https://en.wikipedia.org/w/index.php?title=1918_flu_pandemic&oldid=719921705

Billings, M. (1997). *The influenza pandemic of 1918*. Retrieved from https://virus.stanford.edu/uda/

Brainerd, E., & Siegler, M. V. (2002). *The economic effects of the 1918 influenza epidemic*. Retrieved from http://www.birdflubook.org/resources/brainerd1.pdf

Garrett, T. A. (2007). *Economic effects of the 1918 influenza pandemic: Implications for a modern-day pandemic*. Retrieved from https://www.stlouisfed.org/~/media/Files/PDFs/Community%20Development/Research%20Reports/pandemic_flu_report.pdf

1. What is the main idea of this paragraph?
2. What kind of information is used to illustrate the author's point?

Cause-and-Effect Essay Structure

A cause-and-effect essay follows the standard essay structure described in Unit 2 (pages 38–41) with an introduction, two or more body paragraphs, and a conclusion. The introduction contains a thesis statement that outlines the key points to be focused on in the essay. Each body paragraph contains a single controlling idea that is directly related to the thesis statement. The conclusion summarizes the main points of the essay.

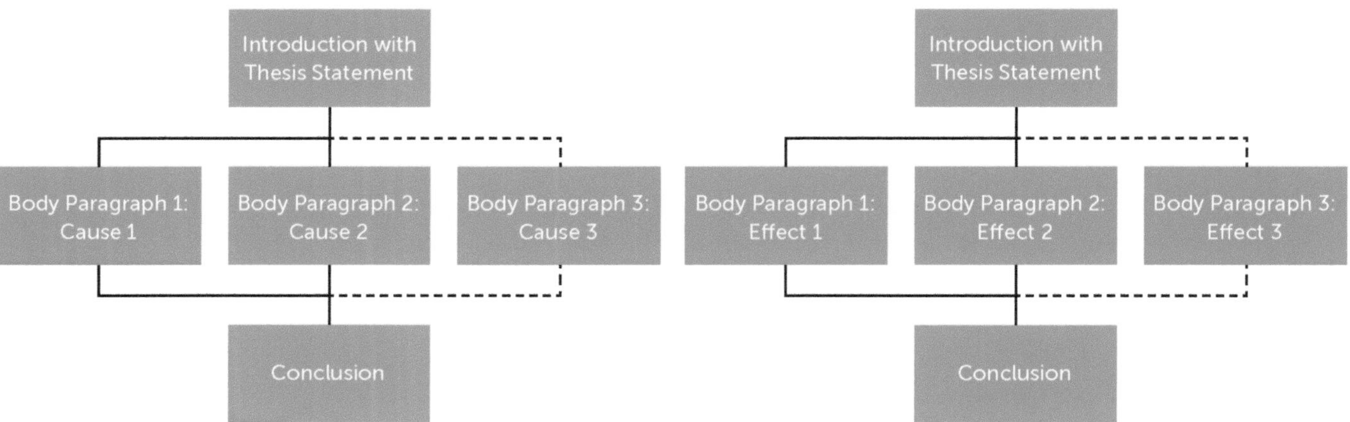

FIGURE 4.1 Compare-and-effect essay structure

Activity B | The following essay illustrates the cause-and-effect essay structure shown above in Figure 4.1. Read the essay closely, paying attention to the organizational pattern, and answer the questions that follow.

The 2013–2016 Ebola Outbreak: Why Was it So Devastating?

In December 2013, the worst-ever Ebola outbreak began, and it lasted well into 2016. As a result of the epidemic, more than 28,000 people, mainly in West Africa, were infected with the virus; more than 11,000 people died (World Health Organization [WHO], 2016). These deaths left more than 16,000 children without one or both parents or without their primary caregiver (UNICEF, 2015). These deaths had and will have a significant economic impact on the countries most affected by this epidemic. Experts expect these countries to see a significant reduction in their GDP, an indicator of a nation's economic performance. The estimates range from a reduction in the GDP by 4.9 percent in Guinea up to 18.7 percent in Liberia between 2014 and 2017 (United Nations Development Group–Western and Central Africa, 2015).

Because of these devastating consequences, we must examine what caused this epidemic and what led to its rapid spread across the region.

The Ebola virus itself has certain characteristics that caused this epidemic to be so deadly. First of all, there is no cure nor vaccine for the virus. Once a patient has been infected and becomes ill, doctors and nurses can only treat the symptoms. This means helping the patient stay as strong as possible so that the body can fight the infection by itself. Consequently, 90 percent of all Ebola patients die (Médecins Sans Frontières [MSF], n.d.). Furthermore, the infection is very difficult to diagnose for two reasons. The early symptoms of the disease are similar to those of other common diseases, such as cholera and malaria (Stylianou, 2014; Weizman, 2015). Also, only an analysis of a patient's sample can confirm an Ebola infection (MSF, n.d.). Finally, although one cannot catch Ebola from breathing the air near an Ebola patient, the patient's sweat and blood are extremely infectious. That means if relatives or health care workers look after an Ebola patient without knowing it, they can easily become infected (MSF, n.d.). Therefore, the features of the virus itself represent one reason that the epidemic became so serious.

Another reason for the severity of the epidemic was the state of the local health care systems. Even before the Ebola outbreak began, health care facilities in Guinea, Liberia, and Sierra Leone were not well equipped. They had trouble dealing with less serious but more common diseases, such as malaria and cholera (Weizman, 2015). Therefore, when the outbreak hit, the health care systems did not have the basic resources and equipment to treat or transport patients (Weizman, 2015). Furthermore, the ratio of doctors to patients is much lower in these countries compared to developed countries. For example, Liberia has one doctor per 70,000 people, Sierra Leone has one doctor per 45,000 people, and Guinea has one doctor per 10,000 people. In contrast, there is one doctor for every 410 people in the United States and one doctor for every 260 people in Germany (Stylianou, 2014). This low doctor–patient ratio led to overcrowding of facilities. As a result, there were long line-ups and waiting periods for people who needed medical attention (Weizman, 2015). Because many Ebola patients were actually health workers themselves, the situation got worse, and there were more shortages (WHO, 2015). All health workers (not just doctors and nurses) were 21 to 32 times more likely to be infected with the Ebola virus. Fifty percent of all these infected health care workers were nurses or nurse's aides. In total, more than 800 health workers contracted Ebola, and more than 60 percent of those workers died (WHO, 2015). In brief, a struggling health care system was unable to deal with the epidemic.

The Ebola outbreak was extremely devastating to West African countries. This was in part because there is no vaccine or effective treatment for the virus and because it is also very challenging to diagnose an infection. Furthermore, the ill-equipped health care systems in the hardest-hit countries combined with the fact that many victims were also health workers made the situation worse. We cannot prevent future outbreaks of Ebola, but we can certainly learn from this devastating outbreak in order to better handle future outbreaks of this or other infectious diseases if and when they occur.

References

Médecins Sans Frontières. (n.d.). *FAQ: The top ten questions about Ebola*. Retrieved from http://www.msf.ca/en/faq-top-ten-questions-about-ebola

Stylianou, N. (2014, November 27). How world's worst Ebola outbreak began with one boy's death. *BBC News*. Retrieved from http://www.bbc.com/news/world-africa-30199004

UNICEF. (2015). *Impact of Ebola*. Retrieved from http://www.unicef.org/emergencies/ebola/75941_76129.html

United Nations Development Group–Western and Central Africa. (2015). *The socio-economic impact of Ebola virus disease in West African countries*. Retrieved from http://www.africa.undp.org/content/dam/rba/docs/Reports/ebola-west-africa.pdf

Weizman, M. J. (2015, August 15). Analysis of the 2014 Ebola outbreak in Guinea, Sierra Leone, and Liberia. *Peace & Conflict Monitor*. Retrieved from http://www.monitor.upeace.org/innerpg.cfm?id_article=1089

World Health Organization. (2015, May 21). *Health worker Ebola infections in Guinea, Liberia and Sierra Leone*. Retrieved from http://www.who.int/hrh/documents/21may2015_web_final.pdf

World Health Organization. (2016, March 30). *Ebola situation report*. Retrieved from http://apps.who.int/ebola/current-situation/ebola-situation-report-30-march-2016

1. What is the main idea of the essay?
2. How is the topic introduced?
3. Are both causes and effects mentioned in the essay? If so, where are causes discussed and where are effects mentioned?
4. What evidence is used to explain or illustrate the causes and/or effects discussed in the body paragraphs?
5. What connectors does the writer use to link information on causes and/or effects?
6. What technique does the writer use to conclude the essay?

Language Tip

Using Cause-and-Effect Connectors

Connectors play an important role in helping your reader understand the connections between ideas in your text. In a cause-and-effect essay, appropriate connectors communicate the direction of the causal relationship quickly to the reader: is the focus on the cause or the effect of something?

accordingly	because	for	so
as	because of + NOUN	for this/that reason	therefore
as a result	consequently	hence	thus
as a result of + NOUN	due to/because of the fact that	since	

The list of connectors above includes some common examples, but note that these are not the only cause-and-effect connectors used in English.

Activity C | Writing Task: Cause or Effect Paragraph | Write a short paragraph in which you describe the causes or the effects of a serious disease that you are familiar with.

Activity D | Exchange your paragraph with a partner. Read your partner's paragraph and use the following questions to provide feedback.

1. What is the main idea of this paragraph?
2. Does it focus on causes or effects?
3. Does the paragraph contain good details to illustrate the causes or effects?
4. What do you like best about this paragraph?
5. How would you improve this paragraph?

Activity E | Revisit your Unit Inquiry Question on page 110. What new ideas have you thought of that will help you answer your question? Share your ideas with a partner or small group. At this point, you may consider revising your Unit Inquiry Question.

ACADEMIC READING

Vocabulary

Vocabulary Skill: Using Vocabulary Learning Strategies

Many students find it challenging to learn new vocabulary in a way that allows them to use it in their writing. Choosing the right strategy or strategies depending on your needs is one way to make the task of learning new words easier.

- **Choosing words**: Decide which words you want to learn. In each unit of this textbook, 10 AWL and 10 mid-frequency level words have been chosen for you to give you the opportunity to learn them in context. When you choose your own words to learn, select words that are worth knowing for your purposes of learning English.
- **Choosing what aspect to focus on**: Understanding meaning is of course important when you learn new words. However, there are other aspects to knowing words well:
  - » *knowing the grammatical functions of a word*: What structural patterns does the word fit into?
  - » *recognizing collocations*: Which words does the new word typically occur with?

    Tip: A collocations dictionary, such as the *Oxford Collocations Dictionary for students of English*, will provide this information. (See *Vocabulary Skill* in Unit 5, page 154 for more information on collocations.)
  - » *understanding limits of use*: When is it appropriate to use the word (e.g., in writing, orally, formally, or informally)?
- **Planning repetition**: We need to see new words more than once before we learn them. Plan a schedule to revisit and review each new word.
- **Analyzing word parts**: Many English words are made up of different parts: the stem or root of the word and the affixes (parts before or after the stem). *Inequality*, for example, is made up of *in-* + *equal* + *-ity*. Analyze the parts that make up new words to understand them better.
- **Using context**: Awareness of the context in which you encounter a new word helps you to understand its meaning. Ask yourself these questions when you are trying to guess the meaning of a word from context:
  - » What is the topic of the text?
  - » Is the word a verb, a noun, an adjective, or an adverb?
  - » What does the context of the sentence and the paragraph tell you about the meaning of the word?
  - » Which words come directly before and after the word whose meaning you are trying to determine?
- **Using parallels with other languages**: When you learn a new word in English, try to find similarities with other languages you know.
  - » Does the word have the same stem as a word in another language (e.g., *equality* in English and *égalité* in French)?
  - » Does the English word look different from words in another language you know, but function in the same way in its meaning and grammar?

    Tip: Assume words work similarly in the different languages you know unless you see information in the context in which you see the word or in your dictionary that tells you the words do not work in the same way.

Source: Based on Nation, I. S. P. (2001). *Learning vocabulary in another language.* Cambridge, UK: Cambridge University Press.

Activity A | Review the list of vocabulary learning strategies below and select the ones you have used before. Discuss with a partner or small group why you have or have not used certain strategies in the past.

1. Carefully choosing words to learn
2. Choosing what aspects of the word to focus on
3. Planning repetition
4. Analyzing word parts (stems and affixes)
5. Using context to guess the meaning
6. Using parallels with other languages

Activity B | Apply each of the vocabulary learning strategies at least once as you work with the new words in this unit. Take notes of how and when you applied them and discuss your experience with a partner or small group.

1. Carefully choose one unfamiliar word from Reading 1 that is not bolded (i.e., not an AWL or mid-frequency word for this unit). Why did you choose this word?

   Word: ____________ Why? ____________________

2. Now choose two AWL and two mid-frequency words and look them up in your dictionary with a focus on aspects of each word other than meaning. What did you discover?

   AWL:

   Word 1: ____________ Discovery: ____________________

   Word 2: ____________ Discovery: ____________________

   Mid-frequency words:

   Word 1: ____________ Discovery: ____________________

   Word 2: ____________ Discovery: ____________________

3. Plan how often and when you want to review your new words from this unit.

   ____

   ____

   ____

   ____

4. Find one AWL or mid-frequency word of which you can analyze the stem and/or the affixes to help understand or remember the meaning of this word.

   ____

5. Choose a word you do not know in Reading 1 (that is not bolded) and try to guess its meaning from context.

   Word: ____________________

   What helped you to guess the meaning? ______________________________

   ____

6. Check to see if any of the AWL or mid-frequency words in the unit work in the same way in terms of meaning and grammar in English as in another language you know.

   English word: ____________________ Same as: ____________________

Learning Strategy

Creating Mental Connections

Good learning strategies help you improve your English. When are learning new words that you want to use in your writing or your speech, creating mental connections is an excellent strategy to use. To help you learn these new words, try the following approaches to creating mental connections:

- **Grouping**: Group or organize new vocabulary words in one or more of the following ways.
  1. part of speech (e.g., noun, verb)
  2. topic (e.g., media, technology, tourism, or immunity)
  3. practical function (e.g., reporting verbs—see Unit 1, page 8)
  4. similar meaning (e.g., *respond* and *react*)
  5. opposite meaning (e.g., *cause* and *effect*)

  Note: There are many other ways to group words depending on the context in which you see them.

- **Associating and elaborating**: Connect the new words to words you already know. For example, you can write the key concept in the centre of a concept map and show links between the concept and other words or phrases using lines, as illustrated in the semantic map for *immunity* in Figure 4.2.

- **Placing new words into a new context**: Create a new sentence or a story to help you remember the new word. This is different from guessing a word in the context in which you see it for the first time.

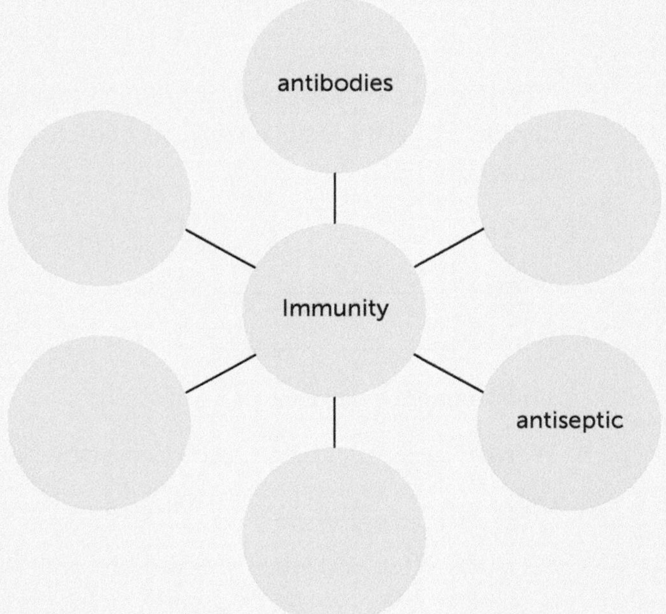

FIGURE 4.2 Semantic map

Try using these strategies to create new connections when you try to learn the new vocabulary words in this unit.

Source: Based on ideas in Oxford, R. L. (1990). *Language learning strategies: What every teacher should know.* Boston, MA: Heinle & Heinle.

Vocabulary Preview: The Academic Word List

Activity C | Read the example sentences below and try to figure out the meaning of the words in bold. Work with a partner or small group to explain the meaning in your own words. Example sentences drawn from Reading 1 are indicated with an asterisk (*).

1. a. She has **acquired** a good knowledge of English. (oxforddictionaries.com)
   b. Abstract art is an **acquired** taste. (oxforddictionaries.com)

   Meaning:

   ____

   ____

2. a. The south of the country was worst **affected** by the drought. (*Oxford Advanced Learner's Dictionary*)
   b. The condition **affects** one in five women. (*Oxford Advanced Learner's Dictionary*)

   Meaning:

   ____

   ____

3. a. Once pathogens are inside the body, the body sends **chemical** signals to coordinate an attack and to transport specialized cells to the infection. (*)
   b. Heat and **chemicals** such as soap, vinegar, and rubbing alcohol kill pathogens that are outside of the body. (*)

   Meaning:

   ____

   ____

4. a. Break the problem down into its **component** parts. (*Oxford Advanced Learner's Dictionary*)
   b. If any one of these **components** fail, the whole system fails. (oxforddictionaries.com)

   Meaning:

   ____

   ____

5. a. Vaccination allows a person to develop immunity against an illness without actually **contracting** the disease. (*)
   b. If you think you've **contracted** an infectious disease, contact your doctor. (oxforddictionaries.com)

   Meaning:

   ____

   ____

6. a. The immune system uses **physical** barriers to keep pathogens out. (*)
   b. The ordeal has affected both her mental and **physical** health. (*Oxford Advanced Learner's Dictionary*)

   Meaning:

   ____

   ____

7. a. These days we **rely** heavily on computers to organize our work. (*Oxford Advanced Learner's Dictionary*)
   b. The charity **relies** on donations to provide its services free to clients. (oxforddictionaries.com)

   Meaning:

   ____

   ____

8. a. When you are exposed to a pathogen and have not been vaccinated, you get sick because the pathogen reproduces faster than your immune system can **respond**. (*)
   b. The government **responded** by banning all future demonstrations. (*Oxford Advanced Learner's Dictionary*)

   Meaning:

   ____

   ____

9. a. The skin also secretes oil and sweat. Many pathogens cannot **survive** in this kind of environment. (*)
   b. Many birds didn't **survive** the severe winter. (*Oxford Advanced Learner's Dictionary*)

   Meaning:

   ____

   ____

10. a. Antibiotics are medicines that **target** pathogens and keep them from growing or reproducing. (*)
    b. An online store can offer a much bigger selection because it can **target** a much bigger audience. (oxforddictionaries.com)

    Meaning:

    ____

    ____

Vocabulary Preview: Mid-frequency Vocabulary

Activity D | Read the following sentences from Reading 1 and choose the correct meaning for each bolded word.

1. Scientists have developed many different ways to control the spread of disease. Cleaning supplies, medicine, and **vaccines** are technologies that help to prevent against sickness or treat people who are already sick.
   a. a substance that treats diseases
   b. a substance that causes diseases
   c. a substance that protects from diseases
2. Vaccines **artificially** produce immunity.
   a. in a way that copies something natural
   b. in a way that is entirely natural
   c. in a way that is extremely skillful
3. If the pathogen enters your body after you are vaccinated, your memory B cells make **antibodies** right away.
   a. a type of injection to fight disease
   b. a medication to fight infections
   c. a substance produced by the body to fight disease
4. The skin blocks any **invading** pathogens.
   a. unfamiliar but peaceful
   b. new and unpleasant
   c. entering without permission
5. The skin also secretes sweat, which makes the skin **acidic**.
   a. alkali
   b. with a pH of less than seven
   c. having a very sour taste
6. Just as a castle's walls have doors and windows, your skin also has openings, for example, your eyes, nose, ears, mouth. **Membranes** in these organs use a sticky liquid to trap pathogens before they move into the body.
   a. a thin cover inside the body
   b. an opening or hole in the body
   c. a kind of pathogen
7. **Antibiotics** work in a variety of ways. For example, penicillin makes bacteria unable to form cell walls.
   a. a kind of operation
   b. a medication that kills bacteria
   c. a drug with serious side effects
8. These medicines target bacteria or **fungi** and keep them from growing or reproducing.
   a. a very small animal
   b. a plant with nice flowers
   c. a mould-like organism

9. Antibiotic resistance occurs when bacteria **mutate** so that they are no longer affected by antibiotics. This makes the bacteria resistant to the effects of medication.
   a. to develop a new structure
   b. to improve a design
   c. to make less effective

10. Without a strong cell wall, the microbe's **nutrients** leak out, and the microbe bursts.
   a. the parts of food that make it taste good
   b. a kind of poison
   c. something that nourishes plants and animals

Reading 1

The reading "Immunity" is an excerpt from the textbook *Holt McDougal Biology* by Stephen Nowicki. This textbook is used in biology classes in Canadian high schools.

Activity A | How does the human immune system work? Complete the first two columns of the KWL chart below with information you already know (K) about the immune system and what you want (W) to learn about it. After you have read the text, return to this chart to write down what you learned (L) about the immune system from this text.

Know	Want to Know	Learned

Activity B | The reading contains three figures related to the topic of the text. Study the figures and try to predict what this reading might be about.

Activity C | Read the following textbook excerpt straight through. Then read it again and highlight important information related to what you know, want to know, or did not know about the immune system. You may want to use three separate colours of highlighters. Add information that is new to you to the third column in the KWL chart above and use it to answer the questions that follow the text.

READING

Immunity

Immune System

1 The immune system is the body system that fights off infection and pathogens[1]. Just as a castle has several lines of defence, so does your body's immune system. The immune system **relies** on **physical** barriers to keep pathogens out. However, when pathogens get past the physical barriers, the warrior cells of the immune system travel through the lymphatic[2] and circulatory systems to reach the site of infection.

2 Your skin is your body's first line of defence. Like a castle's outer wall, the skin surrounds and protects your insides. The skin **physically** blocks **invading** pathogens. The skin also secretes oil and sweat, which make the skin **acidic** and can cause the cells of pathogens to burst. Many pathogens cannot **survive** in this kind of environment.

3 Just as a castle's walls have doors and windows, your skin also has openings. For example, your eyes, nose, ears, mouth, and excretory organs are open to the environment, and so they need extra protection. Mucous **membranes** in these organs use cilia (hair-like structures) that are covered with a sticky liquid to trap pathogens before they move into the body, as shown in Figure 4.3.

4 Even with skin and mucous membranes to protect you, some pathogens still get into the body. Once pathogens are inside, the immune system relies on the circulatory system to send **chemical** signals to coordinate an attack and to transport specialized cells to the infection.

[...]

[1] bacteria, viruses, or other microorganisms that can cause disease

[2] connected with lymph or involved in moving it around the body; lymph is a clear liquid containing white blood cells that helps to clean the tissues of the body and helps to prevent infections from spreading

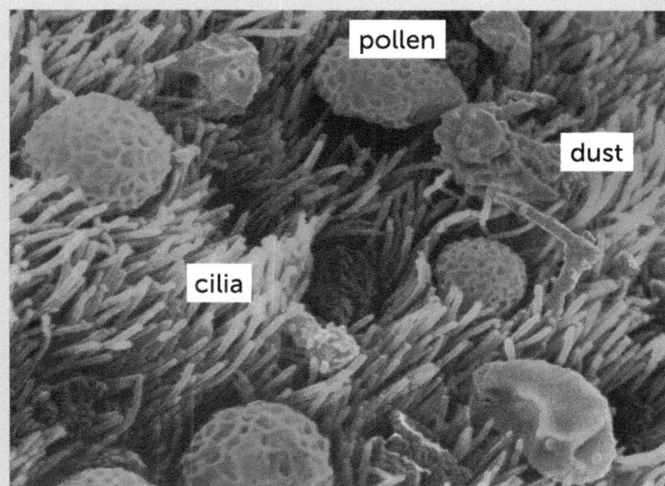

FIGURE 4.3 Cilia that line the throat capture foreign particles

Immunity and Technology

5 Because infectious diseases are spread from person to person, the risk of getting sick increases when there are many people in one area. Luckily, scientists have developed many different ways to control the spread of disease. Cleaning supplies, medicine, and vaccines are technologies that help to prevent against sickness or treat people who are already sick.

Many Methods Are Used to Control Pathogens

6 Because pathogens can have such a negative effect on health, scientists have developed many ways to kill pathogens that our immune system might otherwise have a hard time fighting off. One way to prevent infection is to keep your environment clean. Cleaning can kill pathogens before they ever have a chance to enter your body and make you sick.

7 Heat and **chemicals** kill pathogens that are outside of the body. Antiseptics are chemicals, such as soap, vinegar, and rubbing alcohol that kill pathogens. Rubbing alcohol, for example, weakens cell membranes. Without a strong cell membrane, the microbe's **nutrients** leak out, and the microbe bursts. Antiseptics are not specific, meaning that they kill many different types of pathogens.

8 Once pathogens enter the body, sometimes they can be killed with medicines. **Antibiotics** are medicines that **target** bacteria or **fungi** and keep them from growing or reproducing. Antibiotics work in a variety of ways. For example, penicillin makes bacteria unable to form cell walls. The bacteria cannot divide successfully, and they burst, as shown in Figure 4.4.

9 Unlike antiseptics, antibiotics target one type of bacterium or fungus. As antibiotic use has become more common, antibiotic resistant bacteria have evolved. [...] Antibiotic resistance occurs when bacteria **mutate** so that they are no longer **affected** by antibiotics. Mutations make the bacteria resistant to the effects of antibiotics. When bacteria become resistant, scientists must find new medicines that can kill these mutant bacteria.

Vaccines **Artificially** Produce Acquired Immunity

10 Vaccination cannot cure a person who is sick because vaccines only work to prevent infection. Vaccination allows a person to develop memory cells and **acquired** immunity against an illness without actually **contracting** the disease. A vaccine is a substance that contains the antigen of a pathogen. The antigen causes your immune system to produce memory cells, but you will not get sick. You do not get sick because the pathogen is weakened, and it cannot reproduce or attack your cells. When you are exposed to a pathogen and have not been vaccinated, you get sick because the pathogen reproduces faster than your immune system can **respond**. You stop being sick when your B or T cells win the fight over the infection. If the pathogen enters your body after you are vaccinated, your memory B cells make **antibodies** right away, as shown in Figure 4.5. If you have not been vaccinated, your body must go through the entire immune response, and the pathogen has enough time to make you feel sick.

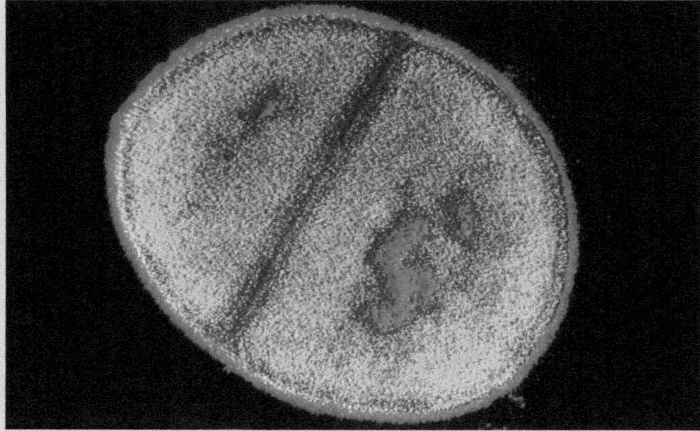

FIGURE 4.4 Antibiotics have killed the bottom cell by weakening its cell wall and causing it to burst

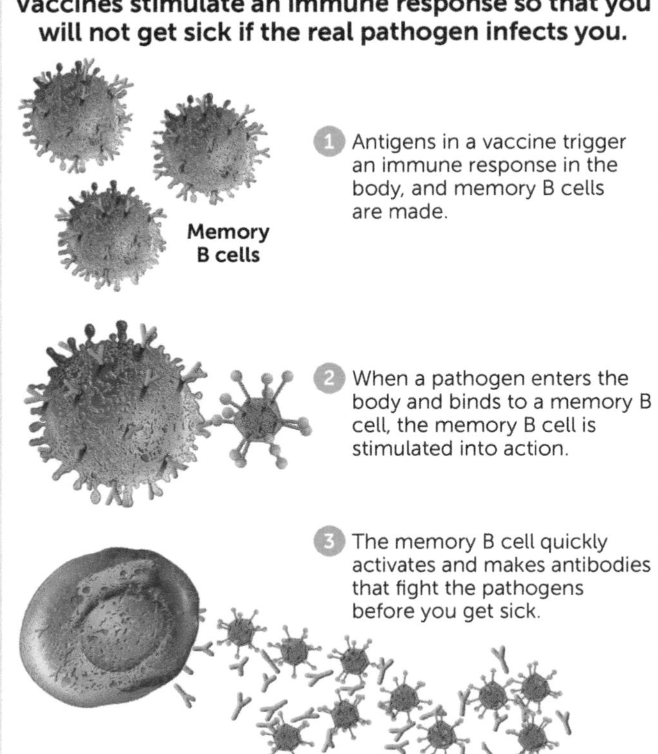

FIGURE 4.5 Vaccine response

11 There are four main types of vaccines.

- Some vaccines contain whole dead bacteria or viruses.
- Live attenuated vaccines contain weak living pathogens.
- **Component** vaccines use only the parts of the pathogen that contain the antigen, such as the protein coat of a virus that has had its genetic material removed.
- Toxoid vaccines are made from inactivated bacterial toxins, which are chemicals a bacterium produces that cause a person to become ill.

Source: Adapted from Nowicki, S. (2015). *Holt McDougal biology* (pp. 885-886, 894, 896). Boston, MA: Houghton Mifflin Harcourt.

Activity D | The following questions are based on the textbook excerpt you just read. Discuss your answers with a partner or small group.

1. How does the body try to prevent pathogens from entering the human body?

   ____

   ____

   ____

2. Complete the chart below with information about how technology helps to prevent the spread of diseases.

Technology	How It Prevents the Spread of Diseases
Antiseptics	
Antibiotics	
Vaccines	

Critical Thinking

Bloom's Taxonomy—*Analysis*

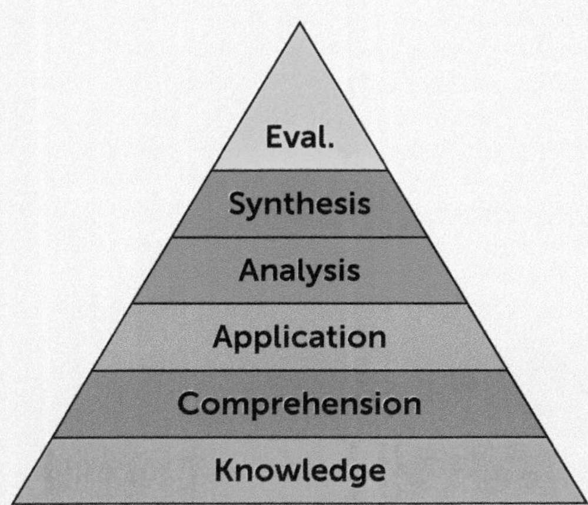

The fourth level of thinking in Bloom's taxonomy is *analysis*. When you analyze a situation or text, you break it down into its smaller parts and think about how the smaller parts relate to the whole. Determining causes and effects requires careful analysis because of the specific logical relationship between them.

As you read or think about a topic, ask yourself questions like

- What are the different parts of this text or situation?
- Can I put the relevant details or information into categories?
- How are the details or pieces of information related to each other?
- How are the details or pieces of information related to the main idea(s)?
- Why...? (Most questions that start with *why* will prompt analysis.)

Source: Bloom, B. S., Engelhart, M. D., Furst, E. J., Hill, W. H., & Krathwohl, D. R. (1956). *Taxonomy of educational objectives: The classification of educational goals. Handbook 1: Cognitive domain*. London, UK: Longman.

Reading 2

The next reading, "Asking for an Outbreak of Preventable Diseases" is an excerpt from an article published in the Canadian newsmagazine *Maclean's*. This magazine is published every week and contains articles on a wide range of topics.

Activity A | Read the excerpt and highlight all the relevant details about the issue. Make notes in the margin about how the details are related to each other and to the main idea. Use that information to answer the questions that follow.

READING

Asking for an Outbreak of Preventable Diseases

With vaccination rates plummeting, are anxious parents putting everyone at risk?

1 On April 8, 2012, Pierre Lavallée took a call from Quebec's public health office. Lavallée was into his fifth and last year as principal at Marie-Rivier high school in Drummondville, a town of about 67,000 an hour's drive east of Montreal. He learned that a school employee had gone to the emergency room with a fever and rash the day before. Doctors quickly isolated the woman and rushed her to intensive care, where she was diagnosed with

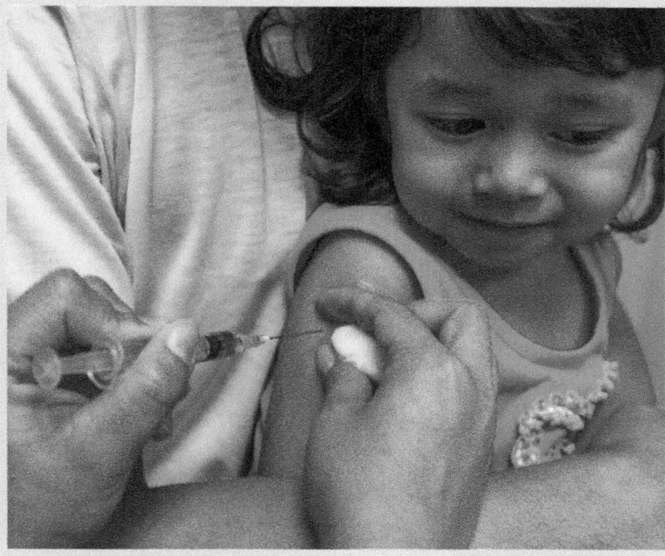

measles,[2] a highly contagious and potentially deadly virus. According to the World Health Organization, measles was eradicated from the Americas in 2002. [...] Thus began what the Quebec government calls by far the worst measles outbreak in the Americas in 20 years. Over the next eight months, 763 cases were reported in the province, the vast majority in Mauricie and Centre-du-Quebec, a region that includes Drummondville. Roughly 11 percent of those who were infected were hospitalized. Even a few who were inoculated as children caught the virus. [...]

2 Since routine immunization began, infectious diseases that once plagued us—measles, mumps,[3] diphtheria,[4] polio—have all but disappeared. For a growing number of people who haven't seen them first-hand, anxiety about vaccines is replacing fear of the disease. Parents are increasingly delaying their kids' shots, or cherry-picking certain vaccines and refusing others. A small, vocal minority avoids all vaccines, often out of the discredited belief that childhood immunization can cause autism. [...]

---

[2] an infectious disease, especially of children, that causes fever and small red spots that cover the whole body

[3] a disease, especially of children, that causes painful swellings in the neck

[4] a serious infectious disease of the throat that causes difficulty in breathing

3 Public health experts say that about 95 percent of a population has to be vaccinated to provide what's called "herd immunity." This is reached when enough people are vaccinated to stop a contagious disease. As vaccination rates continue to fall, preventable diseases might start to reappear. "Measles is the one we'd expect to see first, because it's so infectious," says Dr. Kumanan Wilson, Canada Research Chair in public health policy at the Ottawa Hospital Research Institute, University of Ottawa. "Hopefully we will see this resolved before polio or worse emerge."

4 Today in Canada, measles is extremely rare. In the last decade, the country typically saw fewer than a dozen cases per year, according to Dr. John Spika, director general of the Centre for Immunization and Respiratory Infectious Diseases at the Public Health Agency of Canada (PHAC); [...] Quebec first started seeing a small number of measles cases in early 2011, but they followed a typical pattern: travellers returning from other parts of the world, like France. A measles epidemic has been intense there since 2008 due to low vaccination rates. "We saw a few cases, and then they died out," Spika says. "It wasn't until April that it became self-sustained." [...]

5 Public health workers wondered what made this school susceptible. ... About 85 percent of people at the school were immunized—lower than the 95 percent health officials aim for. However, the rates were not a lot lower than schools elsewhere in the province, where vaccination rates vary from 63 to 93 percent.

6 That picture continues across Canada. Only Ontario, New Brunswick, and Manitoba require that kids receive some vaccinations before attending school (all including measles), but even in those provinces, parents can opt out on medical or religious grounds, or simply for reasons of conscience. [...] In Canada, it's hard to know for sure how good our coverage is, because no national tracking method exists. Experts have been working on a public health information system called Panorama for almost a decade now. This system could follow vaccination uptake; until it becomes fully operational, vaccinations are tracked by public health agencies, physicians' offices, and

by patients themselves. (Quebec is planning to use the data it gathers as part of its current vaccination campaign to create a more effective province-wide registry.)

7 For now, we can only estimate coverage across Canada. The PHAC says that about 62 percent of Canadian two-year-olds were up to date for all recommended vaccines when they checked most recently in 2009. It seems the measles outbreak at Marie-Rivier could have happened in countless other places—in some ways, it was just their bad luck. [...]

8 Vaccines do carry potential risks. In a study of Ontario toddlers, Wilson found that about one in 168 who got the MMR shot (measles, mumps, and rubella[5]) at 12 months went to hospital between four and 12 days afterwards. Most had fever and other viral symptoms, but few were sick enough to be hospitalized. After receiving the MMR vaccine, about one in a million patients will develop encephalitis, a potentially fatal inflammation of the brain. But about one in 1000 patients with measles will develop encephalitis, a much higher rate. (No encephalitis cases or deaths from measles were reported in Quebec.) [...]

9 Edda West is the coordinator of the Vaccination Risk Awareness Network. According to West, some parents are concerned about vaccine safety because they feel there has been an "explosion" of childhood illnesses and conditions ever since the 1980s, which is about the same time as a steep increase in the numbers of vaccines routinely given to infants and young children. West also believes that we need more long-term studies that are "free of conflicts of interest" in order to determine the safety of vaccines.

10 A little over a decade ago, undervaccinated kids were more likely to come from families that had trouble accessing health care, or from strict religious communities that forbade the practice. Today's unvaccinated children are "more likely to be white, to belong to households with higher income, [and] to have a married mother with a college education," says a 2009 study in the *New England Journal of Medicine*, which notes that parents of unvaccinated kids are more likely to seek alternative health care, and to use the Internet as an information source.

11 They also tend to live close to one another—maybe drawn together by an alternative school, church or politician, or to live near like-minded neighbours—which creates vulnerable pockets across the country. Beyond the financial cost of an outbreak, it puts others at risk, like babies too young to be immunized and those who can't be vaccinated for health reasons.

12 If vaccination rates dip too low, the consequences will be serious for everyone. In 2010, the *Canadian Medical Association Journal* published an editorial about a polio outbreak in Tajikistan, which was certified polio-free in 2002. That country may not seem to have much in common with Canada; but with an 87 percent uptake of the polio vaccine, its rate is actually quite close to some Canadian regions. (The WHO recommends a minimum of 90 percent coverage.) "This dreadful disease has no cure and causes paralysis and even death," the editorial states, noting that Tajikistan's outbreak should be "ringing alarm bells. We are only one asymptomatic[6] infected traveller away from an outbreak because of low vaccination rates." [...] Until a powerful reminder resurfaces, it's easy to forget the consequences of missed vaccines. [...]

Source: Adapted from Lunau, K., & Patriquin, M. (2012, January 9). Asking for an outbreak of preventable diseases. *Maclean's*. Retrieved from http://www.macleans.ca/society/health/asking-for-an-outbreak/

[5] a mild infectious disease that causes a sore throat and red spots all over the body

[6] having no symptoms of an illness

Activity B | The following questions are based on the magazine article you just read. Discuss your answers with a partner or small group.

1. What was unusual about the measles outbreak in Québec in 2012?

   ____

2. Have we achieved "herd immunity" in Canada for vaccine-preventable diseases? Why or why not?

   ____

   ____

3. Why did the measles outbreak happen at the Marie-Rivier high school in Drummondville and not at another school?

   ____

4. Why do some parents decide not to have their children vaccinated?

   ____

5. Are those reasons the same for parents today as for parents in the past? Explain your reasons for your answer.

   ____

   ____

6. How is the polio outbreak in Tajikistan linked to the situation in Canada?

   ____

   ____

Activity C | Writing Task: Paragraph Exploring Causes | What causes some people not to be vaccinated against diseases that can be prevented by vaccines? Write a short paragraph in which you explain some of these reasons.

Activity D | Compare your paragraph to the sample paragraph "Why People Do Not Get Vaccinated" in Appendix 2. Then answer the following questions about the sample paragraph.

1. What is the main idea of the paragraph?
2. What details does it include to illustrate why people are not vaccinated against some diseases?
3. With a partner, discuss how the sample paragraph fulfills the requirements of a paragraph exploring causes. Does your paragraph fulfill these requirements?

PROCESS FUNDAMENTALS

Before You Write

Flow Chart

In Unit 2 (pages 55–56), you learned about two general brainstorming techniques: listing and freewriting. Depending on the topic you want to write about, it can be useful to use the listing technique in a format that helps guide your thinking about a particular type of question.

A flow chart is particularly useful if you want to list the causes and effects of an event, a situation, or a person's reaction in an organized way because the flow chart allows you to visualize the causal relationships. You write the event, situation, or reaction you want to analyze in the centre. Then you write any reasons or causes for it on the one side and its effects or consequences on the other side. Notice the arrows, which help you to focus on the direction of the relationship: A leads to B; B leads to C. Remember, you still need to evaluate and choose the ideas most relevant to your topic after completing the flow chart.

Activity A | Thinking about your own experiences, what you have heard from others, and what you have read, brainstorm causes and effects for the outbreak of an infectious disease and complete the flow chart below.

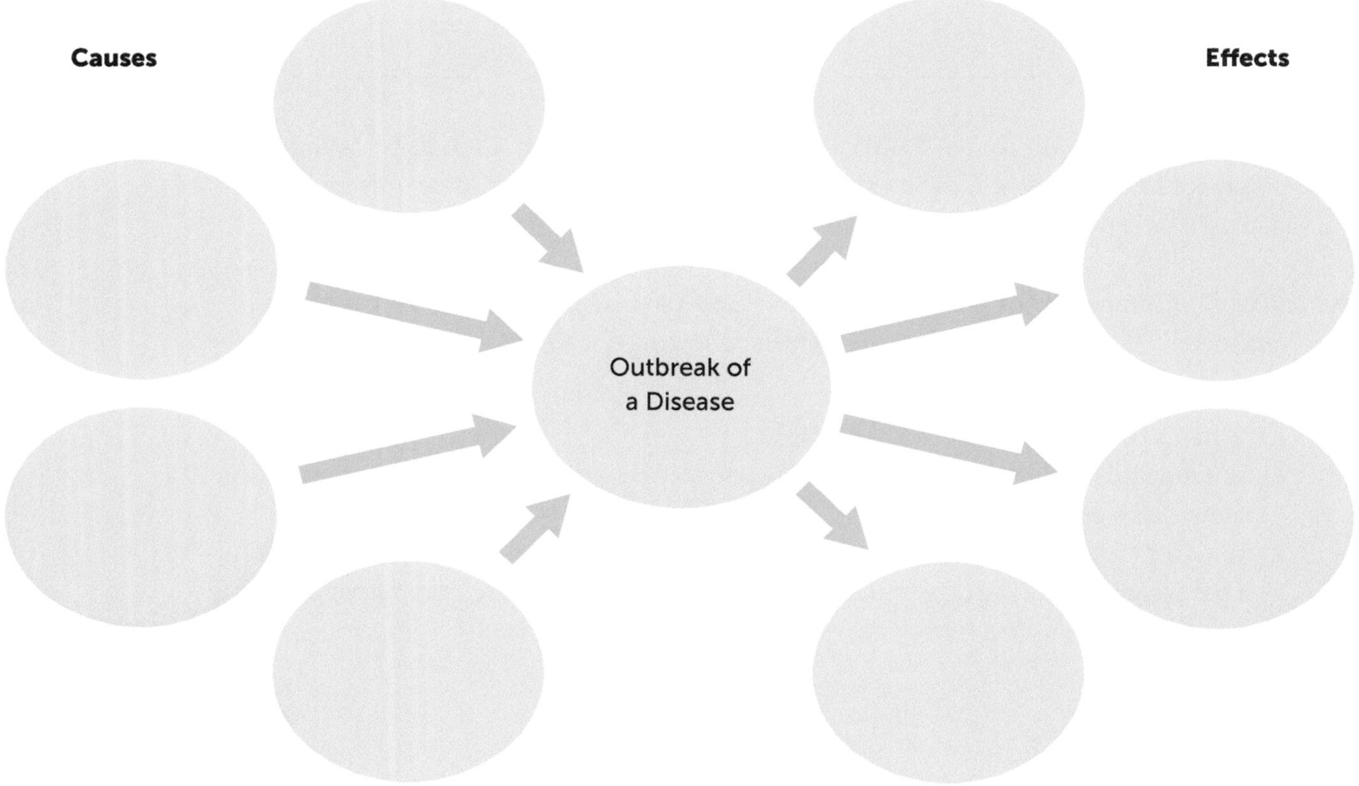

Activity B | Look back at your Unit Inquiry Question. Thinking about your own experiences, what you have heard from others, and what you have read, brainstorm causes and effects on your topic using the flow chart below.

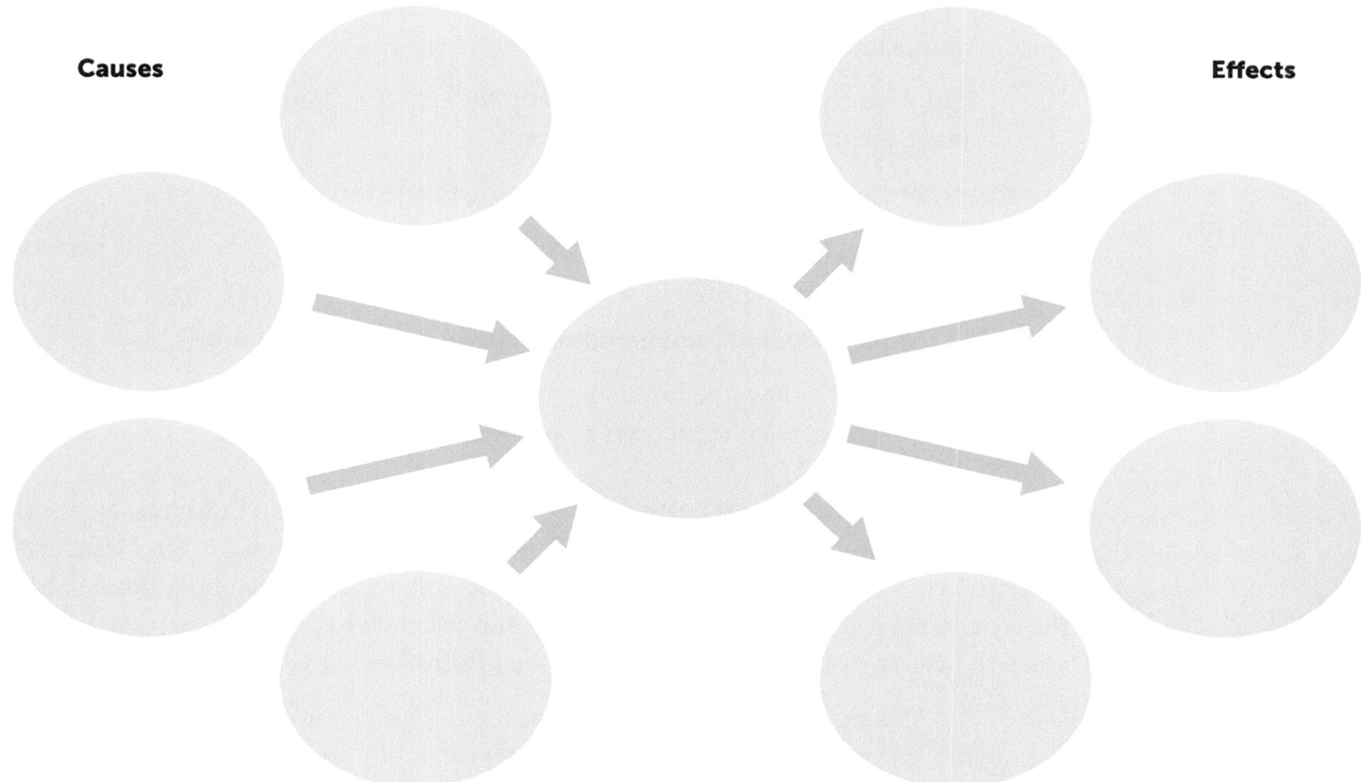

Activity C | Look at the flow chart you created for your Unit Inquiry Question in Activity B. Create a rough outline for an essay based on this flow chart. As you learn more about your topic, use your outline to add more ideas and details to support your topic. This rough outline will help you identify gaps in your knowledge. If you end up writing an essay on your Unit Inquiry Question, this rough outline may be helpful in guiding your planning.

Integrating Information from an Outside Source

Sentence Patterns for Integrating Source Material, Part 2

In Unit 3 (pages 92–93), you learned how to use reporting verbs, such as *state*, *explain*, and *argue*, to indicate to the reader that what follows is someone else's information or idea. You can also use expressions without a verb to indicate the source of information. These are the most commonly used expressions:

1. In [Name(s)]'s words, [direct quotation from the source]

   In Nowicki's words, "just as a castle has several lines of defence, so does your body's immune system."

   Tip: Use "In [Name(s)]'s words" only for verbatim quotes (i.e., when you are using the original author's exact words).

2. According to [Name(s)], [idea/information from the source]

   According to Nowicki, the body's immune system is similar to a castle because it also has several different ways in which it defends itself.

3. In [Name(s)]'s view/opinion, [idea/information from the source]

   In Nowicki's view, the body's immune system is similar to a castle because it also has several different ways in which it defends itself.

Activity A | The statements below have been taken from Reading 1 (Source: Nowicki, S. [2012]. Holt McDougal Biology [p. 896]. Boston, MA: Houghton Mifflin Harcourt). To practise paraphrasing, rewrite them using one of the expressions above. Remember, the statements below are in quotation marks and taken word for word from the text, so you will have to paraphrase them to write the information in your own words.

1. "Just as a castle's walls have doors and windows, your skin also has openings. For example, your eyes, nose, ears, mouth, and excretory organs are open to the environment, and so they need extra protection."

   ____

   ____

   ____

2. "Because infectious diseases are spread from person to person, the risk of getting sick increases when there are many people in one area."

   ____

   ____

   ____

3. "Vaccination cannot cure a person who is sick because vaccines only work to prevent infection."

   ____

   ____

   ____

Preventing Plagiarism

Editing and Revising Responsibly

Is This Plagiarism?

Alpha is taking English 301 this semester and is having difficulty with grammar and vocabulary in writing. Therefore, Alpha decides to ask Beta, whose English is much better than his, to check all his essays before he submits them to the instructor. At the end of the course, Alpha is very happy with his English 301 grades because his essays are much better after Beta corrected his problems with grammar and vocabulary.

Did Alpha commit plagiarism? Did Beta do anything wrong? Consider the details of the above scenario in the context of the definitions and rules regarding plagiarism established by your academic institution. Discuss your answer to this question with a partner or small group. You may use the following questions to guide your discussion:

1. How important is correct grammar and vocabulary in an English paper? Why?
2. Do you think Alpha learned how to use better grammar and vocabulary? Why or why not?
3. Did Beta do anything wrong? Explain your reasoning.
4. What would you do to prevent plagiarism in this scenario?

Now consider the following changes to the scenario:

a. Alpha asks Beta to review and correct essays for a course other than English.
b. Alpha visits the school's writing centre and asks a writing assistant for help with his English 301 essays.
c. Alpha and one of his English 301 classmates check each other's essays before submitting them to their instructor.

Do these changes affect your answers to questions 1–3 above? Why or why not?

Note: For information on your institution's plagiarism policy, search the college or university's website for a statement on academic integrity and/or its academic code of conduct.

Thesis Skill

Writing a Cause-and-Effect Thesis Statement

Writing a cause-and-effect thesis is similar to writing a thesis that answers a question as you learned in Unit 2 (pages 58–60). The difference, however, is that it has to clearly show the causal relationship for your topic. A thesis generally focuses on either the effects of an event or situation or on the causes that led to an event or situation. It usually does not do both.

Activity A | Which of the following thesis statements express a causal relationship? For each statement that expresses a causal relationship, indicate if it focuses on explaining the causes or the effects of something.

1. The body's immune system is a complex system with interrelated parts.
2. Controlling the spread of diseases is very important for public health.

3. When the body is infected with a pathogen, it is affected in a number of different ways.
4. There are a number of factors that can lead to the rapid spread of a disease among the population.

Activity B | Writing Task: Cause-and-Effect Thesis | Look back at your Unit Inquiry Question and the notes you took while brainstorming using a flow chart. Create the first draft of a working thesis statement. Remember to focus on the causal relationship in your topic.

____

____

____

Introductions

Strategies for Introducing Cause and Effect

Take another look at the essay on the Ebola pandemic on pages 112–114. How was the topic in that essay introduced? How does the focus of the introduction relate to the rest of the essay?

The essay focuses on the factors that led to the outbreak and spread of the Ebola pandemic. To introduce the reader to the topic, the writer explained some of the effects of this pandemic. This is an effective way to make the reader curious about the causes of the disease—the topic of the essay. If the topic of the essay were the effects of the Ebola pandemic, the writer could begin with a focus on some of the causes to arouse the reader's interest in the effects of the pandemic.

As with all introductions, it is important to provide a good link to the thesis statement, as you learned in Unit 2 (page 60). From the first sentence of the introduction to the end, each sentence should take the reader one step closer to the thesis statement at the end.

Consider the following example of such an introduction.

As we saw with the recent Ebola pandemic, a disease can spread rapidly. According to the World Health Organization [WHO] (2014a), the number of cases increased dramatically from fewer than a hundred to over six hundred and spread from one to four countries in the first few months of the pandemic. A month later, there were over 6000 cases and more than 3000 people had died (WHO, 2014b). It is hard to imagine such a drastic change in such a short time period. We can only understand how that was possible if we examine what caused the disease to spread so quickly.

References

World Health Organization. (2014a, August 29). *Ebola response roadmap situation report 1*. Retrieved from http://apps.who.int/iris/bitstream/10665/131974/1/roadmapsitrep1_eng.pdf?ua=1

World Health Organization. (2014b, September 26). *Ebola response roadmap update*. Retrieved from http://apps.who.int/iris/bitstream/10665/135029/1/roadmapupdate26sept14_eng.pdf?ua=1

Activity A | For each thesis statement below, analyze whether it focuses on causes or effects. If it focuses on causes, think of the effects you could include in your introduction to make the reader curious about the topic. Similarly, if the thesis statement deals with effects, brainstorm some causes to include in the introduction. Share your ideas with a partner or small group.

1. An infection with the flu virus can have serious consequences for an elderly person.
2. There are several factors that lead to improved effectiveness of vaccines.
3. When parents choose not to have their own children vaccinated, the serious effects may be felt by many other people's children.

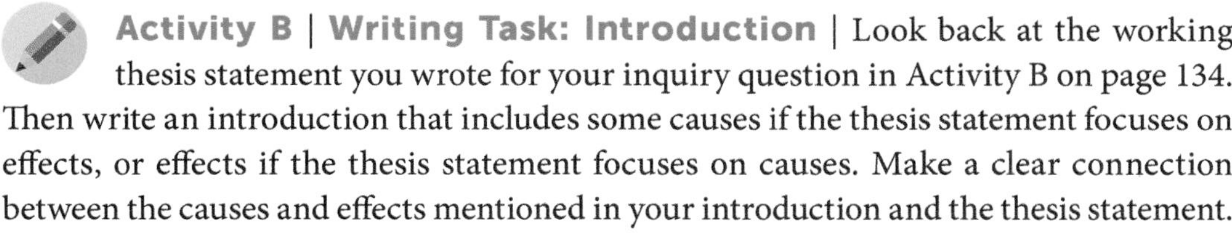

Activity B | **Writing Task: Introduction** | Look back at the working thesis statement you wrote for your inquiry question in Activity B on page 134. Then write an introduction that includes some causes if the thesis statement focuses on effects, or effects if the thesis statement focuses on causes. Make a clear connection between the causes and effects mentioned in your introduction and the thesis statement.

Conclusions

Thought-Provoking Comment

A good way to conclude your essay and leave your reader thinking about the topic is to end the conclusion with a thought-provoking comment. The challenge is to write a statement that encourages the reader to think further about the topic, so the comment cannot be too simplistic, obvious, or general. A good comment reinforces what you have written about in the essay but also takes the reader beyond what has already been said without introducing new ideas, which should not be done in a conclusion. The following conclusion shows how a comment can be used to do this.

Consider the following example of such a conclusion.

One of the major factors that facilitated the spread of the Ebola virus at a dramatic rate was the fact that humans do not have immunity to this disease unless they have survived a previous infection with the virus. Furthermore, there is no cure, leaving the medical community helpless in treating this disease. However, the failure of experts to recognize the signs of an outbreak early on and take all necessary measures to limit its impact meant that the disease spread more quickly and widely than it should have. The question is whether we have learned from our mistakes in managing the Ebola crisis and will be better prepared when the next outbreak of this or another deadly disease occurs.

Activity A | Read the four sentences below. Which ones are good thought-provoking comments and which ones are too simplistic, obvious, or general? Share your ideas with a partner or small group.

1. The future is uncertain, so we need to carefully consider our actions.
2. The question is whether anything more can be done to limit the spread of future epidemics.
3. This is a serious problem, so we should do more to solve it.
4. As vaccines are so effective, it's difficult to understand why we do not see a 100 percent approval rate among parents of young children.

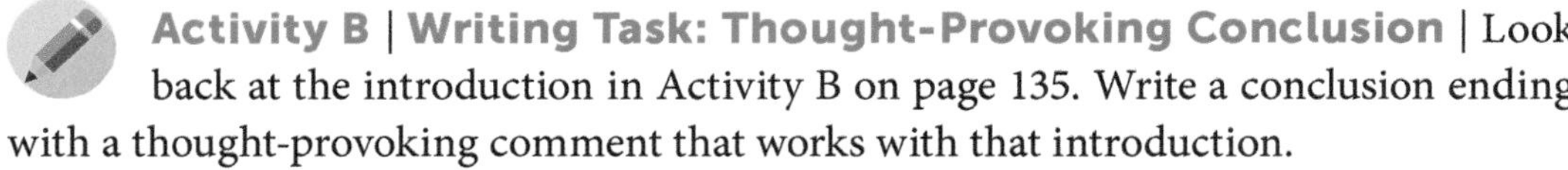

Activity B | Writing Task: Thought-Provoking Conclusion | Look back at the introduction in Activity B on page 135. Write a conclusion ending with a thought-provoking comment that works with that introduction.

WRITING FUNDAMENTALS

Composition Skill

Revising

When you have finished writing an essay, you may consider your assignment complete. However, the most challenging part of your task remains: revision. Revision involves checking and improving your content and organization.

After you finish your first draft, do not look at your writing for a day or two (if you have time). Then check your content and organization. Pretend that this is someone else's essay and ask yourself these questions to check the content and organization of the essay:

1. Are all the ideas in the essay related to the thesis?
2. Is all the support in each body paragraph related to the topic sentence of that paragraph?

3. Is the support detailed enough?
4. Is there convincing evidence to support the ideas?
5. Are the ideas presented in a clear and logical order, or should the order of paragraphs, supporting ideas, or evidence be changed?
6. Have connectors been used well, or should connectors be added and/or removed?

Make any necessary changes based on your review. Then check the content and organization of the essay again to make sure the problems you identified have been solved.

Activity A | Read the paragraph below and revise it for content and organization. Discuss your ideas for revision with a partner or small group.

Thanks to the development of the oral polio vaccine, polio has practically been eradicated around the world. Before the invention of polio vaccines, the disease was feared by many people because it often led to permanent paralysis. In fact, polio survivors are one of the largest groups fighting for the rights of the disabled ("History of Poliomyelitis," n.d.). It has taken time for this reduction to happen. In 1957, Albert Sabin began human trials for an oral vaccine, which was eventually licensed in 1962 ("History of Poliomyelitis," n.d.). This oral vaccine was even more effective than the Salk's original, and it meant that polio was no longer a feared disease. Before that, the first polio vaccine was introduced in 1955 by Alfred Salk and by 1961, the number of cases of poliomyelitis in the United States was reduced dramatically to only 161, compared to 58,000 during a major epidemic in 1952. ("History of Poliomyelitis," n.d.). Since the introduction of the vaccines, there have been very few polio cases around the world. In fact, in 2015, only 25 cases of polio were reported, most of them in Pakistan ("Poliomyelitis Eradication," n.d.). While polio still exists in some places, the polio vaccines have led to the virtual eradication of the virus.

References

History of poliomyelitis. (n.d.). *Wikipedia* Retrieved May 27, 2016, from https://en.wikipedia.org/w/index.php?title=History_of_poliomyelitis&oldid=722275377

Poliomyelitis eradication. (n.d.). *Wikipedia*. Retrieved May 26, 2016, from https://en.wikipedia.org/w/index.php?title=Poliomyelitis_eradication&oldid=722240567

Activity B | Writing Task: Paragraph Revision | Reread one of the paragraphs you wrote for this unit and use the guiding questions above to revise it for content and organization. Exchange paragraphs with a partner and give each other feedback on your revisions.

Sentence and Grammar Skill

Using Adverbials

In Unit 1 (pages 28–30), you learned that there are two different types of clauses: independent and dependent. All dependent clauses start with a subordinator. Adverbial subordinators introduce dependent clauses that provide additional information about the circumstances of the information in the independent clauses.

1. **Time**: When?

   When babies are born, their bodies have not yet had time to develop immunity against any diseases.

   After a person receives a vaccine, the body develops immunity against that disease.

   Before babies can be vaccinated, they rely on herd immunity to protect them against infections.

   As vaccines improve, the number of side effects is reduced.

   As soon as an outbreak of a disease is detected, health professionals start working toward preventing it from spreading.

   Since the polio vaccine was invented in the 1950s, the disease has been eradicated in most countries around the world.

   Until a reliable AIDS vaccine is discovered, humans will have to use other methods to prevent the spread of this disease.

   Whenever scientists discover a new vaccine for a disease, it must undergo careful testing to minimize side effects.

2. **Location**: Where?

   People need to have access to adequate health care facilities **where** they live.

   Vaccines should be distributed **wherever** they are most needed.

3. **Reason**: Why?

   Because/since/as vaccines are expensive to develop, governments need to provide incentives for companies to work on developing new vaccines.

4. **Purpose**: What is the goal?

   Governments should fund medical research **so that** scientists can develop an effective Ebola vaccine.

   Note: If the subjects are the same in the two clauses, you can also use *in order to.*

   Scientists have been working hard **in order to** develop an effective Ebola vaccine.

5. **Contrast**: How are the two statements incompatible?

   Whereas/while smallpox has been eradicated, many other diseases still pose a threat to humans.

6. **Concession**: Is the result unexpected?

   Some parents decide not to have their children vaccinated **although/even though/though** vaccines are the safest way to protect children against many infectious diseases.

Punctuation

When the dependent clause precedes the independent clause, the dependent clause is followed by a comma.

> **Whereas** smallpox has been eradicated, many other diseases still pose a threat to humans.

When the dependent clause follows the independent clause, no comma is used.

> Some parents decide not to have their children vaccinated **although** vaccines are the safest way to protect children against many infectious diseases.

Activity A | Look at each pair of sentences below and think about the most logical connection between the two ideas. Then choose the most appropriate connector to rewrite the two sentences as one. Remember to use a comma after the dependent clause if it comes before the independent clause. Write your combined sentence on a separate sheet of paper.

1. The flu vaccine can protect people against the flu. Not everyone decides to get the flu vaccine.
2. The flu virus mutates. The flu vaccine is not 100 percent effective.
3. Some people are allergic to eggs. They cannot receive the flu vaccine.
4. Governments encourage people to get the flu vaccine. Governments can reduce health care costs for flu patients.
5. The effectiveness of the annual flu vaccine is very low one year. The flu vaccination rate is low the following year.
6. A vaccine can protect against the flu. There is no vaccine against the common cold.

Activity B | Reread one of the paragraphs you wrote for this unit and check your use of adverbials in that paragraph:

- Did you use the most appropriate connector?
- Did you punctuate the sentences correctly when you used connectors?

Make any necessary changes to your connector use in that paragraph.

UNIT OUTCOME

Writing Assignment: Cause-and-Effect Essay

Write a cause-and-effect essay of 350 to 450 words on a topic related to immunity. (Your instructor may give you an alternative length.) Use either APA- or MLA-style in-text citations and a References or Works Cited list.

You may write an essay that answers your Unit Inquiry Question. If you choose to do so, look back at the work you have done in this unit:

- the latest version of your Unit Inquiry Question on page 110;
- the working thesis you wrote in Activity B on page 134;
- the introduction you wrote in Activity B on page 135;
- the ideas you brainstormed in Activity B on page 131; and
- the conclusion you wrote in Activity B on page 136.

Decide whether you want to include drafts of any of the above in your essay. You may have to revise your writing to integrate these elements into your essay.

If you do not want to write about your Unit Inquiry Question, you may develop a new question or write an essay that answers one of the following questions instead:

- What are the causes or the effects of the spread of epidemics? Focus on one particular disease to explain the causes or effects.
- What are the effects on herd immunity if some people are not vaccinated against disease?
- What are the effects of weakened immunity due to HIV/AIDS or another disease?

Use the skills you have developed in this unit to complete the assignment. Follow the steps set out below to ensure that you practise each of your newly acquired skills to write a well-developed cause-and-effect essay.

1. **Brainstorm**: Use a flow chart to generate ideas related to the topic you will write about.
2. **Find outside sources of information**: Select appropriate information from Readings 1 and 2 to support your argument as you learned in Unit 2 (page 56).
3. **Write a thesis statement**: Develop a focused thesis statement.
4. **Outline**: Fill in the outline on page 141 to plan your first draft.
    - Develop your body paragraphs using the question technique you learned in Unit 2 (pages 62–63).
    - Include information from Readings 1 and 2 in each body paragraph, if appropriate.

Introduction	Describe causes or effects related to the topic of your essay: A clear link between your question and your thesis statement: Thesis statement:
Main Body Paragraphs	Topic sentence 1: Information to be included: Concluding sentence 1 (optional):
	Topic sentence 2: Information to be included: Concluding sentence 2 (optional):
Conclusion	Summary of main ideas and thought-provoking comment:

5. **Prepare a first draft**: Use your outline to write the first draft of your essay. Use AWL and mid-frequency vocabulary from this unit where appropriate. In your first draft, you should
   - focus on getting your ideas down on paper without worrying too much about grammar.
   - skip a section if you get stuck and come back to it later. For example, consider writing the body paragraphs before writing the introduction and conclusion.
6. **Ask for a peer review**: Exchange your first draft with a classmate. Use the Cause-and-Effect Essay Rubric on pages 142–143 to provide suggestions for

improving your classmate's essay. Ask questions to help him or her develop the body paragraphs more effectively as you learned in Unit 2 (pages 62–63). Read your partner's feedback carefully. Ask questions if necessary.

7. **Revise**: Use your partner's feedback to write a second draft of your essay.
8. **Self-check**: Review your essay and use the Cause-and-Effect Essay Rubric to look for areas in which you could improve your writing.
   - Edit your essay for use of adverbials. Make sure you have used the right adverbials and have punctuated your sentences correctly.
   - Check that you have used appropriate phrases with or without reporting verbs to show when you are referring to other people's ideas.
   - Edit your essay for correct APA- or MLA-style citations. Make sure you include a References or Works Cited section. Include page numbers for direct quotations.
   - Use spelling and grammar checking features on your word-processing software to catch mistakes.
   - Try reading your essay aloud to catch mistakes or awkward wording.
9. **Compose final draft**: Write a final draft of your essay, incorporating any changes you think will improve it.
   - When possible, leave some time between drafts.
10. **Proofread**: Check the final draft of your essay for any small errors you may have missed. In particular, look for spelling errors, typos, and punctuation mistakes.

Evaluation: Cause-and-Effect Essay Rubric

Use the following rubric to evaluate your essay. In which areas do you need to improve most?

E = **Emerging**: frequent difficulty using unit skills; needs a lot more work
D = **Developing**: some difficulty using unit skills; some improvement still required
S = **Satisfactory**: able to use unit skills most of the time; meets average expectations for this level
O = **Outstanding**: exceptional use of unit skills; exceeds expectations for this level

Skill	E	D	S	O
The introduction uses the strategies discussed in this unit to introduce cause and effect.				
The thesis statement is clear.				
Each body paragraph starts with a clear topic sentence.				
The essay and all its paragraphs have unity (see Unit 3, page 97).				
Each body paragraph develops one controlling idea (see Unit 3, pages 94–95).				
The ideas are well organized.				

Cause-and-effect connectors have been used to show causal relationships.				
Information from readings in this unit has been integrated appropriately using the sentence patterns for integrating sources (see also Unit 3, pages 92–93).				
AWL and mid-frequency vocabulary items from this unit are used when appropriate and with few mistakes.				
Adverbials have been used appropriately.				
Commas have been used correctly with adverbials.				
APA- or MLA-style in-text citations and a References or Works Cited list are formatted correctly.				

Unit Review

Activity A | What do you know about the topic of immunity that you did not know before you started this unit? Discuss with a partner or small group. Be prepared to report what you have learned to the class.

Activity B | Look back at the Unit Inquiry Question you developed at the start of this unit and discuss it with a partner or small group. Then share your answers with the class. Use the following questions to guide you:

1. What ideas did you encounter during this unit that contributed to answering your question?
2. How would you answer your question now?

Activity C | Use the following checklist to review what you have learned in this unit. First decide which 10 skills you think are most important—circle the number beside each of these 10 skills. If you learned a skill in this unit that isn't listed below, write it in the blank row at the end of the checklist. Then put a check mark in the box beside those points you feel you have learned. Be prepared to discuss your choices with the class.

Self-Assessment Checklist	
☐	1. I can talk about immunity.
☐	2. I can write a cause-and-effect inquiry question.
☐	3. I can use cause-and-effect connectors to show causal relationships.
☐	4. I can evaluate a peer's writing and give feedback for improvement.
☐	5. I can use peer feedback to improve first drafts.
☐	6. I can use a variety of vocabulary learning strategies.
☐	7. I can use AWL and mid-frequency vocabulary from this unit.
☐	8. I can use a flow chart to find causes and effects.

Self-Assessment Checklist	
☐	9. I can prepare an essay outline using the ideas generated through brainstorming.
☐	10. I can use phrases without reporting verbs to integrate information from outside sources into my own writing.
☐	11. I can avoid plagiarism by being responsible when editing and revising my own writing.
☐	12. I can cite my sources using APA or MLA style
☐	13. I can write a clear cause-and-effect thesis statement.
☐	14. I can write an effective introduction for a cause-and-effect essay.
☐	15. I can write an effective conclusion that ends with a thought-provoking comment.
☐	16. I can revise my writing for content, organization, and language.
☐	17. I can use adverbials to express different types of relationships.
☐	18. I can use commas well with adverbials.
☐	19. I can write a cause-and-effect essay of four of more paragraphs.
☐	20.

Activity D | Put a check mark in the box beside the vocabulary items from this unit that you feel you can now use with confidence in your writing.

Vocabulary Checklist	
☐ acidic (adj.) 4000	☐ invading (adj.) 4000
☐ acquired (adj.) AWL	☐ membrane (n.) 5000
☐ affect (v.) AWL	☐ mutate (v.) 5000
☐ antibiotic (n.) 5000	☐ nutrient (n.) 5000
☐ antibody (n.) 5000	☐ physical (adj.) AWL
☐ artificially (adv.) 4000	☐ rely (v.) AWL
☐ chemical (adj./n.) AWL	☐ respond (v.) AWL
☐ component (n.) AWL	☐ survive (v.) AWL
☐ contract (v.) AWL	☐ target (v.) AWL
☐ fungus (pl. fungi) (n.) 5000	☐ vaccine (n.) 5000

UNIT 5

Climatology

Environmental Science

KEY LEARNING OUTCOMES

- Creating an inquiry question for exploring solutions to a problem
- Brainstorming using an idea web
- Understanding collocation
- Writing a problem–solution thesis statement
- Hedging claims
- Citing indirect sources
- Understanding and using conditional sentences effectively
- Achieving coherence
- Concluding an essay by issuing a warning
- Writing a problem–solution essay

EXPLORING IDEAS

Introduction

Canadian Prime Minister Justin Trudeau speaking at the United Nations Climate Change Conference in Paris, November 30, 2015.

Leaders from 195 countries, including Canada, met in Paris in 2015 for the United Nations Climate Change Conference. The result of the conference, called the Paris Agreement, was historic. For the first time, world leaders adopted a universal and legally binding plan to limit global warming.

Activity A | How much do you know about climate change? Take this quiz and discuss with a partner or small group. You will find answers to these questions in this unit's readings. When you are finished this unit, take the quiz again to see what you have learned.

1. What is the "greenhouse effect"?
2. What are the main greenhouse gases associated with global warming?
3. What are some human activities that contribute to climate change?
4. What are some examples of extreme weather conditions that result from climate change?

Activity B | Analyze the problem of climate change by filling out the concept matrix below.

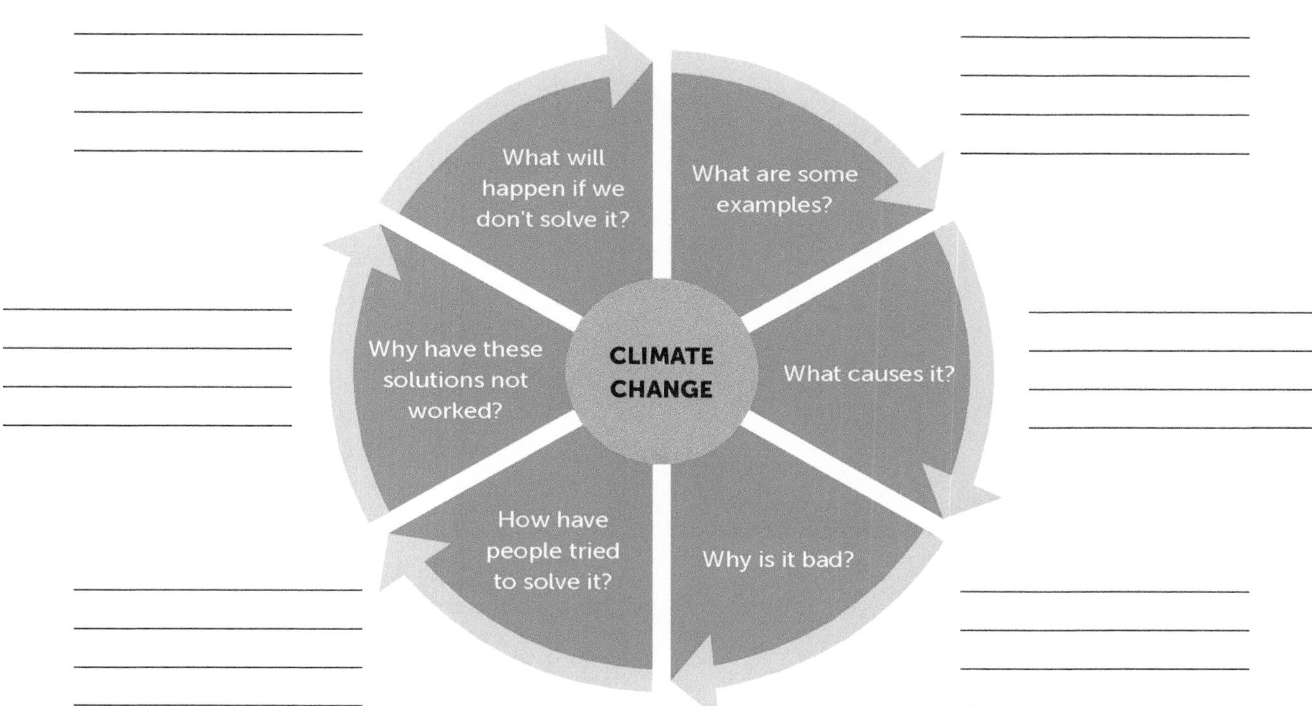

FIGURE 5.1 Concept matrix for climate change

Activity C | Writing Task: Problem Paragraph | Write a short paragraph about the problem of climate change. Refer to the concept matrix you filled out in Activity B above.

Fostering Inquiry

Finding Solutions

Finding an effective solution to a problem is an important academic skill, because much academic writing at higher levels is problem-based. Finding solutions is complex. It involves analyzing both the causes and effects of a problem, then considering different ways to solve the problem. A solution might

1. address the underlying cause of the problem. For example, you might propose a way to prevent the problem from occurring in the first place.
2. address the negative effects of the problem. For example, you might propose a way to make the consequences less serious or help people cope with them.
3. outline a general approach to arriving at a solution, rather than articulating a specific action. This is common when discussing large and complex problems that have no obvious or easy solutions.
4. be a combination of the above.

Activity A | What do you want to know more about in relation to climate change and the field of environmental science? For example, *How can we ensure adequate supplies of water for people, animals, and crops during a drought?* or *What are some ways that individuals can reduce their carbon footprint?*

1. Write down two or three questions you have about climate change solutions.
2. In a small group, share your questions.
3. Choose one question to be your guiding inquiry question for this unit. Your inquiry question can be different from the other group members' questions. The focus of your question may change as you work your way through this unit.
4. Write your inquiry question here and refer to it as you complete the activities in this unit.

My Unit Inquiry Question:

____

____

____

____

____

Activity B | Writing Task: Freewriting | Write for at least five minutes on the topic of your Unit Inquiry Question. Do not stop writing during this time. After five minutes, read what you have written and circle two or three ideas that you would like to explore further in order to answer your Unit Inquiry Question.

Structure

Problem–Solution Essay

The purpose of a problem–solution essay is to describe a problem (or problems) and propose one (or more) solution(s). This type of writing is common on post-secondary exams in different disciplines as well as on English language proficiency tests like the IELTS or TOEFL.

A problem–solution essay may include various rhetorical strategies to achieve its purpose. For example, a thorough description of a problem requires an analysis of its causes and effects. To offer an effective solution to a problem, the writer must either address its underlying causes or mitigate its negative effects. A writer may also draw comparisons to or highlight contrasts with other problems or solutions in order to illustrate a point.

Activity A | With a partner or small group, read the example of a student paragraph on the topic of cattle farming. Answer the questions that follow.

Many Canadians enjoy eating a nice juicy steak or pouring milk over their cereal in the morning, but may not realize that raising cattle for beef and dairy generates a lot of greenhouse gases, which contribute to global warming. The biggest culprit is methane (CH_4), a natural by-product of digestion in cows. It is responsible for about 40 percent of agricultural greenhouse gas emissions in Canada (Environment and Climate Change Canada, 2016). In fact, a single dairy cow produces roughly the same amount of methane in one year as the greenhouse gas emissions from a car driven 20,000 kilometres (Agriculture and Agri-Food Canada, 2012). Cattle farming is a way of life in North America, and eating meat is often seen as part of living "the good life." Beef and dairy products are readily available and relatively cheap. However, with global warming threatening not only Canada but the entire planet, we must find ways to reduce greenhouse gas emissions any way we can. Perhaps one solution to this problem would be to place a tax on these products, making them more expensive and thereby reducing the demand for beef and dairy. Similar taxes on cigarettes have been successful in reducing the number of smokers. The revenue generated from the tax could be returned to the farmers to replace some of their lost income and help them invest in green technologies for their farms.

References

Agriculture and Agri-Food Canada. (2012, Dec. 17). *Reducing methane emissions from livestock* [fact sheet]. Retrieved from http://www.agr.gc.ca/eng/science-and-innovation/results-of-agricultural-research/technical-factsheets/archived-content-reducing-methane-emissions-from-livestock/?id=1305058576718

Environment and Climate Change Canada. (2016, April 15). *About Canada's greenhouse gas inventory.* Retrieved from https://www.ec.gc.ca/ges-ghg/default.asp?lang=En&n=3E38F6D3-1

1. What problem is described in this paragraph?
2. What solution does the author propose?
3. Are there any causes or effects discussed in the paragraph? Name them.
4. Are there any comparisons made in the paragraph? Explain.

Language Tip

Hedging

Academic writing strives to be credible—in other words, the goal of a piece of academic writing is to make its readers believe that the author is right about something. One way academic writers do this is by *hedging*, or using language to soften or moderate their claims. A very strong or extreme statement is easy to disagree with and can make you seem less credible to a reader. Consider the following statement:

a. *Climate change is the most serious problem the planet has ever faced.*

This sentence presents an author's opinion that the reader may not share; for example, the reader may feel that there are other global problems just as serious as climate change.

Consider the following alternative statements, which all use hedging language to avoid making such an extreme claim that is too easily challenged:

b. *Climate change is **a** very serious problem facing the planet today.*

c. *Climate change is **one of** the most serious problems we face today.*

d. *Climate change is **perhaps** the most serious problem the planet faces.*

e. ***Many people feel that** climate change is the most serious problem facing the planet today.*

Common language used to hedge includes

1. verbs, such as *appears, suggests, tends;*
2. modal verbs, such as *may, might, can,* or *could;*
3. adverbs of frequency, such as *often, typically, frequently, usually;*
4. adverbs of certainty, such as *perhaps, maybe, probably;* and
5. clauses that qualify the claim, such as *it is possible that, many people agree that, it seems that, it is likely that.*

Keep in mind that you do not want to weaken your claims too much! Use the strongest wording you can that still protects your claim from being rejected by a skeptical reader.

Problem–Solution Essay Structure

A problem–solution essay follows the standard essay structure described in Unit 2 with an introduction, two or more body paragraphs, and a conclusion. The introduction briefly introduces a problem and leads to a thesis statement that proposes a solution. Each body paragraph contains a single controlling idea directly related to the thesis statement.

Like compare-and-contrast or cause-and-effect essays, problem–solution essays present many ideas that are related in complex ways, so the organization can be difficult. There are two common patterns for problem–solution essays: the block pattern and the chain pattern (see Figure 5.2). The block pattern describes one or more problems first, then proposes the solution(s). This pattern is common when the essay focuses on one problem and one solution. The chain pattern, which is often used when discussing multiple problems and solutions, presents a problem and its solution in each body paragraph. The choice of organizational pattern depends on your purpose for writing and the number of problems or solutions you will discuss.

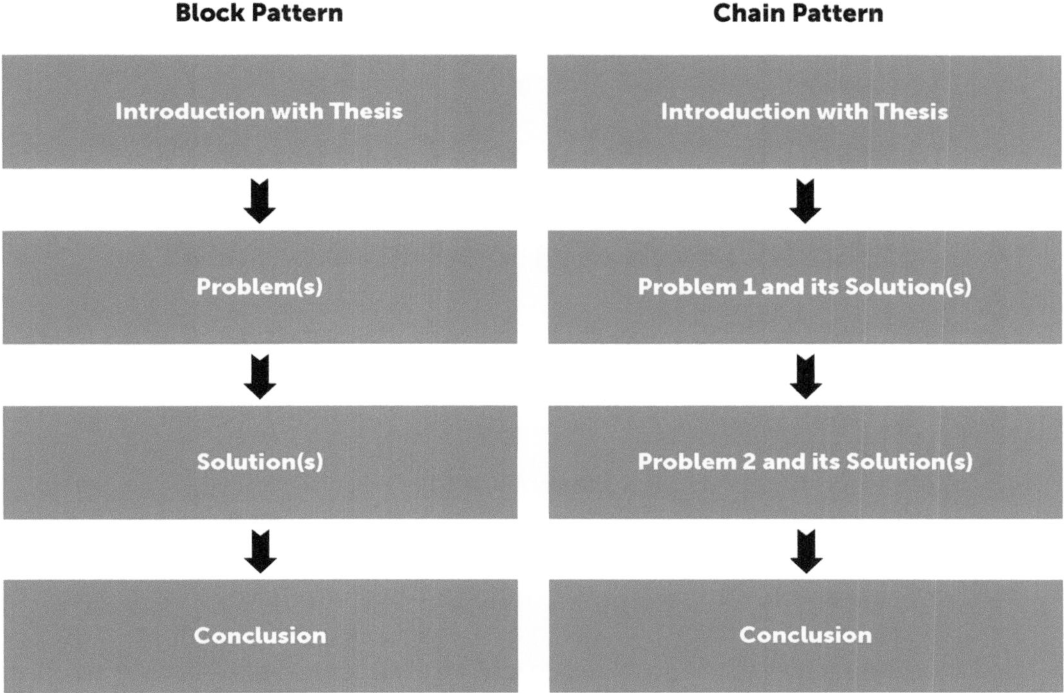

FIGURE 5.2 Problem–solution essay structure

Activity B | The following essay illustrates one of the organizational patterns shown in Figure 5.2. Read the essay closely, paying attention to the organizational pattern and answer the questions that follow.

Reducing the Risk of Wildfires through Reforestation

In May 2016, a giant wildfire in Alberta spread quickly and grew out of control. The fire crossed both the Hangingstone and the Athabasca rivers, joined with other smaller fires, and at its peak, covered 241,000 hectares (an area equal to 2410 square kilometres). The entire population of the town of Fort McMurray (approximately 80,000 people) had to be evacuated from their homes. The town lost more than 2400 buildings (French, 2016). The fire may likely turn out to be "the costliest disaster in Canadian history" (Morgan, 2016). Wildfires like the one in Fort McMurray are becoming more common and increasingly destructive. While it is impossible to pinpoint a single cause, most scientists agree that this increase is related to global warming. According to Mike Flannigan, who directs the Western Partnership for Wildland Fire Science,

"the area burned in Canada has increased over the past 40 to 50 years. This is due to human-caused climate change" (as cited in Schwartz, 2016). To reduce the risks of wildfires that burn out of control, we need a solution that addresses this root cause.

Wildfires are a natural phenomenon and have always occurred. The boreal forests in Canada have grown, burned, and regrown in a natural cycle for 6000 years, according to Merritt Turetsky, a researcher at the University of Guelph (as cited in Cruickshank, 2016). However, rising temperatures have led to reduced precipitation, dry conditions, and an increase in lightning strikes. All these things make wildfires more prone to breaking out and harder to fight. The so-called fire season, a period of time when wildfires are more likely to occur, is getting longer (Schwartz, 2016). The increase in wildfires upsets the natural balance of carbon capture and release in trees. When many trees burn quickly, much of the carbon that is stored in them is suddenly released into the air, and there are fewer trees left to draw greenhouse gases out of the air. The Fort McMurray fire alone released about as much as five percent of the annual greenhouse gas emissions in Canada from all other sources (Cruickshank, 2016).

Reducing greenhouse gas emissions is of course crucial for a long-term solution to climate change. In the meantime, though, we should also pursue ways to offset or compensate for the greenhouse gases we do emit. One way to do this is mass reforestation. Reforestation involves planting trees to replace those lost through forest fires or deforestation.[1] Since trees absorb carbon from the atmosphere, a greater number of trees can capture more carbon and help to reduce the greenhouse effect, among many other environmental benefits. Large-scale reforestation is neither easy nor cheap, however. It will require major public investment as well as co-operation from private industry

[1] cutting down trees for logging, agriculture, or other development

(Heyman, Parfitt, & Bercov, 2010). In addition to directly reforesting large areas of land, governments can look for innovative ways to encourage individuals to plant trees. For example, in Java, Indonesia, couples who want to get married or divorced must plant a certain number of tree seedlings ("Five tree fee," 2007). Small-scale programs such as this could make a big difference if they are carried out in communities around the world.

The Fort McMurray fire should be a warning to us all. It surprised everyone in how big and how quickly it grew. Its effects will be felt for a long time. Fortunately, this disaster caused few human deaths. However, we may not be so lucky in the future if we continue to face longer fire seasons, drier and hotter conditions, and other unpredictable and extreme weather. Offsetting carbon emissions through reforestation may be one of our best tools in the fight against climate change. If we fail to act, we will surely see fires even more devastating than the one at Fort McMurray.

References

Cruickshank, A. (2016, May 11). Carbon release in wake of Fort McMurray wildfire spikes greenhouse gases. *Edmonton Sun*. Retrieved from http://www.edmontonsun.com/2016/05/11/carbon-release-in-wake-of-fort-mcmurray-wildfire-spikes-greenhouse-gasses

Five tree fee for a Java wedding. (2007, December 3). *BBC News*. Retrieved from http://news.bbc.co.uk/2/hi/asia-pacific/7124680.stm

French, J. (2016, May 13). Timeline: Fort McMurray wildfire—A small fire turns into The Beast. *Edmonton Sun*. Retrieved from http://www.edmontonsun.com/2016/05/13/timeline-fort-mcmurray-wildfire----a-small-fire-turns-into-the-beast

Heyman, G., Parfitt, B., & Bercov, A. (2010, May 11). *BC's reforestation crisis*. Retrieved from https://www.policyalternatives.ca/publications/commentary/bcs-reforestation-crisis

Morgan, G. (2016, May 13). Alberta insurance rates to rise as Fort McMurray fire expected to be costliest disaster in Canadian history. *Financial Post*. Retrieved from http://business.financialpost.com/news/fp-street/alberta-insurance-rates-to-rise-as-fort-mcmurray-fire-expected-to-be-costliest-disaster-in-canadian-history

Schwartz, Z. (2016, May 4). Did climate change contribute to the Fort McMurray fire? *Maclean's*. Retrieved from http://www.macleans.ca/society/science/did-climate-change-contribute-to-the-fort-mcmurray-fire/

1. What problem is described in the essay?
2. How does the author introduce the essay?
3. Which organizational pattern does the essay use: the block pattern or the chain pattern?

4. What language does the author use to hedge his or her claims?

Paragraph	Hedging Language
1	
3	
4	

5. What kind of information does the author include to describe the problem?
6. Which type of solution is proposed? (Check more than one if you think they apply.)
   - ☐ solution that addresses the cause of the problem
   - ☐ solution that addresses the negative effects of the problem
   - ☐ general approach to finding a solution
7. How does the author conclude the essay?

Activity C | Revisit your Unit Inquiry Question on page 148. What new ideas have you thought of that will help you answer your question? Share your ideas with a partner or small group. At this point, you may consider revising your Unit Inquiry Question.

ACADEMIC READING

Vocabulary

Vocabulary Skill: Understanding Collocation

One of the most useful things to know about vocabulary is that words go together in predictable ways; that is, there are words that "like" to work together. This act of words working together is known as *collocation*. Even if your sentences are grammatically accurate, they might sound strange if you are using words together in unexpected ways. Knowing which words tend to appear together will help you to produce more natural-sounding texts.

Fill in the blanks in the following sentences with the first word that comes to mind.

a. Take a look at my ________________ new car!

b. If you don't ________________ your medicine, you will not get better.

c. The fastest way to end up in jail is to ________________ a crime.

If you wrote *brand* in the first blank, *take* in the second, and *commit* in the third, you were using your knowledge of English collocation. Of course, it might be possible to say "very new," or "extremely new," but the phrase "brand new" is common and expected. It is a strong collocation.

There are four main sources of information about collocation:

1. English texts that you read;
2. your dictionary (learner's dictionaries include one or more example sentences for most words and some provide information about strong collocations of a word);
3. computerized corpora (large collections of digital texts, which can be searched with concordance software to find particular words and phrases in context); and
4. Internet and word processing search functions (even without special concordance software, it is easy to search for a particular word in most web pages or digital texts).

Learning Strategy

Noticing

Good learning strategies help you to improve your English. When you are learning new vocabulary words, noticing how they are used in English texts will help you use them more effectively yourself. *Noticing* in this context means paying attention to a particular aspect of the word. For example, in this unit you are learning about collocations, or groups of words that frequently appear together. When you look up a word in the dictionary, look at the example sentences and observe what other words appear near the target word. Which preposition comes before or after it? Is it part of a phrase that you have seen many times before? When you are reading and you see a word you are trying to learn, notice which other words appear near it and how the word behaves grammatically in the sentence. When you are reading a text about a specific topic, you are likely to see a few keywords over and over. Noticing how these keywords are used in different sentences in the text can give you a lot of information about how to use the word yourself.

Source: Based on ideas in Oxford, R. L. (2011). *Teaching and researching language learning strategies*. Harlow, UK: Pearson.

Activity A | Look up the following AWL and mid-frequency vocabulary words from this unit in your dictionary, and scan Reading 1, "Climate Change," on pages 158–161 to see them in context. Write down one or more collocations containing each word. Note that a collocation can include more than two words.

1. drought ______________________
2. precipitation ______________________
3. infrared ______________________
4. source ______________________
5. vapour ______________________

Vocabulary Preview: The Academic Word List

Activity B | Study the following AWL words and their definitions. Then fill in the blanks in the sentences that follow by choosing the best word for each. Be sure to use the correct form of the word in the sentence.

factor (n.) one of several things that cause or influence something
occur (v.) to happen
predict (v.) to say that something will happen in the future
release (v.) to stop holding something or stop it from being held so that it can move, fly, fall, etc. freely
shift (v.) (of a situation, an opinion, a policy, etc.) to change from one state, position, etc. to another
significantly (adv.) in a way that is large or important enough to have an effect on something or to be noticed
somewhat (adv.) to some degree
source (n.) a place, person, or thing that you get something from
trend (n.) a general direction in which a situation is changing or developing
whereas (conj.) used to compare or contrast two facts

1. Global warming ________________ because greenhouse gases such as CO_2 trap heat in the Earth's atmosphere.
2. So-called "climate change deniers" do not believe that human activity is causing global warming; ________________ the majority of scientists believe that temperatures are rising because of an increase in greenhouse gas emissions.
3. The balance of greenhouse gases in the atmosphere was fairly stable before the Industrial Revolution; since then, the balance has been ________________.
4. Industrial agriculture and the burning of fossil fuels are two ________________ that contribute to global warming.
5. Scientists continue to study the phenomenon of climate change very closely in the hopes of finding ways to reverse the warming ________________.
6. One problem with ________________ how temperatures will change is that we don't know how much extra heat will be retained by oceans as sea levels rise.
7. It may be ________________ surprising that global warming can cause both drought and flooding.
8. Many people agree that switching to renewable ________________ of energy, such as solar and wind, must be part of the solution to global warming.
9. Trees are natural climate change fighters because they remove carbon dioxide from the air and ________________ oxygen.
10. Unless we find a way to ________________ reduce greenhouse gas emissions, global temperatures will rise to dangerous levels.

Vocabulary Preview: Mid-frequency Vocabulary

Activity C | Indicate how well you know each word listed below by circling a number between 0 and 4 (see the legend below). You will have a chance to check the meaning of words that you scored 0, 1, or 2 when you complete the first reading.

Legend

0: I have never seen or heard this word before.
1: I think I have seen the word before, but I don't know what it means.
2: I think I know what the word means, but I am not sure.
3: I know what the word means. (Write a short definition or give a synonym in the space provided.)
4: I know what the word means and I can use it in a sentence. (Write a short definition or give a synonym and write a sentence containing the word in the space provided.)

adversely	0 1 2 3 4	
drought	0 1 2 3 4	
ecosystem	0 1 2 3 4	
erode	0 1 2 3 4	
greenhouse	0 1 2 3 4	
hemisphere	0 1 2 3 4	
infrared	0 1 2 3 4	
nourish	0 1 2 3 4	
precipitation	0 1 2 3 4	
vapour	0 1 2 3 4	

Reading 1

The reading "Climate Change" is an excerpt from the textbook *Environmental Science* by Michael R. Heithaus and Karen Arms. This textbook is used in environmental studies classes in Canadian high schools.

Activity A | Discuss the following questions with a partner or small group.

1. What is the climate like where you are from? If you are not originally from Canada, how is the climate in your country of birth similar to or different from the climate in Canada?
2. What do you think would happen if the average temperature increased by two degrees Celsius where you are from?
3. Are there any industries or activities where you are from that generate greenhouse gases?

Activity B | Look back at Activity C on page 157. How many words did you know well? Make a list of any words that you scored 0, 1, or 2. Pay attention to these words when you see them in Reading 1. After reading the text, go back and complete the vocabulary table in Activity C. Use your dictionary to check your answers.

Activity C | Annotate the following textbook excerpt while you are reading. Highlight and make notes on causes, effects, comparisons, and contrasts. Underline any new collocations that you think will be useful when writing about this topic. Use your annotations to answer the questions that follow the text.

READING

Climate Change

1 Have you ever gotten into a car that has been sitting in the sun with all its windows closed? Even if the day is cool, the air in the car is much warmer than the air outside. The reason warmth builds up inside a car is that the sun's light energy streams into the car through the clear glass windows. The carpets and upholstery[1] in the car absorb the light and convert it into energy in the form of heat. This energy does not pass through glass as easily as light energy does. Sunlight continues to stream into the car through the glass, but the energy in the form of heat cannot get out. This energy continues to build up and is trapped inside the car. A greenhouse works the same way. By building a house of glass, gardeners trap the sun's light energy and grow delicate plants in the warm air inside the greenhouse even when there is snow on the ground outside.

The Greenhouse Effect

2 Earth is somewhat comparable to a greenhouse. Earth's atmosphere acts like the glass in a greenhouse. As shown in Figure 5.3, solar radiation enters the atmosphere as high-energy wavelengths of light that warm Earth's surface. Some of the energy escapes into space. The rest is absorbed by gases in the troposphere[2]

[1] soft covering on furniture such as armchairs and sofas

[2] the lowest layer of the earth's atmosphere, between the surface of the earth and about 6–10 kilometres above the surface

and warms the air. This process of warming Earth's surface and lower atmosphere is called the *greenhouse effect*.

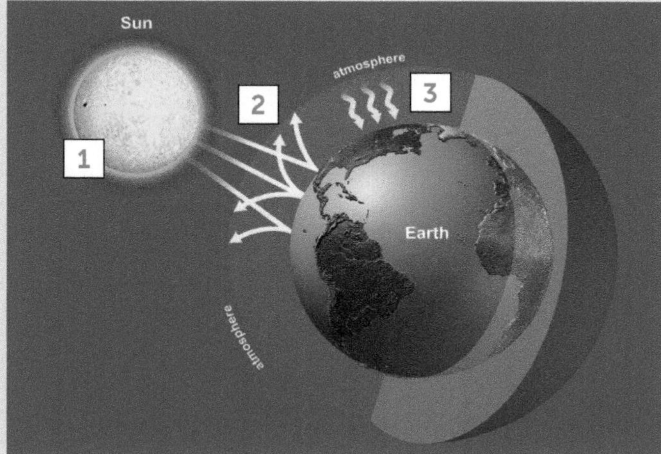

1. *Most of the sun's rays that reach the Earth's surface are absorbed by the ground.*
2. *Once heated, the ground emits infrared rays into the atmosphere. Some infrared rays pass through the atmosphere and are lost in space.*
3. *Greenhouse gases trap some of the infrared* rays and send them back to Earth, further heating its surface.*

FIGURE 5.3 How the greenhouse effect works

3 Not every gas in our atmosphere absorbs and radiates the sun's energy in this way. Gases that do absorb and radiate infrared radiation from the sun are called **greenhouse gases**. The major greenhouse gases are water vapour, carbon dioxide, methane, and nitrous oxide. Of these, water vapour and carbon dioxide account for most of the absorption of energy that occurs in the atmosphere.

Greenhouse Gases and the Earth's Temperature

4 Most atmospheric scientists think that because greenhouse gases absorb and rerelease infrared radiation to Earth's surface, increased greenhouse gases in the atmosphere will result in an increase in global temperature. A comparison of CO_2 in the atmosphere and average global temperatures for the past 400,000 years supports this view.

5 Today, we are releasing more CO_2 than any other greenhouse gas into the atmosphere. Millions of tons of CO_2 are released into the atmosphere each year from power plants that burn coal or oil and from cars that burn gasoline. Millions of trees are burned in tropical rain forests to clear the land for farming. Thus, the amount of CO_2 and other greenhouse gases in the atmosphere is increasing. Figure 5.4 shows the sources of some major greenhouse gases.

Carbon dioxide, CO_2: burning fossil fuels and deforestation

Methane, CH_4: animal waste, biomass burning, fossil fuels, landfills, livestock, rice paddies, sewage, and wetlands

Nitrous oxide, N_2O: biomass burning, deforestation, burning of fossil fuels, and microbial activity on fertilizers in the soil

Water vapour, H_2O: evaporation, plant transpiration

FIGURE 5.4 Major greenhouse gases and their sources

Global Climate Change

6 Figure 5.5 shows that the average temperature at Earth's surface increased during the twentieth century. This gradual increase is known as **global warming**. Because the rise in temperature correlates to the increase in greenhouse gases in the atmosphere, most scientists conclude that the increase in greenhouse gases, and other factors, have caused the increase in temperature. Thousands of experiments and computer models support this hypothesis. The increase in temperature is predicted to continue. This does not mean that temperatures are rising at a constant rate, or that they are rising in all parts of the world. As with changes in CO_2 levels, short-term

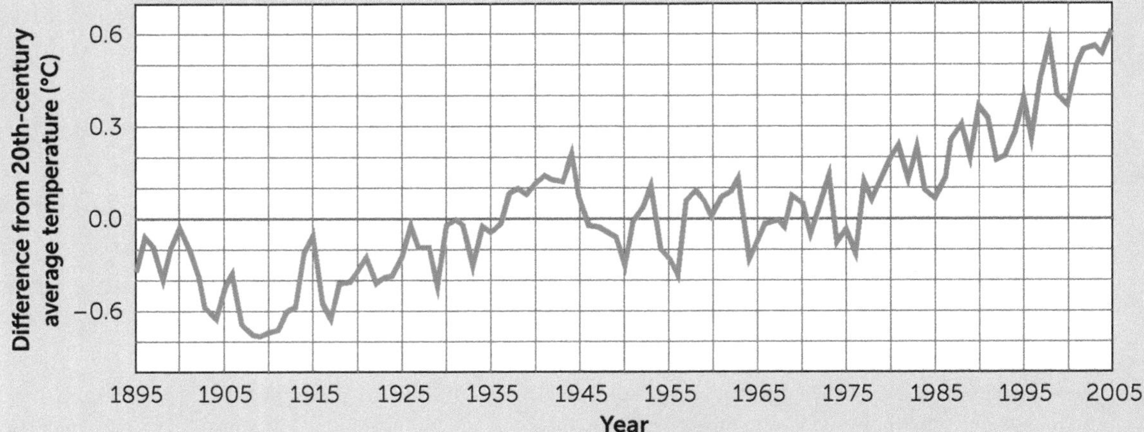

FIGURE 5.5 Global surface temperature

This graph shows that the average surface temperature of Earth warmed during the 20th century. For example, the average global surface temperature in the year 2005 was 0.61°C above the 20th-century average temperature.

variations in temperature are superimposed[3] on larger trends. For example, the patterns of precipitation, frequency of fires, and extreme weather events are also predicted to change. So, most scientists use the term *global climate change* rather than global warming.

The Consequences of a Warmer Earth

7 In North America, tree swallows, Baltimore orioles, and robins are nesting about two weeks earlier than they did 50 years ago. In Britain, at least 200 species of plants are flowering up to 55 days earlier in the year than they did 40 years ago. Although correlations are not proof of causation, scientists know that the time at which birds nest and plants flower are both strongly influenced by temperature.

8 The possible effects of climate change include a number of potentially serious environmental problems, including changes in weather patterns and rising sea levels. The possible effects of a warmer Earth will not be the same everywhere. For instance, some ecosystems are less sensitive to changes in climate than others are. Countries, too, will vary in their ability to respond to problems caused by changes in climate.

Rising Sea Levels

9 Sea level has been measured in many locations over the past 100 years. Although there is some uncertainty about the total amount, sea levels are rising and will continue to rise. Sea level rises because as water warms, it expands. Also, ice that is currently over land is melting and the water is flowing into the ocean. Scientists are particularly concerned about melting of glaciers over land in Greenland and Antarctica. The rise in sea levels could flood coastal wetlands and other low-lying areas. Enormous numbers of people who live near coastlines could lose their homes and sources of income. Beaches could be extensively eroded. The salinity[4] of bays and estuaries[5] might increase, adversely affecting marine fisheries. Also, coastal freshwater aquifers[6] could become too salty to be used as sources of fresh water.

Global Weather Patterns

10 If Earth warms up significantly, the surface of the oceans will absorb more energy in the form of heat, which may make hurricanes and typhoons more intense. Some scientists are concerned that climate

[3] put on top of something else so that the two can be seen combined

[4] the amount of salt contained in something

[5] the wide parts of rivers as they flow into seas

[6] layers of rock or soil that can absorb and hold water

change will also cause a change in ocean current patterns, such as a slowing of the Gulf Stream. Such a change could significantly affect the world's weather. For instance, some regions might have more rainfall than normal, whereas other regions might have less. Severe flooding could occur in some regions while droughts and fires devastate other regions.

Human Health Problems

11 Warmer average global temperatures pose potential threats to human health. Greater numbers of heat-related deaths could occur. Since trees and flowering plants, such as grasses, would flower earlier and for longer than they do now, people who are allergic to pollen would suffer from allergies for more of the year. Warmer temperatures could also enable mosquitos—vectors[7] of diseases such as malaria and Dengue Fever—to establish themselves in areas that are too cold for them currently.

Agriculture

12 Agriculture would be severely impacted by climate change if extreme weather events, such as droughts, become more frequent. Higher temperatures could result in decreased crop yields. The demand for irrigation[8] could increase, which would further deplete aquifers that have already been overused.

Effects on Plants and Animals

13 Climate change could alter both the range of plant species and the composition of plant communities. Trees could colonize cooler areas. Forests could shrink in the warmer part of their range and lose diversity. Increased frequency of fires may shift whole ecosystems.

14 Climate change may cause a shift in the geographical range of some animals. For example, birds in the Northern Hemisphere may not have to migrate as far south for winter. Warming in the surface waters of the ocean might cause a reduction of zooplankton, which many marine animals, such as whales and seals, depend on for food. Warming in tropical waters may kill the algae that nourish corals, thus destroying coral reefs. As more CO_2 dissolves into oceans, the water could become more acidic, which could disrupt the ocean food webs.

Source: Excerpted from Heithaus, Michael R. and Arms, Karen (2013), *Environmental science* (pp. 339–344). Boston, MA. Houghton Mifflin Harcourt.

[7] insects, etc. that carry a particular disease from one living thing to another

[8] the practice of supplying water to an area of land through pipes or channels so that crops will grow

Activity D | The following questions are based on the textbook excerpt you just read. Discuss your answers with a partner or small group

1. What are three greenhouse gases discussed in the text, and what are the main human activity-related sources of each of these gases? Fill in the table below.

Greenhouse Gas	Source(s) from Human Activity

2. Why are these gases called "greenhouse gases"?
3. The text mentions many consequences of global warming. List five specific negative effects of global warming noted in the text.

____

____

____

____

____

4. From your list above, which do you think is the most serious problem? Why? Discuss with a partner.

Activity E | Writing Task: Problem Paragraph | Write a short paragraph in which you describe one problem that is caused by global warming. Title your paragraph by naming the problem. Remember to include references to the source of your information if you use words or ideas from the textbook excerpt or from any outside research you may choose to do.

Activity F | Compare your paragraph to the sample paragraph "Destruction of the Arctic Tundra" in Appendix 2. Then answer the following questions about the sample paragraph.

1. What problem is described in the paragraph?
2. What does the author use to describe the problem? Check all that apply.
   - ☐ facts and background information
   - ☐ explanation of cause(s)
   - ☐ explanation of effect(s)
   - ☐ comparisons or contrasts
   - ☐ other: _______________
3. How many of the items in question 2 are you able to check off for your own paragraph?

Reading 2

The reading "Is Geoengineering the Solution to Saving the Earth?" comes from the Canadian newsmagazine *Maclean's*. This magazine is published every week and contains articles on a wide range of topics.

Activity A | Read and annotate the magazine article. Underline or make a note about the main idea of the article. Make a note in the margin beside each major supporting idea. Underline any new collocations that you think will be useful when writing about this topic.

READING

Is Geoengineering the Solution to Saving the Earth?

1 On a snowy March day in 2012, Oliver Morton, a British science writer and *Economist* editor, sat in a University of Calgary conference hall and listened to the two questions that came to frame the contents of his new book, *The Planet Remade: How Geoengineering Could Change the World.* "Ask yourself this," said Princeton physicist Richard Socolow. "Do you believe the risks of climate change merit serious actions aimed at mitigating them, and do you think that reducing human-generated carbon dioxide emissions to near zero is very hard?"

2 Morton, who answered yes and yes, soon realized the consequence of that dual affirmation. If carbon emissions bring the risk of climate catastrophe and little can be done about them in time, then—for reasons as much moral as practical—geoengineering had to be considered. The term broadly encompasses the use of science and technology on a massive scale to bend Earth's climate to human ends. Its champions have suggested, and even—in the case of American entrepreneur Russ George, who dumped 100 tonnes of iron sulphate into the Pacific off Haida Gwaii in 2012—experimented with ideas ranging from feeding iron to ocean plankton[1] (to encourage them to absorb more carbon) to giant mirrors in space or atmospheric veiling to reflect sunlight away from the planet.

Chinese residents wear masks for protection as smoke billows from stacks in a neighbourhood next to a coal-fired power plant on November 26, 2015, in Shanxi, China.

3 Climate change skeptics, naturally, are not interested in what geoengineering might accomplish, and oppose it for its usually astronomical costs. Among environmentalists, rejection is more visceral—Al Gore has called it "delusional in the extreme"—because tinkering with the Earth's natural systems is simply more of the hubris[2] that brought us to the brink of disaster in the first place.

4 Morton sympathizes with the green side, but he thinks they are far too optimistic about cutting emissions. In 2013, humans burned three trillion cubic metres of gas over the year, three million barrels of oil monthly and 300 tonnes of coal every *second*. How fast can that possibly change? Bring a new nuclear power plant on stream every week, and it would take 20 years to replace the coal-fired plants; replacing the coal output with power from solar panels would take 150 years at current installation rates. And the oil and gas would still burn.

5 The real moral issue—the true reason geoengineering has to be considered, according to Morton—is the plight of the global poor. There are seven billion humans now, many of them still in grinding poverty; there will be two or three billion more before the population curve turns downward. A world that aims, as it should, "to support nine billion in comparative comfort will need a great deal of energy. The idea you can reduce carbon emissions suddenly, in a way that's politically feasible[3] and economically non-disastrous—no." Nor would fast action bring fast results. "Emissions reduction is the absolutely necessary answer to people suffering in the future, but it won't make any difference for people suffering over the next couple of decades."

---

[1] very small plants and animals that live in the ocean

[2] extreme and unwarranted belief in one's abilities

[3] possible and likely to be achieved

6 That doesn't mean he's beating the drum for[4] most geoengineering proposals. They essentially break down into two sorts. The first is carbon capture, removing CO_2 from the atmosphere, an approach Morton finds ineffectual because the projects so far either pull out too little CO_2 or emit too much. The second approach is to live with the carbon until emissions are driven down by renewables and nuclear power, while countering its greenhouse effect by blocking sunlight.

7 Morton finds the mirrors-in-space idea so prohibitively expensive that he disposes of it in a few sentences, and holds up atmospheric veiling as the sole serious possibility. It's not a new idea—Canadian scientist and Harvard professor David Keith, a major figure in *The Planet Remade*, first wrote about it in 1992—partly since scientists know veiling's cooling power from studying the aftermath of large volcanic eruptions. "Using aircraft to put a very thin veil of sulphur aerosols,[5] finer than dust, across the stratosphere[6] would diminish, just a bit, the amount of sunlight that reaches the Earth's surface," says Morton. It might be the most effective means of averting disaster until we move off fossil fuels.

8 Or it might not. If Morton has a single point he returns to over and over, it's that we don't know. We need to start thinking about geoengineering, and in a clear-eyed way. Do not contrast a geoengineered Earth with a natural Earth, Morton urges, because that "natural" planet grows more mythic by the day. The real point of comparison is between what we are haphazardly creating—a greenhouse Earth—and a geoengineered planet. "Any decisions we make will be made under fairly radical conditions of uncertainty, because we don't fully understand the risks of either," concludes Morton. "But our future options are a lot more constrained if you rule out geoengineering from the get-go."[7]

Source: Bethune, B. (2016, January 12). Is geoengineering the solution to saving the earth? *Maclean's*. Retrieved from http://www.macleans.ca/society/science/is-geoengineering-the-solution-to-saving-the-earth/

[4] supporting

[5] a substance enclosed under pressure and released as a fine spray by means of a propellant gas

[6] the layer of Earth's atmosphere between about 10 and 50 kilometres above the surface of Earth

[7] outset; beginning of something

Critical Thinking

Bloom's Taxonomy—*Synthesis*

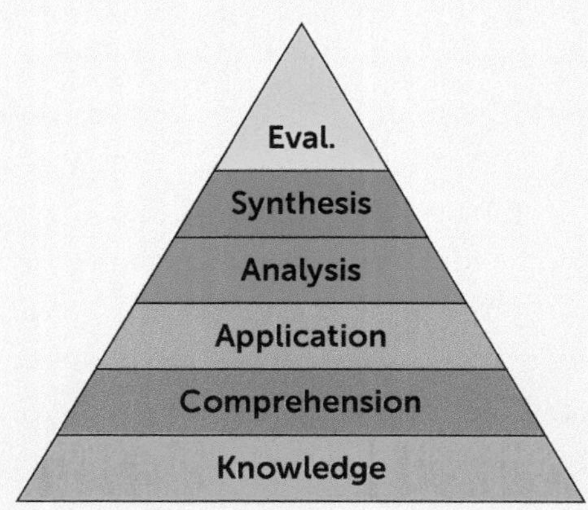

The fifth level of thinking in Bloom's taxonomy is *synthesis*. In this level, you go beyond organizing ideas and analyzing situations. Synthesis involves using and combining ideas in order to create new ideas. For example, when you analyze a problem from various perspectives and then propose a solution based on that analysis, you are synthesizing information.

As you read multiple texts about a topic, ask yourself the following questions to promote synthesis:

- What do these ideas "add up to" if I combine them?
- What other ideas, of my own or from other sources, can I add to this?
- What can I predict based on what I have read from these sources?
- How can I create or design a new version of what these texts are talking about?

Source: Bloom, B. S., Engelhart, M. D., Furst, E. J., Hill, W. H., & Krathwohl, D. R. (1956). *Taxonomy of educational objectives: The classification of educational goals. Handbook 1: Cognitive domain*. London, UK: Longman.

Activity B | Writing Task: Solution Paragraph | Look back at the problem paragraph you wrote in Activity E on page 162. Write a paragraph in which you propose a solution to that problem.

Activity C | Exchange both paragraphs with a partner. Read your partner's paragraph and use the following questions to provide feedback.

1. Is the solution proposed in the second paragraph directly related to the problem described in the first paragraph?
2. Does the solution address the cause of the problem or the effect(s) of the problem? Or does it suggest a general approach to finding a solution?
3. Do you think the solution is a good one? Why or why not?
4. What do you like best about the solution paragraph?
5. How would you improve the solution paragraph?

PROCESS FUNDAMENTALS

Before You Write

Webbing

Webbing is a brainstorming technique that is useful when you are analyzing and synthesizing ideas related in complex ways. The main ideas appear near the centre of the web, and the smaller ideas are connected to them as the web expands. Webbing is a good technique to use when brainstorming ideas for a problem–solution essay, because it is possible to show how a lot of ideas are connected to each other. Often, your brainstorm will result in more ideas than you can use in a single coherent essay. In that case, you must decide which ideas to include and which ideas not to include in your essay.

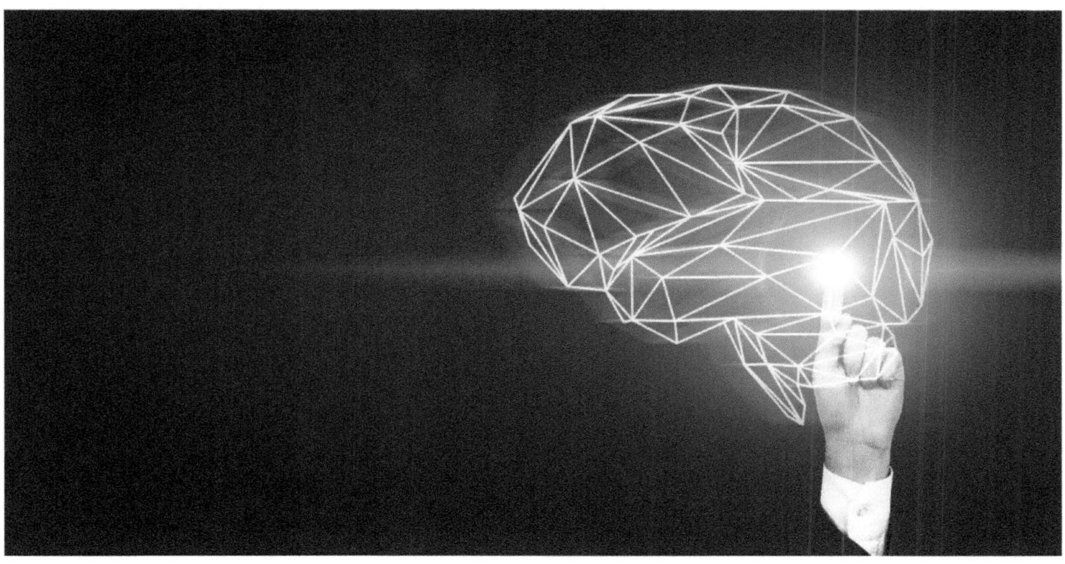

Activity A | Look at the web below, which shows how the ideas for the sample essay "Reducing the Risk of Wildfires through Reforestation" were brainstormed. Which of the ideas in the web appear in the essay? Cross out any ideas that the writer decided not to include.

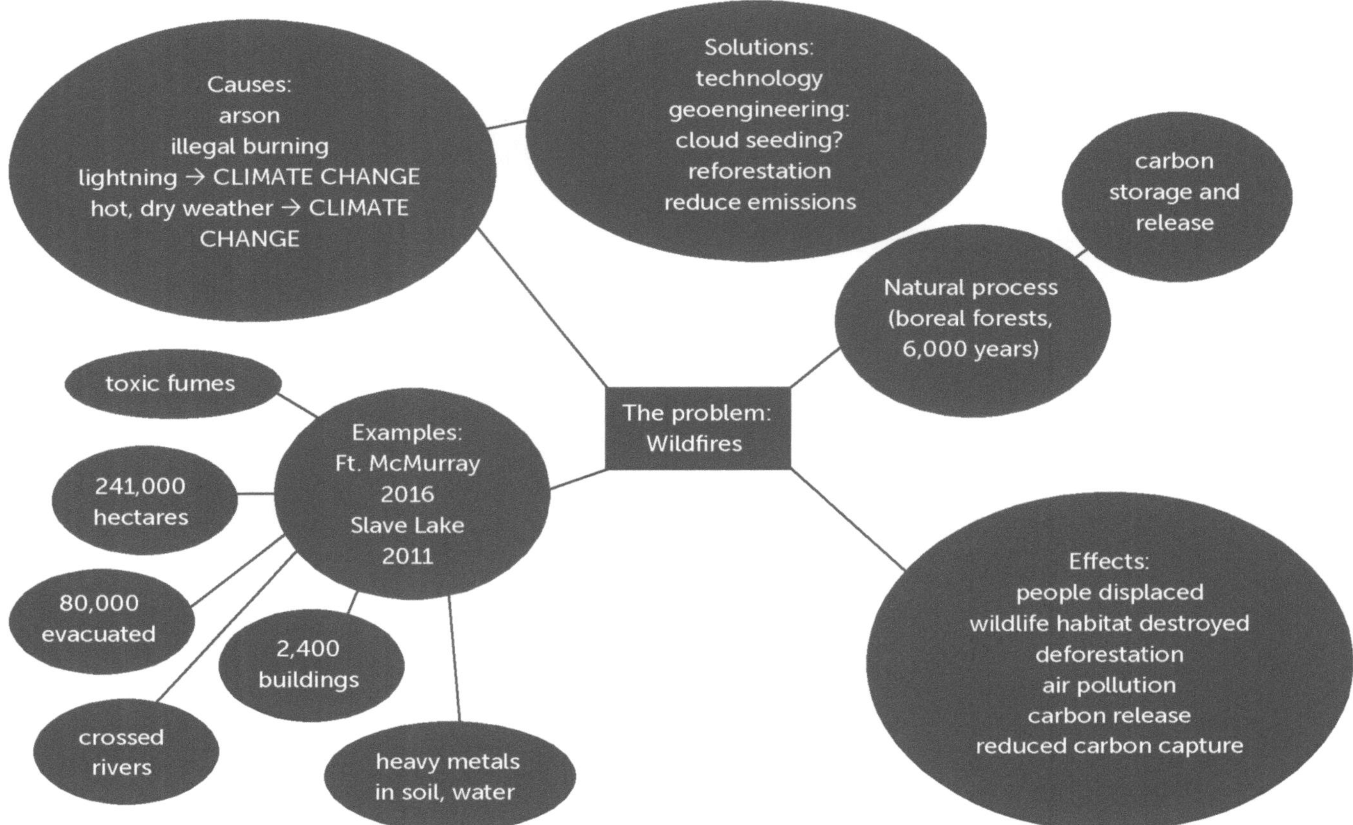

FIGURE 5.6 Wildfires idea web

Activity B | Look back at your Unit Inquiry Question on page 148. Thinking about your own experiences, what you have heard from others, and what you have read, brainstorm ideas related to the problem and its possible solutions. Create a web to show the relationship between the ideas.

Activity C | Using the web you generated for your Unit Inquiry Question in Activity B, create a rough outline for an essay based on this brainstorming web. As you learn more about your topic, use your outline to add more ideas and details to support your topic. This rough outline will help you identify gaps in your knowledge. If you end up writing an essay on your Unit Inquiry Question, this rough outline may be helpful in guiding your planning.

Integrating Information from an Outside Source

Citing Indirect Sources

In the first four units, you have learned how to select, paraphrase, quote, and cite information from outside sources in your writing. Sometimes, though, you will want to cite information that has already been cited in another source—that is, the original source of the information is not the text you are reading, but one that is referred to in the text you are reading.

For example, Brian Bethune is the author of Reading 2 ("Is Geoengineering the Solution to Saving the Earth?"), but the article is about a man named Oliver Morton. Many of the ideas reported in the article are Morton's, not Bethune's. If you are writing about the topic of geoengineering and you refer to Morton's ideas that you read about in Bethune's article, you need to cite an indirect source.

Activity A | Reread the sample essay ("Reducing the Risk of Wildfires through Reforestation") on pages 151–153. Find two examples of citing indirect sources in the essay and fill in the information in the table below.

Paragraph #	Original Source of the Information	Author of the Text that Cites the Information

Both APA and MLA guidelines suggest that, when possible, you should try to find the original source of the information and cite it rather than citing indirectly. If the text you are reading cites a written source—for example, a research article or website that is easily located, you should find and refer to this original written source.

However, it is not always possible to locate an original source. For example, it might be that an expert gives an interview or opinion to a reporter for a newspaper or magazine article. There is no other written source to refer to than the article itself, which was written by the reporter. In this case you need to cite the indirect source.

Citing Indirect Sources in APA

Include the name of the original source in your sentence. In your in-text citation, give the secondary source and add the phrase "as cited in . . . " When quoting word for word, include the page number, if available.[17] Include the secondary source in your References list.

Example

According to Mike Flannigan, who directs the Western Partnership for Wildland Fire Science, "the area burned in Canada has increased over the past 40 to 50 years. This is due to human-caused climate change" (as cited in Schwartz, 2016).

Reference

Schwartz, Z. (2016, May 4). Did climate change contribute to the Fort McMurray fire? *Maclean's*. Retrieved from http://www.macleans.ca/society/science/did-climate-change-contribute-to-the-fort-mcmurray-fire/

Citing Indirect Sources in MLA

Include the name of the original source in your sentence. In your in-text citation, give the secondary source and add the phrase "qtd. in . . . " When quoting word for word, include the page number, if available. Include the secondary source in your Works Cited list.

Example

According to Mike Flannigan, who directs the Western Partnership for Wildland Fire Science, "the area burned in Canada has increased over the past 40 to 50 years. This is due to human-caused climate change" (qtd. in Schwartz).

Work Cited

Schwartz, Zane. "Did Climate Change Contribute to the Fort McMurray Fire?" *Maclean's*, 4 May 2016, www.macleans.ca/society/science/did-climate-change-contribute-to-the-fort-mcmurray-fire/ Accessed 12 May 2016.

Activity B | Writing Task: Citing Indirect Sources | In each excerpt that follows (from Reading 2), author Brian Bethune has reported something that was originally said by another person. After each paragraph, write your own sentence in which you quote or paraphrase the information from the indirect source. Be sure to cite the indirect source correctly in either APA or MLA format, and indicate which format you have used.

Example

The real moral issue—the true reason geoengineering has to be considered, according to Morton—is the plight of the global poor. There are seven billion humans now, many of them still in grinding poverty; there will be two or three

[17] Note that online sources often do not have page numbers.

billion more before the population curve turns downward. A world that aims, as it should, "to support nine billion in comparative comfort will need a great deal of energy. The idea you can reduce carbon emissions suddenly, in a way that's politically feasible and economically non-disastrous—no."

Source: Bethune, B. (2016, January 12). Is geoengineering the solution to saving the earth? *Maclean's*. Retrieved from http://www.macleans.ca/society/science/is-geoengineering-the-solution-to-saving-the-earth/

Oliver Morton claims that it is not possible to reduce carbon emissions quickly enough to maintain a decent standard of living for all people on Earth (as cited in Bethune, 2016). [APA]

1. "Ask yourself this," said Princeton physicist Richard Socolow. "Do you believe the risks of climate change merit serious actions aimed at mitigating them, and do you think that reducing human-generated carbon dioxide emissions to near zero is very hard?"

   Source: Bethune, B. (2016, January 12). Is geoengineering the solution to saving the earth? *Maclean's*. Retrieved from http://www.macleans.ca/society/science/is-geoengineering-the-solution-to-saving-the-earth/

2. Among environmentalists, rejection is more visceral—Al Gore has called it "delusional in the extreme"—because tinkering with the Earth's natural systems is simply more of the hubris that brought us to the brink of disaster in the first place.

   Source: Bethune, B. (2016, January 12). Is geoengineering the solution to saving the earth? *Maclean's*. Retrieved from http://www.macleans.ca/society/science/is-geoengineering-the-solution-to-saving-the-earth/

Preventing Plagiarism

Using Internet Sources Responsibly

Is This Plagiarism?

Alpha is taking an environmental studies course this semester that requires a lot of essays. Having learned that synthesizing information from multiple sources is important, she visited many websites and found a lot of interesting and relevant information to include in the final essay. Some of the websites did not include an author's name, and others had such nice sentences that Alpha knew it was impossible to write them as well. In the end, Alpha copied and pasted the sentences directly into her final essay, placing them together logically and coherently to make a very well-written essay.

Did Alpha commit plagiarism? Consider the details of the above scenario in the context of the definitions and rules regarding plagiarism established by your academic institution. Discuss your answer to this question with a partner or small group. You may use the following questions to guide your discussion:

1. How much information in Alpha's passage is original, and how much is taken from outside sources?
2. How much of Alpha's language is original, and how much is taken directly from outside sources?
3. Do you think Alpha cited the sources correctly? If she did, would this make her paper a good one? Explain.
4. What would you do to prevent plagiarism in this scenario?

Note: For information on your institution's plagiarism policy, search the college or university's website for a statement on academic integrity and/or its academic code of conduct.

Thesis Skill

Writing a Problem–Solution Thesis Statement

A problem–solution thesis statement mentions the problem and proposes the solution to be discussed in the essay. The thesis may be stated in one or more sentences. As with any type of writing, there may be variation depending on the specific writing task and the ideas set out in the essay. Keep in mind that a problem–solution thesis statement does not have to contain the words *problem* and *solution*, as long as it clearly proposes a way to address a negative situation.

Activity A | Read the following sentences. Which are examples of a problem–solution thesis statement? Discuss your answers with a partner or small group.

a. Climate change is a big problem.
b. One solution to the problem of wildfires is *cloud-seeding*, injecting chemicals into clouds to induce rainfall.
c. Even if we reduce carbon emissions to zero today, the Earth's temperature will continue to rise for the next century.
d. As a short-term solution to global warming, we might consider geoengineering.

e. The Arctic is seeing the effects of climate change earlier than other places in the world.
f. In order to help farmers in drought-stricken areas, more efficient irrigation systems are necessary.

Activity B | Look back at the sample essay "Reducing the Risk of Wildfires through Reforestation" on pages 151–153 and answer the questions below. Discuss your answers with a partner or small group.

1. Can you identify one or more sentences that state the thesis of the essay? Underline it (them) in the text, and indicate the paragraph number(s) here:

   ____

2. Does the thesis mention both the problem and the solution, or only the solution?

In short essays that you write for school, it is often expected that the thesis will be explicitly stated and will appear at the end of the introduction. In other types of writing, however, the thesis is sometimes implied or appears elsewhere.

Activity C | Writing Task: Problem–Solution Thesis Statement | Look back at your Unit Inquiry Question and the notes you have taken while brainstorming and reading throughout this chapter. Create the first draft of a working thesis statement that mentions a problem and proposes a solution. You may also revise your inquiry question, if you wish. When you are done, exchange your thesis statement with a partner and discuss.

Keep the following in mind as you think about your solution:

- An effective solution will either address the underlying cause of the problem or mitigate the effects of the problem.
- It is possible to suggest a general approach to solving a problem rather than specifying one particular course of action.

Introductions

Presenting an Example of the Problem or Solution

An example can help bring your topic alive for your reader. Presenting a concrete example of the problem or solution you plan to discuss is one strategy for introducing a problem–solution essay. You could use a real-life example of the problem occurring or the solution being implemented. Alternatively, it could be a hypothetical, but specific, example of a more general type of problem or solution. For example, if you propose geoengineering as a solution to global warming, you might describe a specific type of geoengineering proposal in your introduction (e.g., putting mirrors in outer space). As always, it is important to make an explicit connection to your thesis. If you have

already written a draft of your thesis, you will usually have to revise it slightly so that it follows naturally from your introduction.

Activity A | Look at the following brainstorming notes and notice how they led to the drafting of a working thesis. Then read the sample introduction that presents an example of the solution. How was the wording of the thesis revised in the introduction? Discuss your answer with a partner.

Notes:

problem—deforestation (mass cutting of trees)

causes: housing developments, logging, agriculture, wildfires

effects: soil erosion, landslides, loss of habitat, global warming

solution: get people to plant trees and stop cutting trees! Need lots of small-scale programs in different places.

working thesis: In order to solve the problem of deforestation, we need to encourage local communities to plant trees and to preserve existing forestland.

Local officials in Java, Indonesia, instituted an interesting policy a few years ago. Any couple who wanted to get married was required to pay for the planting of five trees. If a couple wanted to get divorced, they had to pay for the planting of 25 trees. The officials said they came up with the idea as a way to get local citizens involved with the fight against climate change, since Indonesia has been criticized for massive deforestation activities ("Five tree fee," 2007). This is an excellent example of an innovative program that operates on a small scale, but if enacted in many places around the world, can contribute to a solution to the problem of deforestation.

Reference

Five tree fee for a Java wedding. (2007, December 3). *BBC News*. Retrieved from http://news.bbc.co.uk/2/hi/asia-pacific/7124680.stm

Activity B | Look back at the sample essay "Reducing the Risk of Wildfires through Reforestation" on pages 151–153. Read the introduction and answer the following questions. Discuss your answers with a partner or small group.

1. Does the introduction present an example of the problem or of the solution that will be discussed in the essay?
2. How does the writer connect the example to the thesis?

Activity C | Writing Task: Example Introduction | Look back at your thesis statement from Activity C on page 171. Then write an introduction that presents an example of the problem or solution that you would discuss in the essay. Make a clear connection between the example and the thesis statement. You may have to reword the thesis statement to improve the flow of the introduction.

Conclusions

Issuing a Warning

The purpose of a problem–solution essay is to propose a solution to a problem. A problem, by definition, is bad—if a situation did not have negative effects, there would be no need to deal with it. A natural way of concluding a problem–solution essay is to issue a warning about what will happen if the problem is not solved. For example, the negative effects of a problem might get even worse. Alternatively, new problems might arise.

Activity A | Read the sample conclusion below. Underline the sentence that issues a warning.

Deforestation threatens wildlife, leads to soil erosion, and makes communities vulnerable to devastating landslides. Deforestation also robs the Earth of its main method of removing carbon dioxide from the atmosphere, disrupting an age-old process that has helped to keep carbon dioxide levels stable. At current rates of deforestation, all of the Earth's rainforests will be destroyed within 100 years (Kukreja, n.d.). The solution is clear: protect our forestland through aggressive international regulation of clear-cutting. If we do not take action to reverse course, we will find ourselves in a dry and barren wasteland, more like Mars than the bountiful Earth we love.

Reference

Kukreja, R. (n.d.). Deforestation facts [Blog post]. *Conserve Energy Future*. Retrieved from http://www.conserve-energy-future.com/various-deforestation-facts.php

Activity B | Look back at the sample essay "Reducing the Risk of Wildfires through Reforestation" on pages 151–153. Read the conclusion and answer the following questions. Discuss your answers with a partner or small group.

1. What warnings are issued in the conclusion?
2. What kind of language does the author use to make the warnings?

Activity C | Writing Task: Warning Conclusion | Look back at the example introduction you wrote in Activity C on page 173. Now write a warning conclusion to fit with that introduction.

WRITING FUNDAMENTALS

Composition Skill

Achieving Coherence

In Unit 3, you learned that essays and paragraphs must have *unity*—that is, all information in a paragraph should be directly related to its topic sentence, and all paragraphs should be directly related to the thesis of the essay. Unity is an important characteristic of a coherent text.

Another characteristic of a coherent text is the smooth and logical flow of information in a way that a reader expects. In a paragraph, for example, a reader expects that the idea in the topic sentence will be explained and developed. To explain the idea in your topic sentence, you must present new information. However, that new information must be connected logically to something that is already known by the reader. This "known information" is typically something that has been mentioned previously in your essay or paragraph.

A common way to connect new information to known information is to refer to known information in the subject of the sentence and new information in the predicate of the sentence.

Look again at the second paragraph in this section on coherence (copied below). Notice how the information flows through the text, from known to new. **New** information is bolded the first time it is mentioned. When it is referred to later, as <u>known</u> information, it is underlined.

> <u>Another characteristic of a coherent text</u> is the smooth and logical flow of information in **a way that a reader expects**. In a paragraph, for example, <u>a reader expects that</u> **the idea in the topic sentence will be explained and developed**. To <u>explain the idea in your topic sentence</u>, you must **present new information**. However, that <u>new information</u> must be connected logically to **something that is already known by the reader.** <u>This "known information"</u> is typically something that has been mentioned previously in your essay or paragraph.

Notice that "another characteristic of a coherent text" is underlined in the first sentence, indicating that it is known information. Even though it appears in the first sentence of the paragraph, it refers to information introduced in the previous paragraph. In this way, the topic sentence of a paragraph can be used to achieve coherence by referring to an idea from the previous paragraph.

Activity A | Compare the two paragraphs below, adapted from Reading 2, which present the same information. Trace the flow of information in each. Highlight the new information and underline known information, then draw an arrow connecting the new information to the known information. Remember that known information is often referred to in different words for variety—for example, with a pronoun, an example, or paraphrased language. Which paragraph seems more coherent?

Paragraph A

That doesn't mean [Morton is] beating the drum for most geoengineering proposals. There are two sorts of geoengineering proposals. Morton finds it ineffectual to remove CO_2 from the atmosphere, also known as carbon capture, because the projects so far either pull out too little CO_2 or emit too much. Countering the greenhouse effect of carbon by blocking sunlight until emissions are driven down by renewables and nuclear power is another approach.

Paragraph B

That doesn't mean [Morton is] beating the drum for most geoengineering proposals. They essentially break down into two sorts. The first is carbon capture, removing CO_2 from the atmosphere, an approach Morton finds ineffectual because the projects so far either pull out too little CO_2 or emit too much. The second approach is to live with the carbon until emissions are driven down by renewables and nuclear power, while countering its greenhouse effect by blocking sunlight.

Activity B | Writing Task: Paragraph Revision | Choose one of the paragraphs you have written for this unit. Trace the flow of known to new information through the paragraph using the method described in Activity A. Then revise the paragraph to improve the coherence of the information flow as necessary.

Sentence and Grammar Skill

Using Conditional Sentences

In this unit, you wrote a concluding paragraph issuing a warning. Warnings are often made using conditional sentences. Conditional sentences are made up of two parts: the *condition*—circumstances that must exist for something to happen—and the *result*—what will happen if the condition is (or is not) met.

> <u>If the polar ice caps melt</u>, **sea levels will rise**.
> *condition* *result*
>
> **Sea levels will rise** <u>if the polar ice caps melt</u>.
> *result* *condition*

The condition is expressed in a dependent clause that begins with the subordinator *if*. The result is expressed in an independent clause. Notice that the condition can be expressed first or last.

There are several types of conditional sentences. Here we will focus on three types.

Activity A | In each conditional sentence below, underline the verbs in both clauses. How do the verbs differ in each sentence? What is the difference in meaning? Discuss your answers with a partner or small group. Then check your answers in the chart.

a. If governments care about protecting the environment, they focus on long-term solutions instead of short-term political gains.
b. If governments care about protecting the environment, they will focus on long-term solutions instead of short-term political gains.
c. If governments cared about protecting the environment, they would focus on long-term solutions instead of short-term political gains.

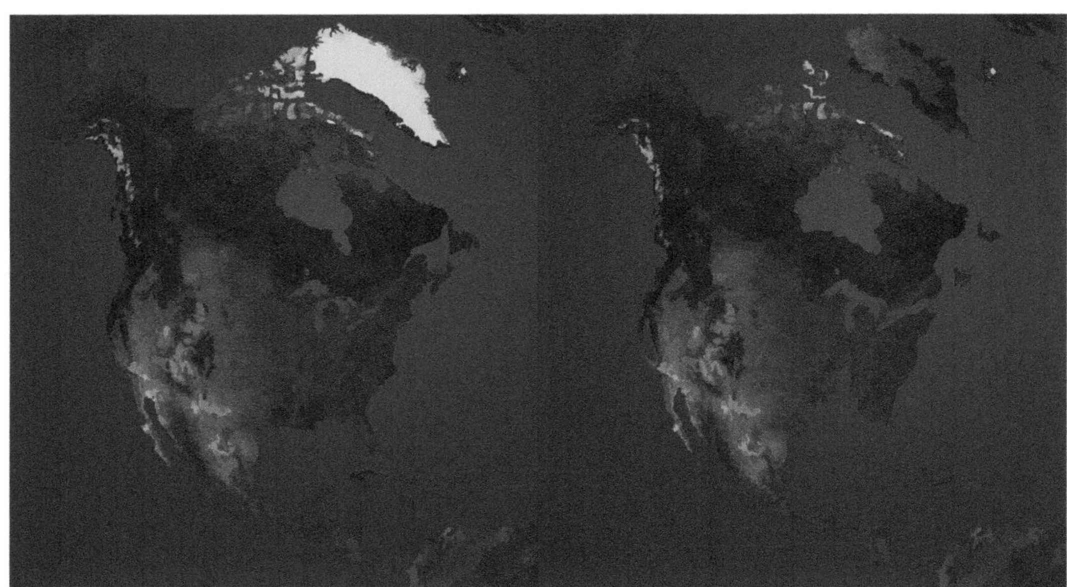

Three Types of Conditional Sentences

1. General truth

Look again at Sentence a. on the facing page. This type of sentence expresses a result that is always or generally true, given the condition. In other words, in our example, *If governments care about protecting the environment, they focus on longterm solutions instead of short-term political gains*, any time it is true that governments care about protecting the environment, it is also true that they focus on long-term solutions. The verb in the condition clause and the verb in the result clause are both in the simple present tense.

> If you heat water to 100 degrees, it boils.

meaning = Every time X happens, Y also happens.

form = *If* + clause in simple present, clause in simple present.

2. Future prediction

Look again at Sentence b. on the facing page. This type of sentence expresses a result that will happen in the future, if the condition is met. The verb in the condition clause is in the simple present tense and the verb in the result clause in the simple future tense.

> If the polar ice pack melts, sea levels will rise.

meaning = It is possible that X will happen. In the case that X happens, Y will also happen.

form = *If* + clause in simple present, clause in future simple

NOTE: The future tense is never used in the condition clause.

3. Untrue condition

Look again at Sentence c. on the facing page. This type of sentence expresses a result that is not true, because the condition is not met. In other words, the writer is indicating that governments don't care about protecting the environment, and therefore they don't focus on long-term solutions.

> If I had a million dollars, I would invest in green technology.

meaning = X is not true, so Y is not true or will not happen.

form = *If* + clause in past tense, clause with *would* + verb

The verb in the condition clause is in the simple past to show that the condition is not met. The verb in the result clause is made up of the modal verb *would* + simple present.

NOTE: In untrue conditional sentences, the verb *to be* is always conjugated as *were*, not *was*.

> If I were you, I would invest in green technology.
>
> The prime minister would make more investments in green technology if he were serious about addressing climate change.

Activity B | In each conditional sentence below, fill in the blanks with an appropriate form of the verbs in parentheses. Some verbs may be in the negative. Label each sentence as GT (general truth), FP (future prediction), or UC (untrue condition).

1. Major flooding of coastal areas ________________ (occur) if the polar ice pack ________________. (melt) ________
2. Polar bears ________________ (can survive) if there ________________ (be) not enough ice cover in the winter. ________
3. If it ________________ (be) possible to reduce carbon emissions to zero immediately, global temperatures ________________ (rise) more slowly and eventually reverse course. ________
4. Greenhouse gas emissions ________________ (be) much lower if industries ________________ (rely) more on clean, renewable energy sources. ________
5. If local authorities ________________ (control) deforestation in Indonesia, the Sumatran rainforest ________________ (exist) in 20 years. ________

Activity C | Writing Task: Paragraph Editing | Look back at the conclusion you wrote in Activity C on page 174. Did you use a conditional sentence to issue your warning? Is it written correctly? Revise the conclusion if necessary to include a conditional sentence issuing a warning.

UNIT OUTCOME

Writing Assignment: Problem–Solution Essay

Write a problem–solution essay of 350 to 450 words on a topic related to climate change. (Your instructor may give you an alternative length.) Use either APA- or MLA-style in-text citations and a References or Works Cited list.

You may write an essay that answers your Unit Inquiry Question. If you choose to do so, look back at the work you have done in this unit:

- the latest version of your Unit Inquiry Question on page 148;
- the brainstorming web you created on page 166;
- the outline you wrote in Activity C on page 166;
- the working thesis and introduction you wrote in Activity C on page 171; and
- the conclusion you wrote in Activity C on page 174.

Decide whether you want to include drafts of any of these in your essay. You may have to revise your writing to integrate these elements into your essay.

If you do not want to write about your Unit Inquiry Question, you may develop a new question or write an essay on one of the following topics instead:

- steps governments can take to reduce their national greenhouse gas emissions;
- the role of individuals in fighting climate change; or
- ways to help people in coastal areas cope with rising sea levels.

Use the skills you have developed in this unit to complete the assignment. Follow the steps set out below to ensure that you practise each of your newly acquired skills to write a well-developed problem–solution essay.

1. **Brainstorm**: Use a web to generate ideas related to the topic you will write about.
2. **Find outside sources of information**: Select appropriate outside information as you learned in Unit 2. If you cite indirect sources, be sure to use the correct format.
3. **Write a thesis statement**: Develop a focused thesis statement that mentions the problem and/or the solution you intend to discuss.
4. **Outline**: Fill in the outline below to plan your first draft.
   - Decide whether you will organize your ideas using the block pattern or the chain pattern.
   - Develop your body paragraphs using the question technique you learned in Unit 2.
   - Include information from Readings 1 and 2 (or additional outside research) in each body paragraph, if appropriate.

Introduction	Relevant example of the problem or solution: A clear link between your example and your thesis statement: Focused thesis statement:

Main Body Paragraphs	Topic sentence 1: Information to be included: Concluding sentence (optional):
	Topic sentence 2: Information to be included: Concluding sentence (optional):
	(Optional) Topic sentence 3: Information to be included: Concluding sentence (optional):
Conclusion	Summary of main ideas: Warning:

5. **Prepare a first draft**: Use your outline to write the first draft of your essay. Use AWL and mid-frequency vocabulary from this unit where appropriate. In your first draft, you should
   - focus on getting your ideas down on paper without worrying too much about grammar.
   - skip a section if you get stuck and come back to it later. For example, consider writing the body paragraphs before writing the introduction and conclusion.
6. **Ask for a peer review**: Exchange your first draft with a classmate. Use the Problem–Solution Essay Rubric on page 182 to provide suggestions for improving your classmate's essay. Ask questions to help him or her develop the body paragraphs more effectively as you learned in Unit 2. Read your partner's feedback carefully. Ask questions if necessary.
7. **Revise**: Use your partner's feedback to write a second draft of your essay.
8. **Self-check**: Review your essay and use the Problem–Solution Essay Rubric to look for areas in which you could improve your writing.
   - Edit your essay for conditional sentences. Make sure you have used the correct verb forms in the condition and result clauses to express your intended meaning.
   - Check that you have used the best sentence patterns to introduce information from outside sources. (See Units 3 and 4 in this book.)
   - Edit your essay for correct APA- or MLA-style citations. Make sure you include a References or Works Cited section. Include page numbers for direct quotations. Note indirect sources where appropriate.
   - Try reading your essay aloud to catch mistakes or awkward wording.
9. **Compose final draft**: Write a final draft of your essay, incorporating any changes you think will improve it.
   - When possible, leave some time between drafts.
10. **Proofread**: Check the final draft of your essay for any small errors you may have missed. In particular, look for spelling errors, typos, and punctuation mistakes.

Evaluation: Problem–Solution Essay Rubric

Use the following rubric to evaluate your essay. In which areas do you need to improve most?

E = **Emerging**: frequent difficulty using unit skills; needs a lot more work
D = **Developing**: some difficulty using unit skills; some improvement still required
S = **Satisfactory**: able to use unit skills most of the time; meets average expectations for this level
O = **Outstanding**: exceptional use of unit skills; exceeds expectations for this level

Skill	E	D	S	O
The introduction presents a relevant example of the problem or solution and includes a link to the thesis statement.				
The thesis statement is clear and proposes a solution.				
Each body paragraph starts with a clear topic sentence.				
Each body paragraph develops one controlling idea.				
The flow of information in each paragraph is coherent.				
The ideas are organized according to the block or chain pattern.				
The claims are hedged appropriately.				
Information from readings in this unit has been integrated and cited appropriately.				
AWL and mid-frequency vocabulary items from this unit are used when appropriate and with few mistakes.				
The conclusion issues a warning.				
Conditional sentences are used appropriately.				
APA- or MLA-style in-text citations and a References or Works Cited list are formatted correctly.				

Unit Review

Activity A | What do you know about the topic of climate change that you did not know before you started this unit? (Hint: return to the quiz at the beginning of the unit.) Discuss with a partner or small group. Be prepared to report what you have learned to the class.

Activity B | Look back at the Unit Inquiry Question you developed at the start of this unit and discuss it with a partner or small group. Then share your answers with the class. Use the following questions to guide you:

1. What ideas did you encounter during this unit that contributed to answering your question?
2. How would you answer your question now?

Activity C | Use the following checklist to review what you have learned in this unit. First decide which 10 skills you think are most important—circle the number beside each of these 10 skills. If you learned a skill in this unit that isn't listed below, write it in the blank row at the end of the checklist. Then put a check mark in the box beside those points you feel you have learned. Be prepared to discuss your choices with the class.

Self-Assessment Checklist	
☐	1. I can talk about climate change.
☐	2. I can write a problem–solution inquiry question.
☐	3. I can hedge my claims effectively.
☐	4. I can use a block or chain pattern to organize problems and solutions.
☐	5. I can recognize and use collocations effectively to improve my vocabulary.
☐	6. I can use AWL and mid-frequency vocabulary from this unit.
☐	7. I can evaluate a peer's writing and give feedback for improvement.
☐	8. I can use peer feedback to improve first drafts.
☐	9. I can use a web to show relationships among ideas.
☐	10. I can cite indirect sources using APA or MLA style.
☐	11. I can avoid plagiarism by using Internet sources responsibly.
☐	12. I can write a problem–solution thesis statement.
☐	13. I can write an introduction that includes an example of a problem or solution.
☐	14. I can write a conclusion that issues a warning.
☐	15. I can present my ideas coherently.
☐	16. I can use conditional sentences.
☐	17. I can write a problem–solution essay of four of more paragraphs.
☐	18.

Activity D | Put a check mark in the box beside the vocabulary items from this unit that you feel you can now use with confidence in your writing.

Vocabulary Checklist	
☐ adversely (adj.) 4000	☐ precipitation (n.) 5000
☐ ecosystem (n.) 6000	☐ predict (v.) AWL
☐ drought (n.) 5000	☐ release (v) AWL
☐ erode (v.) 5000	☐ shift (v.) AWL
☐ factor (n.) AWL	☐ significantly (adv.) AWL
☐ greenhouse (n.) 4000	☐ somewhat (adv.) AWL
☐ hemisphere (n.) 5000	☐ source (n.) AWL
☐ infrared (adj.) 7000	☐ trend (n.) AWL
☐ nourish (v.) 6000	☐ whereas (conj.) AWL
☐ occur (n.) AWL	☐ vapour (n.) 6000

UNIT 6 Corporate Social Responsibility

Business

KEY LEARNING OUTCOMES

- Creating an inquiry question for examining a controversial issue
- Planning to persuade an audience
- Correcting grammar using your dictionary
- Writing a debatable thesis statement
- Refuting a source
- Acknowledging opposing views
- Using quantifiers with countable and non-countable nouns
- Introducing an essay with a turnaround
- Concluding an essay with a call to action
- Writing a persuasive essay

EXPLORING IDEAS

Introduction

Some people argue that the main purpose of a business is to make as much money as possible for its owners or shareholders. Others argue for *corporate social responsibility*, the idea that a business has a responsibility to consider the common good (e.g., the welfare of its workers, the environmental impact of its activities, or the well-being of the community in which it is located). These are some of the issues you will be thinking about in this unit.

Activity A | Discuss the following questions with a partner or small group.

1. When you look at the picture of the Apple store above, what ideas first come to mind?
2. What do you know about how and where Apple devices are produced?
3. When you are planning to purchase a new product, what factors do you consider to help you choose between different brands?
4. What aspects of a company's activities contribute to creating a positive image for the company?
5. Making money is a goal for all businesses. What other goals do or should businesses have?

Activity B | Reflect on the reasons for and against evaluating a business only in terms of how much profit it generates for its owners or shareholders. Complete the T-chart below, listing your reasons in the appropriate column.

Reasons for Focusing Only on Profits	Reasons against Focusing Only on Profits

Activity C | Writing Task: Short Paragraph Exploring Arguments | Write a short paragraph about the arguments for or against focusing only on profits when evaluating a business.

Fostering Inquiry

Building an Argument

Persuading people to consider your point of view, which may differ from theirs, requires the presentation of appropriate reasons and facts, statistics, and other evidence to support that point of view. Building an argument requires collecting this evidence and organizing it in a clear and convincing manner. Only when you have provided the reasons for your argument and supported them to build a strong argument can you expect to succeed in persuading someone else to accept your position or point of view.

Activity A | What do you want to know more about in relation to corporate social responsibility and the field of business? For example, *What role does business play in a community?* or *What is the relationship between a business and its workers?*

1. Write down two or three questions you have about the relationship between business and society.
2. In a small group, share your questions.
3. Choose one question to be your guiding inquiry question for this unit. Your inquiry question can be different from the other group members' questions. The focus of your question may change as you work your way through this unit.

4. Write your inquiry question here and refer to it as you complete the activities in this unit.

   My Unit Inquiry Question:

   ____

   ____

   ____

   ____

   ____

Activity B | Writing Task: Freewriting | Write for at least five minutes on the topic of your Unit Inquiry Question. Do not stop writing during this time. After five minutes, read what you have written and circle two or three ideas that you would like to explore further in order to answer your Unit Inquiry Question.

Structure

Persuasive Essay

The purpose of a persuasive essay is to take a position on an issue and persuade (or convince) a reader that your position is the correct one. This persuasion can be achieved by supporting the arguments you make as well as addressing opposing views on the issue.

A persuasive essay may use various rhetorical strategies to achieve its purpose. For example, a persuasive essay may argue for a particular solution to a problem, but the difference between a problem–solution essay and a persuasive essay is the fact that the persuasive essay attempts to show why one solution is better than the alternative(s). In other words, a persuasive essay is always arguing *against* an alternative.

In order to persuade an audience, you must be able to

- take a clear *position* (stance, point of view, or side in an argument) on an issue;
- support your position with strong arguments;
- anticipate your audience's questions or objections; and
- provide convincing answers to your audience's questions or objections.

Activity A | With a partner or small group, read the following example of a student paragraph that develops an argument about the role of businesses in society. Answer the questions that follow.

A company must act in socially responsible ways because it relies on the community in which it operates for infrastructure, consumers, and employees, among other things. If its practices are harmful for the community, the business itself will suffer. For example, a company can only succeed if it can recruit and keep good employees. This means that the company has a stake in making sure that a community can nurture the type of people who would make good employees, perhaps through supporting schools and education. Businesses also need effective roads and transportation networks in order to move their goods and to be accessible to their consumers. They benefit from a clean environment, which provides safe drinking water for their employees and customers and saves money on expensive cleanup projects or filtration systems. Thus, it is in a company's best interest to act in the best interest of the community. While it may be true that communities rely on businesses for employment and economic growth, it is also true that businesses owe a lot to their communities.

1. What is the author's position in this paragraph?
2. What kind of information is used to support the author's position?
3. Do you agree with the author?
4. In which line does the author mention a different point of view?

Persuasive Essay Structure

A persuasive essay follows the standard essay structure described in Unit 2, with an introduction, two or more body paragraphs, and a conclusion. The introduction briefly introduces an issue and leads to a debatable thesis statement—that is, one that takes a position on a controversial issue. Each body paragraph contains a single controlling idea directly related to the thesis statement.

Body paragraphs in a persuasive essay usually develop arguments in favour of the thesis statement. Arguments are the reasons you give explaining why your position is the right one, and why your reader should agree with you.

In addition to strong arguments in favour of the thesis, a persuasive essay also mentions opposing views. A persuasive essay is like one side in a debate: it would not be effective if it did not acknowledge and respond to the other side. Usually, in a persuasive essay, opposing views are mentioned at least briefly in the introduction to give context to the debate. Then the writer responds to those opposing views in the body of the essay. This can be accomplished in more than one way.

For example, the writer may wish to address the opposing views early in the essay and then concentrate on developing strong arguments in favour of the thesis. Or, the writer may wish to win readers over with strong arguments in favour of the thesis right away, and then mention the opposing views to demonstrate awareness of these views and respond to them. Alternatively, the writer may employ a counterargument strategy, whereby opposing views are brought up throughout the essay and the writer argues strongly against each one, illustrating its flaws. Any of these three organizational patterns can be effective, as long as the writer's position on the issue is clear throughout the essay. Which strategy you will use depends on the particular issue you are writing about, the specific arguments and counterarguments relevant to that issue, and/or the assignment given to you by your instructor.

	Opposing View(s) First	Argument(s) First	Counterargument Strategy
Paragraphs	1. Introduction with thesis	1. Introduction with thesis	1. Introduction with thesis
	2. Opposing view(s) followed by your response(s)	2. Main argument(s)	2. Opposing view and counterargument
	3. Main argument(s)	3. Opposing view(s) followed by your response(s)	3. Opposing view and counterargument
	4. Conclusion	4. Conclusion	4. Conclusion

FIGURE 6.1 Persuasive essay organizational patterns

Activity B | The following essay illustrates one of the organizational patterns shown in Figure 6.1. Read the essay closely, paying attention to the organizational pattern, and answer the questions that follow.

Don't Be Fooled by "Corporate Citizenship"

Corporate social responsibility (CSR) is widely praised as a model for how businesses can make a profit while also having a positive impact in their communities. Because consumers have become more aware of social and environmental issues, they can "vote with their pocketbooks" by rewarding companies that behave ethically and punishing companies that behave unethically (Trudel & Cotte, 2009). In fact, major companies now have CSR departments devoted to making sure the company does good things, voluntarily. This is a seemingly wonderful example of how the free market succeeds in benefiting companies, workers, consumers, and the community. Unfortunately, however, the main effect of "corporate citizenship" is that businesses now have yet another deceptive marketing stunt available to increase their market share.

It is undoubtedly true that companies should behave in socially responsible ways. Many do, and this can be beneficial for both the companies and society. Ballingall (2012) describes Canadian Tire as a success story. By instituting several environmentally friendly policies, the company was able to cut costs and increase profits. Nobody would argue that outcomes such as these are bad. In fact, the International Chamber of Commerce (2002) even argues that private industry "is the driving force for sustainable economic development and for providing the . . . resources needed to meet social and environmental challenges" (n.p.). Sadly, the ICC is wrong about this. It is wonderful when social and business goals align. In the case of Canadian Tire, the company simply made a good business decision—the fact that it was socially responsible was just a coincidence. When social and business goals are in conflict, however, we cannot expect that companies will voluntarily behave in ways that benefit society. There are countless examples of businesses exploiting workers and the environment in order to increase profits.

In fact, the concept of corporate citizenship is actually dangerous when it encourages companies to cheat for recognition as the most socially responsible. *Greenwashing* is an example of this kind of cheating. Greenwashing occurs when a company makes exaggerated claims about its low environmental impact. Because consumers will pay more for "green" products and services, companies have an incentive to portray themselves as greener than they are (Hoffman & Hoffman, 2008). The reprehensible behaviour of Volkswagen, discovered in 2015, is an example of this greenwashing. A growing number of consumers have become interested in fuel-efficient cars with lower emissions of polluting greenhouse gases. The problem is that such cars tend not to perform as well as traditional cars in terms of speed and power. Volkswagen claimed to have solved this problem and introduced a high-performance, low-emissions car, which became very popular with environmentally conscious consumers. What these consumers did not know was that Volkswagen had designed the cars to cheat on emissions tests. Under actual driving conditions, the cars were releasing 40 times the nitrogen oxide allowed under US regulations (Hotten, 2015).

Volkswagen betrayed public trust to make money. Yet the current trend toward CSR marketing set the stage for Volkswagen to profit from such deception. If they had not been caught, we would point to it as another shining example of corporate citizenship. How many more dishonest companies are out there, but haven't been caught yet? We should not rely on businesses to decide how they will be ethical and then profit from the appearance of ethical behaviour. Instead, we as consumers should decide what we think is ethical and hold businesses to standards that match our expectations. In a democratic society, one of the most important freedoms citizens have is the right to organize and participate in public demonstrations. Instead of shopping your way to a better society, become politically active and take to the streets! March to show your support for what you like and your opposition against actions you cannot accept.

References

Ballingall, A. (2012, June 14). How corporate social responsibility improved these companies' bottom lines. *Maclean's*. Retrieved from http://www.macleans.ca/general/how-corporate-social-responsibility-improved-these-companies-bottom-lines/

Hoffman, J., & Hoffman, M. (2008). *Green: Your place in the new energy revolution*. New York, NY: St. Martins' Griffin.

Hotten, R. (2015, December 10). Volkswagen: The scandal explained. *BBC News*. Retrieved from http://www.bbc.com/news/business-34324772

International Chamber of Commerce. (2002, March). *Business in society: Making a positive and responsible contribution* [report]. Retrieved from https://www.icc.fi/wp-content/uploads/B-in-Society-Booklet.pdf

Trudel, R., & Cotte, J. (2009, Winter). Does it pay to be good? *MIT Sloan Management Review, 50*(2), 61–68.

1. What is the issue debated in the essay?
2. What is the author's position on the issue?
3. Which organizational pattern does the essay use?
    - ☐ argument(s) first
    - ☐ opposing view(s) first
    - ☐ counterargument strategy
4. What words are used to show how the author feels about the issue?
5. What argument(s) are presented in support of the author's position?
6. What opposing view(s) are mentioned?
7. How does the author respond to opposing views? (Check more than one if you think they both apply.)
    - ☐ Author admits that the opposing view is partially right, but explains why it is not important or doesn't apply in this case.
    - ☐ Author shows why the opposing view is wrong.
8. How does the author conclude the essay?

Language Tip

Signalling Stance

An essay is more persuasive when there is a clearly signalled, consistent stance throughout the essay. That is, even though a writer discusses both her own arguments and the arguments of her opponents, the reader always knows which side the writer is taking. One way to accomplish this is through the use of language or punctuation that signals an evaluation of an idea. Look at the two sentences on the right. In each case, how does the author feel about corporate citizenship?

a. Fortunately, businesses these days have taken on the role of corporate citizen, engaging in various activities that benefit society rather than the bottom line.

b. Unfortunately, businesses these days have taken on the role of "corporate citizen," engaging in various activities that benefit "society" rather than the bottom line.

Even though the words in the sentences are nearly identical, the author of the first sentence has signalled a positive stance about corporate citizenship by using the word *fortunately*. The author of the second sentence has signalled a negative stance in two ways—by using the word *unfortunately* and by using quotation marks (sometimes called "scare quotes") to show skepticism about the notions of corporate citizenship and society.

To the right are some words commonly used to signal stance:

Positive Stance	**Negative Stance**
fortunate, fortunately	unfortunately
luckily	sadly
happily	bad, worse, worst
good, better, best	misguided
admirable	misplaced
sensible	unreasonable
intelligent	irrational
convincing	poorly conceived
valid	unfair
appropriate	outrageous

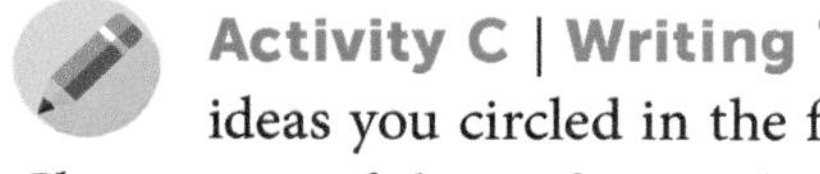

Activity C | Writing Task: Persuasive Paragraph | Look back at the ideas you circled in the freewriting you completed in Activity B on page 188. Choose one of these ideas and write a short paragraph in which you take a position. Use appropriate language to signal your stance.

Activity D | Exchange your paragraph with a partner. Read your partner's paragraph and use the following questions to provide feedback.

1. What is the author's position in this paragraph?
2. What arguments, information, or ideas are used to support the author's position?
3. What words does the author use to signal stance?
4. Do you agree with the author?
5. Does the author mention a different point of view? If so, how does he or she respond?
6. What do you like best about this paragraph?
7. How would you improve this paragraph?

Activity E | Revisit your Unit Inquiry Question on page 188. What new ideas have you thought of that will help you answer your question? Share your ideas with a partner or small group. At this point, you may consider revising your Unit Inquiry Question.

ACADEMIC READING

Vocabulary

Vocabulary Skill: Correcting Grammar Using Your Dictionary

In Unit 2, you saw that a lot of information about the meaning and the use of new words can be found in a good dictionary. This information can also help you identify grammatical problems when you are using new words.

Activity A | Examine the dictionary entries for *contribute* and *contribution*. What kind of grammatical information do the entries provide?

con·trib·ute AWL /kən'trɪbjuːt; *BrE also* 'kɒntrɪbjuːt/ *verb* **1** [T, I] to give sth, especially money or goods, to help sb/sth: **~sth (to/towards sth)** *We contributed £5000 to the earthquake fund.* ◇ **~(to/towards sth)** *Would you like to contribute to our collection?* ◇ *Do you wish to contribute?* **2** [I] **~(to sth)** to be one of the causes of sth: *Medical negligence was said to have contributed to her death.* ◇ *Human error may have been a* ***contributing factor.*** ➲ LANGUAGE BANK AT CAUSE **3** [I, T] to increase, improve or add to sth: **~to sth** *Immigrants have contributed to British culture in many ways.* ◇ **~sth to sth** *This book contributes little to our understanding of the subject.* **4** [T, I] to write things for a newspaper, magazine, or a radio or television programme; to speak during a meeting or conversation, especially to give your opinion: **~sth (to sth)** *She contributed a number of articles to the magazine.* ◇ **~(to sth)** *He contributes regularly to the magazine 'New Scientist'.* ◇ *We hope everyone will contribute to the discussion.*

con·tri·bu·tion AWL /ˌkɒntrɪ'bjuːʃn; *NAmE* ˌkɑːn-/ *noun* **1** [C] a sum of money that is given to a person or an organization in order to help pay for sth SYN **donation**: **~(to sth)** *to* ***make a contribution*** *to charity* ◇ *a substantial contribution* ◇ *All contributions will be gratefully received.* ◇ **~(toward(s) sth/doing sth)** *valuable contributions towards the upkeep of the cathedral* **2** [C] **~(to sth)** a sum of money that you pay regularly to your employer or the government in order to pay for benefits such as health insurance, a pension, etc: *monthly contributions to the pension scheme* ➲ SYNONYMS AT PAYMENT **3** [C, usually sing.] an action or a service that helps to cause or increase sth: **~(to sth)** *He* ***made a*** *very positive* ***contribution*** *to the success of the project.* ◇ *the car's contribution to the greenhouse effect* ◇ **~(toward(s) sth/doing sth)** *These measures would make a valuable contribution towards reducing industrial accidents.* **4** [C] **~(to sth)** an item that forms part of a book, magazine, broadcast, discussion, etc: *an important contribution to the debate* ◇ *All contributions for the May issue must be received by Friday.* **5** [U] **~(to sth)** the act of giving sth, especially money, to help a person or an organization: *We rely entirely on voluntary contribution.*

1. contribute
   a. Is *contribute* a transitive or intransitive verb (see Unit 2)?

   ____

   b. Which preposition is commonly used with *contribute*? Is that always the case?

   ____

   c. Is *contribute* followed by nouns referring to people or nouns referring to things or both?

   ____

2. contribution
   a. Is *contribution* a countable or non-countable noun, or can it be either?

      ____

   b. If it is countable, can it always be used in the plural?

      ____

   c. Which preposition is commonly used with *contribution*? Is that always the case?

      ____

Activity B | Using the dictionary entries for *contribute* and *contribution*, correct the mistakes in the following sentences.

1. Socially responsible businesses contribute their employees to charitable endeavours.
2. Some socially responsible businesses contribute generously for charities related to their business.
3. Every year, that company makes substantial contribution to the Canadian Red Cross.

Vocabulary Preview: The Academic Word List

Activity C | Use the grammatical and other information provided in your dictionary about the words in bold to help you correct the mistakes in grammar or collocation in the following sentences. One of the sentences does not contain an error.

1. A responsible business should establish clear **code** of conduct for its employees.
2. Businesses that **commit** ethical objectives are more profitable.
3. Businesses need to consider local **community** when they establish ethical objectives.
4. The **concept** to ethical objectives is increasing in popularity.
5. Canadian **consumers** should consider workers here and abroad when considering a company's ethics.
6. Ethical objectives should be part of any plan that is **corporate**.
7. If a corporation wants to **establish** for ethical objectives, it needs to consider all its stakeholders.
8. Companies who win their ethical **objectives** benefit in a number of ways.
9. A consumer that is **potential** may have to be convinced to purchase an unfamiliar brand.
10. Before you **purchase** a product to a certain company, consider the company's ethical record.

Vocabulary Preview: Mid-frequency Vocabulary

Activity D | Use your dictionary to decide if the correct form of the bolded word is used in the following sentences. Correct any errors.

1. Long-term employees of a company are **accustom** to certain ways of doing things.
2. If a company has **aspirational** to improve its ethical record, it can start by looking at its impact on the local community.
3. Whether or not ethical objectives are **beneficial** depends on several factors.
4. **Dissatisfying** customers are not likely to do further business with that company.
5. **Dubiously** business practices can damage a company's reputation.
6. Some investors look for **ethics** types of investment.
7. Ethical business objectives should include the elimination of **harassments** of employees.
8. Workplace conditions directly affect employee **morales.**
9. **Multinational** companies have significant economic and political power.
10. If a company sells a faulty product, its customers can seek legal **redressing** for any damages.

Reading 1

The reading "Business Ethics" is an excerpt from the textbook *Business Management* by Loykie Lominé, Martin Muchena, and Robert A. Price. This textbook is used in business classes in Canadian high schools.

Activity A | What do you consider ethical or unethical behaviour for a business? Think of concrete examples where you think a business behaved in an ethical or unethical way. Share these examples with a partner or small group.

Activity B | In addition to simply "doing the right thing," what are some other reasons for a business to behave ethically? What might be the consequences of one business deciding to behave ethically?

Activity C | As you read the excerpt on page 197, think back to one of the businesses that you discussed in Activity A. Are the reasons for this business's ethical behaviour the same as or different from the ones mentioned in the text? Are the consequences of this business's ethical behaviour the same as or different from the ones mentioned in the text? Make notes in the margin indicating whether the authors' ideas are different or similar to your own.

READING

Business Ethics

Why Organizations Set Ethical Objectives

1 It is very common today that businesses are **establishing ethical objectives**. These objectives are goals based on established **codes** of behaviour. When these objectives are met, they allow the business to provide some social or environmental benefit. Even if there are no direct benefits, the business at least does not hurt society or the environment while making a profit. For example, a business may aim to expect all its employees to be treated without discrimination, **harassment**, or even favouritism. Another ethical objective may be that **consumers** are always treated with respect and honesty. Ethical objectives can cover a whole range of activities, and today many businesses are setting them.

2 Businesses may set themselves ethical objectives for some very good commercial reasons. They may include:

1. **Building up customer loyalty**: Repeat customers are vital to most businesses. Customers are more likely to return to a business they trust and respect. Ethical objectives and ethical action foster this.
2. **Creating a positive image**: Both existing and **potential** customers are likely to shop at businesses with good reputations. The opposite is certainly true: customers will avoid businesses with reputations for untrustworthiness.
3. **Developing a positive work environment**: Businesses that have well-motivated staff who enjoy their work at the company have a competitive advantage. Businesses with strong ethical objectives can be attractive to many potential employees and can improve **morale** and motivation.
4. **Reducing the risk of legal redress**: Being unethical can cost a company money because **dissatisfied** customers do not return or unethical behaviour creates a bad reputation. Sometimes unethical behaviour can lead to legal **redress** by the government, by other businesses, or by the customers themselves. Even if a business "wins" in court, the process can be expensive and cause significant damage to the firm's reputation.
5. **Satisfying customers' ever-higher expectations for ethical behaviour**: With improved ICT[1] and the world wide web, business decisions and actions are more visible than ever before. Today, consumers are aware of what is considered ethical and unethical behaviour. Consequently, they often "punish" unethical behaviours by not going to certain businesses. Few businesses can ignore public opinion.
6. **Increasing profits**: Opportunities for businesses to behave ethically are growing. Banks will often not lend to **dubious** businesses. Likewise, clothes manufacturers will not use "sweatshop" workers, and coffee houses use "fair trade" coffee. Many people today seek out and **purchase** from businesses that behave ethically, which can lead to higher profits.

The Impact of Implementing Ethical Objectives

3 When a business implements ethical objectives, many areas of the business environment will be affected. The effects may be on the following:

1. **The business itself**: Business may benefit from having ethical objectives in the long run. However, costs are likely to rise. Employees, who are **accustomed** to certain norms and practices, may resist change in the short term.

[1] information and communications technology

2. **Competitors**: Competitors may have to react to keep their market position.
3. **Suppliers**: If a business implements ethical objectives, this may include the policy of buying only from other ethical businesses. As a result, suppliers may have to respond in order to protect their orders.
4. **Customers**: Customers are likely to trust the business more and develop a strong brand loyalty.
5. **The local community**: Businesses that have ethical objectives generally have a better relationship with the local **community.** This is **beneficial** for the company in terms of employment and goodwill.
6. **Government**: Local, regional, and national governments are increasingly recognizing businesses with ethical objectives because of pressure from voters and other stakeholders. This creates a government–business environment that fosters ethical objectives.

The Difference Between Ethical Objectives and Corporate Social Responsibility

4 Ethical objectives are different from **corporate** social responsibility (CSR), but the two are also closely related. CSR is the **concept** that a business has to operate in a way that will have a positive impact on society. As part of its CSR policy, a business should assess its actions. As a result of such an assessment, the business may wish to implement a particular ethical objective. For example, a business might open a daycare facility for its employees.

The Importance of Corporate Social Responsibility

5 CSR is broader and less specific than ethical objectives. A company **committed** to CSR is intending to act as a good "corporate citizen." This means acting responsibly in all matters and in a way that benefits society as a whole. A business committed to CSR not only obeys laws. It also interacts responsibly and honestly with customers and reduces its impact on the environment. If a business recognizes its CSR, it is very likely that this business has a sustainable business model. If the business builds strong links with society and the environment, people are more likely to see the business as a valued part of the society.

6 Many businesses, and increasingly big businesses, see themselves as role models—as leading citizens. This means setting the standard for everyone for responsible behaviour. In an international context, this might be more difficult because of different ethical values, but it can still be possible if **multinational** companies take action. Although many businesses do not reach their highest **aspirations** for CSR, the movement toward CSR has been significant. There have been dramatic changes in the attitudes and practices of businesses since around 1980.

Source: Adapted from Muchena, M. M., Lominé, L., & Pierce, R. (2014). *Business management* (pp. 45–47). Oxford, UK: Oxford University Press.

Activity D | The following questions are based on the textbook excerpt you just read. Discuss your answers with a partner or small group.

1. Explain each of the following reasons to establish ethical business objectives in your own words.

Reasons for Having Ethical Objectives	Explanation
Building up customer loyalty	

Creating a positive image	
Developing a positive work environment	
Reducing the risk of legal redress	*Win or lose, legal challenges cost time and money.*
Satisfying customers' ever-higher expectations for ethical behaviour	
Increasing profits	

2. The text mentions several potential effects of implementing ethical objectives. Decide if these effects are positive or negative. Give reasons for your answers.

	Effect On	Positive or Negative?	Reason?
The business itself			
Competitors			
Suppliers			
Customers			
The local community			
Government			

3. If a business takes its corporate social responsibility seriously, is that the same as or different from following the rules and laws established for the business? Explain your answer.

Activity E | Writing Task: Persuasive Paragraph | Write a short paragraph in which you attempt to persuade your reader to support or oppose the implementation of ethical business practices in a workplace. Remember to include references to the source of your information if you use words or ideas from the textbook excerpt or from any outside research you may choose to do.

Activity F | Compare your paragraph to the sample paragraph "Economic Benefits of Ethical Business Practices" in Appendix 2. Then answer the following questions about the sample paragraph.

1. What is the main idea of the paragraph?
2. What details does it include to convince the reader to support or oppose the implementation of ethical business practices?
3. Do you find the arguments convincing? Why or why not?
4. Note how unit vocabulary was used in the sample paragraph. Discuss with a partner if and where any of the unit vocabulary could be substituted into your own persuasive paragraph.

Critical Thinking

Bloom's Taxonomy—*Evaluation*

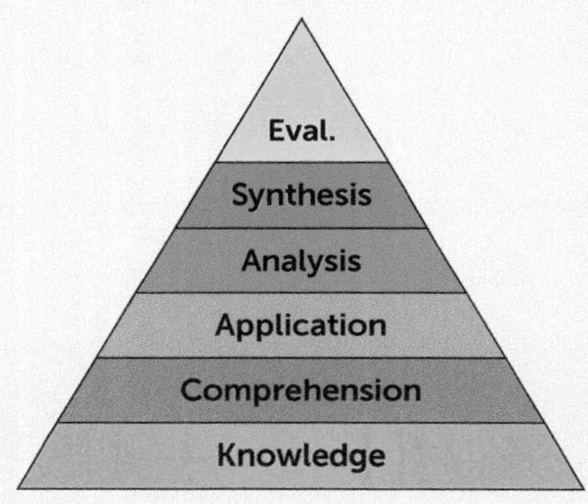

The sixth level of thinking in Bloom's taxonomy is *evaluation*. Evaluation involves using judgment to make decisions and develop opinions. For example, when you write a persuasive essay, you must evaluate multiple positions on an issue to determine which is the best. Doing so requires careful consideration of the support for each position by understanding it at the lower levels of Bloom's taxonomy. In other words, evaluation requires more than just having an opinion; the opinion must be based on critical thinking.

As you consider the position an author has taken on an issue, ask yourself questions like

- Who is the author, and why does he or she want me to take the same position?
- Has the author supported his or her position with logic, facts, or other sufficient evidence?
- Do I agree that ______________________? Why or why not?
- What is the most important thing to consider about this issue? Why is it more important than other things?
- How can I justify or support my own opinion on this issue?

Source: Bloom, B. S., Engelhart, M. D., Furst, E. J., Hill, W. H., & Krathwohl, D. R. (1956). *Taxonomy of educational objectives: The classification of educational goals. Handbook 1: Cognitive domain*. London, UK: Longman.

Reading 2

The following reading, "Two Faces of Apple," discusses the issue of wages and working conditions in factories that manufacture Apple products. It is an excerpt from an article published by the Carnegie Council, a think tank[2] that promotes the importance of ethics in international affairs.

Activity A | Read the excerpt and try to identify the debate (two opposing positions or sides) on the issue. Highlight all the ideas that support one side in this debate. Then highlight (in a different colour) the ideas that support the other side of the debate. Use that information to answer the questions that follow.

---

[2] a group of experts who provide advice and ideas on political, social, or economic issues

READING

Two Faces of Apple

The Good Apple

1 From one perspective, Apple's world could not be rosier. Rising from the ruins of a dying company in 1997, Apple has reached the pinnacle[3] of success in 15 short years. It is among the most valuable and highly profitable companies in the world.

2 Apple's remarkable success lies in the company's ability to create truly innovative products with vast customer appeal. Apple defies the conventional wisdom of the consumer electronics industry, which emphasizes low-cost, "me-too" products,[4] and a continually shortened product life. Instead, Apple has opted for constant product innovation, resulting in fanatic consumer loyalty and a high level of profitability.

The Bad Apple

3 So why does Apple treat its customers and workers by two different standards? When it comes to customers, Apple is a bold innovator that leads the industry in new directions and forces others to follow. However, when it comes to the management of its supply chain and treatment of workers, it hides behind the constraints of prevailing industry practices. It is bad enough that these practices violate local and national laws. It is even more troubling that they also violate Apple's own voluntary self-imposed code of conduct.

4 Most of Apple's worker-related problems are focused on Apple's Chinese manufacturing partner Foxconn. Reports over the past few years have described instances of Foxconn employees committing suicide, presumably from working in an extremely high-stress environment. In addition, there are reports of miserable living conditions, underage

---

[3] most important or successful part of something

[4] a product that is very similar to a competitor's already successful product

workers, below-standard wages, involuntary labour, and health hazards associated with the use of toxic chemicals and inadequate air filtration systems. In 2011, there was also an explosion at the plant in Chengdu that killed three and injured fifteen workers. Other reported instances of questionable conduct include bribery and falsifying records. These activities were also identified in Apple's own previous audits.

Apple's Strategic Profile—Value Culture vs. Cost Culture

5 In my view, Apple's good and bad sides both result from the same business philosophy: skillful exploitation of market power for the sole benefit of the company and its investors. This model does not consider "what is fair." Instead, it only considers how Apple can achieve higher prices for products sold and lower costs for products made.

6 Apple's pricing strategy is driven by a focus on value to its customers. The customer is willing to pay a price that is equal to the product's perceived value to the customer. Hence, as long as the customers are satisfied, Apple is under no obligation to reduce its prices.

7 When it comes to workers' wages and working conditions, Apple uses its dominant market position to acquire these services at the lowest possible price. In this way, it is able to keep the largest share of the profit for itself and yield the lowest possible share to the workers. It is not important that the added costs of better wages and working conditions represent an extremely small proportion of its overall costs. It's all relative. If these additional costs are higher than those of Apple's competitors, they could have a negative effect on the company's stock price in the short run.

8 Apple's business model is no different than its competitors'. Yet as an industry leader, it can—and I argue that it should—set standards of conduct that enrich the "commons"[5] at the same time as it enriches the company's investors.

9 From Apple's perspective, the issues of workers' wages and working conditions have been an unnecessary distraction that must be minimized

[5] society; general public

Undercover filming by the BBC investigative program *Panorama* showed exhausted Apple employees in Chinese factories who said they had worked 12 to 16 hours a day with no days off for long stretches. They lived 12 to a room in dormitories and were forced to attend before and after work meetings without being paid for their time, the BBC said.

Apple said it resents *Panorama*'s suggestion that it is not living up to its promise to customers to improve working conditions.

"We know of no other company doing as much as Apple does to ensure fair and safe working conditions, to discover and investigate problems, to fix and follow through when issues arise, and to provide transparency into the operations of our suppliers," Apple said.

Scott Stratten, a marketing expert and author of *Unselling*, said he doesn't think the company will suffer negative effects from reports about its human rights record.

"People are going to get angry right now. Then Boxing Day will happen. Do you think anybody's going to care what happens to some poor worker overseas when they're trying to get $50 off a flat screen or an iPad?" Stratten said.

"It's a sad commentary. I wish it mattered to people, I really do."

Source: Adapted from CBC News. (2014, December 19). Apple on defence after BBC exposé of working conditions in its factories. *CBC News*. Retrieved from http://www.cbc.ca/news/business/apple-on-defence-after-bbc-expos%C3%A9-of-working-conditions-in-its-factories-1.2879208

or even avoided. There has not been strong and persistent disapproval from customers, investors, and regulators. Thus, Apple does not feel pressure to go beyond the minimum. In their view, there are no measurable benefits that could be expected from doing things differently.

10 Despite extensive media coverage of labour-related problems, Apple has suffered no loss in demand for its products. In fact, demand only continues to grow. Apple also enjoys broad customer loyalty in China even though customers there have a better knowledge of these working conditions. This is not surprising. Product boycotts are usually very short-lived, except those for products that pose a threat to consumers' health and safety, such as contaminated food products.

11 Apple does not have to fear its competitors because they all use factories with similar cost structures and labour practices. On the contrary, competitors are likely to be afraid of Apple since its market power allows it to take the initiative in changing industry practices. If they did this, other companies would be pressured to follow these new practices.

12 That is why, in my opinion, Apple must play a leadership role. This means building a reputation not only as a leading corporate innovator, but also as a leading socially responsible corporate citizen. New Apple CEO Tim Cook could play a pivotal role in shaping Apple's corporate culture. It is crucial to address Foxconn-like working conditions by attacking their root cause rather than merely treating symptoms. One hopes that Apple will once again astonish the world by showing a new approach to building better bridges between private profit and public good.

Source: Adapted from Sethi, S. P. (2012, April 2). *Two faces of Apple*. Retrieved from http://www.carnegiecouncil.org/publications/ethics_online/0068.html

Activity B | The following questions are based on the excerpt you just read. Discuss your answers with a partner or small group.

1. What does the author mean when he refers to "the two faces of Apple"? In other words, what is the first face and what is the second face?
2. What are the author's main criticisms of Apple?
3. What is the debate presented in this excerpt? Write it as a question that has more than one possible answer.
4. What are the two sides in the debate?

   Side A. ______________________________

   Side B. ______________________________

5. What is the author's position?
6. After having read the article along with the sidebar about Apple, which point of view do you agree with? Why? Has your opinion about Apple changed? Why or why not?

PROCESS FUNDAMENTALS

Before You Write

Planning for Your Audience

In Unit 1, you analyzed texts to understand the author's purpose. When you write a persuasive essay, your purpose is to persuade an audience. In order to be effective, you need to think carefully about your audience before you write. Ask yourself questions like the following.

- Who am I writing to?
- What do they know about this issue?
- What kinds of arguments will be convincing to this audience?
- What views will this audience likely have about the issue? How can I respond to these views?
- What is my relationship to the audience? What kind of tone should I use?

Activity A | Consider the following scenarios and answer the questions above for each scenario.

Scenario 1: You are an employee at Canadian Tire. You want to convince your boss to invest money in an after-school program for local children.

Scenario 2: You are a student writing an article for your university's online newspaper. You want to convince students to boycott Apple.

Scenario 3: You are a spokesperson for Apple. You want to convince consumers that you care about workers' rights and safety.

Activity B | Writing Task: Persuasive Paragraph | Choose one of the scenarios above and write a short paragraph to accomplish the given purpose, keeping the audience in mind.

Activity C | Think about your Unit Inquiry Question (see page 188). Imagine you are writing a persuasive essay in response to this question. Plan for persuading your audience by answering the five bulleted questions above.

Activity D | Looking at the answers you formulated about your audience in Activity C, create a rough outline for an essay based on these answers. As you learn more about your topic, use your outline to add more ideas and details to persuade your audience. This rough outline will help you identify gaps in your knowledge. If you end up writing an essay on your current Unit Inquiry Question, this rough outline may be helpful in guiding your planning.

Integrating Information from an Outside Source

Refuting a Source

In the first five units, we have discussed integrating information from outside sources that support your ideas. However, it is also possible to refer to sources that you disagree with. In this case, the source represents an opposing view that you will engage with and respond to. When you refer to an idea from an outside source and explain why it is wrong, you are refuting that source.

Refutations typically contain the following elements:

a. source citation
b. reporting verb(s)
c. source's idea or claim
d. connector that expresses contrast or contradiction
e. word or phrase signalling the author's stance
f. your own view on the idea or response to the source

Activity A | Look at the following examples of refuting the same source. How are they different?

a. Milton Friedman (1970) claimed that "the social responsibility of business is to increase profits." However, this is a misguided notion. In fact, businesses that focus on profits at the expense of societal well-being will face long-term consequences.
b. While Friedman (1970) suggests that businesses' only responsibility is to make money, the truth is that businesses have the moral responsibility to improve the communities that they profit from.

Reference

Friedman, M. (1970, September 13). The social responsibility of business is to increase profits. *The New York Times Magazine*, 32–33, 122–124.

Activity B | For each refutation below, do the following:

a. highlight the source's idea or claim and circle the citation portion of it;
b. highlight the writer's response to the source in another colour;
c. underline any connector that expresses contrast or contradiction, and draw a box around any words that signal stance; and
d. answer the question that follows.

Refutation 1

According to Pendleton (2004), CSR has been "completely inadequate" as a way to address social problems created by large companies in developing countries. However, abundant research has shown that CSR programs are making a real difference in many places. For example, . . .

Reference

Pendleton, A. (2004). *Behind the mask: The real face of corporate social responsibility.* Retrieved from https://www.st-andrews.ac.uk/media/csear/app2practice-docs/CSEAR_behind-the-mask.pdf

Question: Does the student writer think that CSR is an adequate response to social problems?

Refutation 2

Although Ging (2012) argues that businesses can't be expected to "fix the impossible" problem of poverty, this opinion is misguided. In fact, businesses must acknowledge their own role in the problem and take the lead in offering solutions.

Reference

Ging, T. (2012). Corporate social responsibility: The role and reasons for business involvement in sustainable development [Blog post]. *The Specialty Coffee Chronicle.* Retrieved from http://www.scaa.org/chronicle/2012/04/10/corporate-social-responsibility-the-role-and-reasons-for-business-involvement-in-sustainable-development/

Question: Does the student writer think it is impossible for businesses to solve the problem of poverty?

Preventing Plagiarism

Collaborating Responsibly

Is This Plagiarism?

Alpha's instructor for English 301 has assigned students an individual research paper. Each student has one week to research the topic before submitting the paper. Alpha and the other students in the class are used to discussing ideas before writing in-class texts. Alpha finds this process helpful, so he asks two classmates if they want to work together on the research paper. The students choose the same topic and research articles together. Since they each find different sources, they share what they find with each other and have more comprehensive bibliographies on the topic. Finally, the three students write their research papers on their own and then submit them to the instructor.

Did Alpha and his classmates commit plagiarism? Consider the details of the above scenario in the context of the definitions and rules regarding plagiarism established by your academic institution. Discuss your answer to this question with a partner or small group. You may use the following questions to guide your discussion:

1. Did the students break the rules by working together for the research portion of the assignment?
2. Do you think they all used the same information in their papers? Does this matter?
3. Did they use original language to write their papers?
4. Do you think they should get higher grades on their papers because they have more comprehensive bibliographies?
5. What would you do to prevent plagiarism in this scenario?

Note: For information on your institution's plagiarism policy, search the college or university's website for a statement on academic integrity and/or its academic code of conduct.

Thesis Skill

Writing a Debatable Thesis Statement

A debatable thesis statement is a key characteristic of a persuasive essay. That is, the thesis statement takes a clear position on an issue that other people might disagree with. If a thesis statement is not debatable, there is no need to argue for it, and there are no opposing views to respond to.

Activity A | Look again at the thesis statement from the sample essay "Don't Be Fooled by 'Corporate Citizenship.' "

> Unfortunately, however, the main effect of "corporate citizenship" is that businesses now have yet another deceptive marketing stunt available to increase their market share.

1. On what debate is this thesis statement taking a position?
2. In what ways is this statement debatable? What are some alternate positions?

Now look at an example of a statement that is not debatable:

> Many businesses these days have policies on corporate social responsibility.

This is a fact that could be supported with examples of companies' CSR policies, but does not require an argument. There is no opportunity to take a position or stance on an issue. The author is not *for* or *against* CSR policies and is not responding to people who might disagree.

Activity B | Decide which thesis statements below are debatable. For each debatable thesis statement, write a statement that expresses a different position on the issue. Cross out the thesis statements that are not debatable.

1. Consumers should not buy from companies that pollute the environment or exploit their workers.
2. Businesses should focus on what they are good at—making products, delivering services, and generating profit for shareholders—instead of trying to solve society's problems.
3. There is a great debate about whether businesses can make money and be socially responsible at the same time.
4. This essay will explain what corporate social responsibility is.
5. Government regulation is the right way to ensure that businesses behave in socially responsible ways.
6. Proponents of CSR believe it is a win–win situation: companies can profit while doing something to help the environment.

Activity C | Writing Task: Debatable Thesis Statement | Look back at your Unit Inquiry Question on page 188 and the notes you took while planning your writing for a specific audience. Create the first draft of a working thesis statement. Remember to take a clear position on a debatable issue. You may also revise your inquiry question, if you wish. When you are done, exchange your thesis statement with a partner and discuss.

____

____

____

Introductions

Turnaround

Take another look at the sample essay "Don't Be Fooled by 'Corporate Citizenship'" on pages 190–192. The author's position on corporate social responsibility is that it is merely a deceptive marketing ploy, yet the introduction starts with many positive statements about CSR. Why?

Leading the reader in one direction in the introduction, then changing direction to focus on the author's real thesis, is called a turnaround. It can be useful for a number of reasons:

- It captures the reader's attention with the unexpected turn.
- It can establish common ground with readers.
- In a persuasive essay, it is a way to concede[6] valid opposing views early.

---

[6] admit that something is true, logical, etc.

As with all introductions, it is important to provide an effective link to your thesis statement.

Activity A | Read the sample turnaround introduction below and answer the questions that follow.

> It seems like every day we see another horrifying news story about children being exploited in overseas sweatshops, working 12-hour days to produce sneakers or electronic gadgets. It is outrageous that businesses would put profits ahead of human safety and dignity. These greedy companies also disregard environmental standards, often dumping their industrial waste illegally and polluting the local water supply. Government regulations often seem inadequate and allow big companies to operate in ways that many people find unacceptable. However, we have only ourselves to blame for this situation. Companies will supply what their consumers demand, at the price that consumers are willing to pay. We cannot complain about worker exploitation while we continue to be delighted at how cheaply we can buy the goods produced by those workers. To force companies to act responsibly, consumers should not buy from businesses that pollute the environment or exploit their workers.

1. In what direction does the writer seem to be going at the beginning of the introduction? Write a thesis statement that matches this direction.
2. Where does the turnaround happen? Underline the sentence in which the writer changes direction. Highlight the word that signals the turnaround.

Activity B | Writing Task: Turnaround Introduction | Look back at the working thesis statement you wrote for your inquiry question in Activity B on page 208. Write a turnaround introduction that leads to this thesis statement.

Conclusions

Call to Action

After you have successfully argued your position, you may want to leave your reader with a call to action on the issue you have written about. A call to action is empowering, because it gives people the feeling that they can do something about a problem or make a difference. Thus, it is an appropriate way to conclude essays about social issues that affect many people. Look back at the sample essay on pages 190–192. Notice how the sample essay ends by encouraging people to become politically active, supporting changes they would like to see or protesting unethical business practices.

Volkswagen betrayed public trust to make money. Yet the current trend toward CSR marketing set the stage for Volkswagen to profit from such deception. If they had not been caught, we would point to it as another shining example of corporate citizenship. How many more dishonest companies are out there, but haven't been caught yet? We should not rely on businesses to decide how they will be ethical and then profit from the appearance of ethical behaviour. Instead, we as consumers should decide what we think is ethical and hold businesses to standards that match our expectations. In a democratic society, one of the most important freedoms citizens have is the right to organize and participate in public demonstrations. Instead of shopping your way to a better society, become politically active and take to the streets! March to show your support for what you like and your opposition against actions you cannot accept.

Activity A | Read the sample conclusion above. What action does it call on readers to take? Do you agree that this is a good way to respond to unethical businesses?

Activity B | What are some actions that individuals could take to solve the following problems? Discuss your answers with a group.

1. A local business is dumping waste into a river.
2. It is difficult for consumers to know how socially responsible a company is.
3. Businesses make false claims about corporate social responsibility.

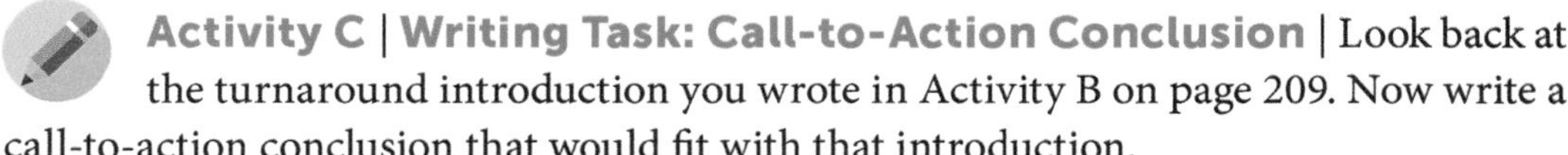

Activity C | Writing Task: Call-to-Action Conclusion | Look back at the turnaround introduction you wrote in Activity B on page 209. Now write a call-to-action conclusion that would fit with that introduction.

WRITING FUNDAMENTALS

Composition Skill

Acknowledging Opposing Views

Since a persuasive essay takes one side in a debate, it is necessary to address the other side. To do so, you must acknowledge critics or opponents and reply to their arguments. Your response to opposing views is very important—it is your chance to convince people to change sides in the debate. Do not simply mention the opposing views and leave them unanswered. If you do so, your reader will be confused about which side you are taking in the debate.

Respond to an opposing view in one of two ways:

1. Refute it, or explain why it is wrong (see *Refuting a Source*, pages 205–206).
2. Concede it, or admit that the idea has some validity (make a concession), but go on to diminish or lessen its importance. For example, you could state that the opposing view
   - is only partially correct;
   - is generally true, but does not apply in this case; or
   - is true but is not as important as something else.

   Like refutations, concessions also use language to signal that they are referring to an opponent's point of view. However, the concession will also contain some language that acknowledges the truth or validity of the point of view before the refutation happens.

   To signal concession, the following are often useful:
   - **It is true that** . . . However, . . .
   - **While it may sometimes be true that** . . . , in this case, . . .
   - . . . **is a valid point,** but it is important to keep in mind that . . .
   - Author (year) points out that . . . Of course **this cannot be denied**. Nevertheless, . . .

Activity A | Annotate the sample concession paragraph below by labelling the following three components: opposing view, concession, response. Pay attention to the words and expressions the writer uses in these components.

> Critics of "voting with your pocketbook" point out that unemployment has risen and wages have fallen in industrialized nations, leaving consumers in those countries with little disposable income. These consumers, they argue, are in no position to voluntarily pay more for goods that can be purchased cheaply at Walmart and other discount retailers. Thus, it is unfair to ask them to stop buying cheap goods for the sake of the environment or of workers in faraway countries. It is sadly true that the economic situation of many families in industrialized countries is bleak. It cannot be denied that "socially responsible shopping" is expensive and creates a burden for poor families. Nevertheless, if we are really concerned about corporate abuses, we must be prepared to make real sacrifices. Certainly, wealthier people should be expected to do more than those living in poverty, but we all need to do our part, since social issues affect us all. There are even ways that we can "vote with our pocketbooks" without spending more money. For example, buying second-hand is a way to save money and avoid rewarding companies that don't live up to our ethical standards.

Activity B | Writing Task: Concession Paragraph | In Activity B of the Introduction to this unit (page 187), you listed reasons for and against a business focusing only on profits. Imagine you are writing an essay on this topic. Which stance will you take? Circle one of the following argumentative thesis statements:

a. Businesses exist to generate profits; this is and should be their rightful focus.
b. Businesses have a responsibility to act in ways that benefit society, rather than focusing only on generating profits.

Now follow the steps below to write a concession paragraph in which you acknowledge and reply to the opposing view (i.e., the thesis statement you did not choose).

Step 1: State an opposing point of view, clearly signalling that it is not your own position. You may want to use one of the five sentence patterns below to do so. (These five examples are only a few of many possible ways to signal an opposing view.)

a. [Some/Many] people [think/feel] that ____________________.
b. [Opponents/Proponents] of ____________ [argue/claim/suggest] that ____________________.
c. Critics of ____________ raise the point ____________________.
d. ____________ rightly point(s) out ____________________.
e. It is frequently argued that ____________________.

____

Step 2: Concede the validity of the opposing view, then respond to your opponents' argument.

Explain why you still hold your position, despite a valid point from the other side. You may want to use one of the five sentence patterns below to concede and respond to opposing views. (Again, these are only a few examples; there are many other ways to do so.)

a. **Although** it may be true that ____________, [your reply here].
b. **Even if** this is sometimes the case, [your reply here].
c. **While** it cannot be denied that ____________, [your reply here.]
d. Admittedly, ____________. **Nevertheless**, [your reply here.]
e. This is a fair point. **However**, it doesn't change the fact that [your reply here.]

Step 3: Combine your sentences from steps 1 and 2 above, then support your argument in a well-developed paragraph.

Sentence and Grammar Skill

Using Quantifiers with Countable and Non-countable Nouns

Nouns in English can be countable or non-countable. Countable nouns have a singular and a plural form and can be used with numbers (e.g., *one, two*) and with indefinite articles (*a, an*).

Non-countable nouns have only one form. They are used with singular verbs and cannot be made plural. Since they are non-countable, these nouns cannot be used with numbers or with indefinite articles. A good learner's dictionary will tell you if a noun is countable or non-countable. As a general rule, non-countable nouns fall into the following categories.

Abstract Concepts	love, hate, happiness
Natural Phenomena	rain, wind, snow
Materials	wood, gold, glass
Activities	walking, hiking, reading
Collective Nouns	baggage, equipment, furniture

Quantifiers, which usually go before a noun, are words that indicate the amount of something (e.g., *little, many*). Some quantifiers can be used only with countable plural nouns; other quantifiers can be used only with non-countable nouns. Some quantifiers can be used with both countable plural and non-countable nouns.

Before Countable Plural Nouns	Before Non-countable Nouns	Before Countable Plural and Non-countable Nouns
few	little	no
a few	a little	hardly any
several	a great deal of	some
quite a few	large amounts of	plenty of
a (large) number of	(too) much	a lot of/lots of
a majority of		almost all
(too) many		all

Examples

Many businesses these days establish ethical objectives.

A great deal of advertising focuses on highlighting a company's socially responsible activities.

A lot of businesses these days establish ethical objectives.

A lot of advertising focuses on highlighting a company's socially responsible activities.

Activity A | Of the choices given below each sentence, circle all the nouns that could be used to fill in the blank. When making your decisions, pay attention to whether the nouns are countable, non-countable, plural, or singular. There may be more than one correct answer for each sentence.

1. Ethical business practices may include limiting how much ________________ a business uses.
   a. resources b. equipment c. raw materials d. water
2. If a company has a good working environment, hardly any of its ________________ will feel unhappy about their workplace.
   a. staff b. employee c. employees d. manager
3. A majority of ethically responsible ________________ focus on certain key areas of their activities to improve their practices.
   a. organization b. business c. institutions d. authority
4. Almost all ________________ that a business hopes to attract can be influenced through strategic marketing strategies.
   a. client b. clientele c. customers d. end user
5. There are very few ________________ that a business relies on that can be considered unlimited.
   a. oil b. space c. assets d. supplies
6. Implementing ethical business objectives requires a great deal of ________________ so that the business can achieve its goals.
   a. strategies b. initiative c. plans d. planning

Activity B | Reread one of the paragraphs you wrote for this unit and check your use of quantifiers with countable and non-countable nouns in that paragraph. Make any necessary corrections, referring to the chart on page 213 and your dictionary to help you.

Learning Strategy

Monitoring Your Work

Good learning strategies help you to improve your English. Monitoring your work is a key strategy that not only helps improve your English but also improves the quality of your work in English. There are two aspects to monitoring your work. First, it involves checking your work for errors in grammar and vocabulary use. You can do this in several ways:

1. Pay attention to areas of grammar that you recently reviewed in class. Did you apply these grammar rules well in your own text?
2. Review your writing along with feedback from your instructor. Note the three most common types of language errors in your recent writing (e.g., verb problems or misused vocabulary). Then check all your new writing for these three error types.
3. Use a dictionary to check the meaning and usage of words that you have not used in a while or that are new to you to make sure you are using them appropriately in terms of meaning and grammar.

In addition, monitoring your work means evaluating how you are improving over time and how your abilities to use English have changed. You can do this in several ways:

1. Compare a text you wrote 6 or 12 months ago to one you wrote recently. What changes do you notice in your writing? Focus on content, organization, and language use.
2. Think of a very difficult text you read 6 or 12 months ago. Read it again now. Do you still find it as difficult to read as when you first read it?
3. Try to remember tasks that you found very difficult or even impossible to do one or two years ago (e.g., discussing an academic topic with classmates or reading academic texts in English). How difficult are these tasks now?

Source: Based on ideas in Oxford, R. L. (2011). *Teaching and researching language learning strategies*. Harlow, UK: Pearson.

UNIT OUTCOME

Writing Assignment: Persuasive Essay

Write a persuasive essay of 350 to 450 words on a topic related to corporate social responsibility. (Your instructor may give you an alternative length.) Use either APA- or MLA-style in-text citations and a References or Works Cited list.

You may write an essay that answers your Unit Inquiry Question. If you choose to do so, look back at the work you have done in this unit:

- the latest version of your Unit Inquiry Question on page 188;
- the debatable thesis statement you wrote in Activity C on page 208;
- the outline you wrote in Activity D on page 204;
- the turnaround introduction you wrote in Activity B on page 209; and
- the call-to-action conclusion you wrote in Activity C on page 210.

Decide whether you want to include drafts of any of the above in your essay. You may have to revise your writing to integrate these elements into your essay.

If you do not want to write about your Unit Inquiry Question, you may develop a new question or write an essay that answers one of the following questions instead:

- Do businesses have the responsibility to improve society?
- Should consumers boycott unethical businesses?
- Should businesses be allowed to set their own ethical objectives, or is this a role for government regulators?

Use the skills you have developed in this unit to complete the assignment. Follow the steps set out below to ensure that you practise each of your newly acquired skills to write a well-developed persuasive essay.

1. **Plan for your audience**: Consider who you are writing to and what kinds of arguments will be persuasive for this audience.
2. **Find outside sources of information**: Select appropriate information from Readings 1 and 2 (as you learned to do in Unit 2). You may consider finding additional sources related to the topic. When searching for information, remember that you can refer to sources that you disagree with, in order to refute them.
3. **Write a thesis statement**: Develop a debatable thesis statement.
4. **Outline**: Fill in the outline below to plan your first draft. Decide where you will acknowledge opposing views and whether you will refute or concede them.
   - Develop your ideas for the body paragraphs using the question technique you learned in Unit 2, keeping your audience in mind. You may wish to have three body paragraphs.
   - Include information from Readings 1 and 2 (or additional outside sources) in each body paragraph, if appropriate.

Introduction	Information or ideas that seem to lead in a different direction than the one you intend to take: A turnaround, where you change direction and connect to your thesis: Debatable thesis statement:

Main Body Paragraphs	Topic sentence 1 (argument for your position or acknowledgement of opposing view): Support for argument or response to opposing view: Concluding sentence 1 (optional):
	Topic sentence 2 (argument for your position or acknowledgement of opposing view): Support for argument or response to opposing view: Concluding sentence 2 (optional):
	(Optional) Topic sentence 3 (argument for your position or acknowledgement of opposing view): Support for argument or response to opposing view: Concluding sentence 3 (optional):
Conclusion	Summary of main ideas and call to action:

5. **Prepare a first draft**: Use your outline to write the first draft of your essay. Use AWL and mid-frequency vocabulary from this unit where appropriate. In your first draft, you should
   - focus on getting your ideas down on paper without worrying too much about grammar.
   - skip a section if you get stuck and come back to it later. For example, consider writing the body paragraphs before writing the introduction and conclusion.
6. **Ask for a peer review**: Exchange your first draft with a classmate. Use the Persuasive Essay Rubric on page 219 to provide suggestions for improving your classmate's essay. Ask questions to help him or her develop his or her body paragraphs more effectively (as you learned in Unit 2). Read your partner's feedback carefully. Ask questions if necessary.
7. **Revise**: Use your partner's feedback to write a second draft of your essay.
8. **Self-check**: Review your essay and use the Persuasive Essay Rubric to look for areas in which you could improve your writing.
   - Edit your essay for use of nouns. Make sure that you have used nouns and quantifiers correctly.
   - Check that you have paraphrased, summarized, and quoted, and that you have used appropriate reporting verbs to introduce quotations.
   - Use your dictionary to help correct grammar mistakes.
   - Edit your essay for correct APA- or MLA-style citations. Make sure you include a References or Works Cited section. Include page numbers for direct quotations.
   - Try reading your essay aloud to catch mistakes or awkward wording.
9. **Compose final draft**: Write a final draft of your essay, incorporating any changes you think will improve it.
   - When possible, leave some time between drafts.
10. **Proofread**: Check the final draft of your essay for any small errors you may have missed. In particular, look for spelling errors, typos, and punctuation mistakes.

Evaluation: Persuasive Essay Rubric

Use the following rubric to evaluate your essay. In which areas do you need to improve most?

E = **Emerging**: frequent difficulty using unit skills; needs a lot more work
D = **Developing**: some difficulty using unit skills; some improvement still required
S = **Satisfactory**: able to use unit skills most of the time; meets average expectations for this level
O = **Outstanding**: exceptional use of unit skills; exceeds expectations for this level

Skill	E	D	S	O
The introduction contains a turnaround that captures the reader's attention.				
The thesis statement takes a clear stance on a debatable issue.				
Each body paragraph starts with a clear topic sentence.				
Each body paragraph develops one controlling idea.				
The writer's arguments are clear and persuasive.				
Opposing points of view are acknowledged and addressed.				
The writer's stance on the issue is consistent and clearly signalled throughout the essay.				
Information from readings in this unit has been integrated and cited appropriately.				
AWL and mid-frequency vocabulary items from this unit are used when appropriate and with few mistakes.				
The conclusion issues a call to action.				
Nouns and quantifiers have been used appropriately.				
APA- or MLA-style in-text citations and a References or Works Cited list are formatted correctly.				

Unit Review

Activity A | What do you know about the topic of corporate social responsibility that you did not know before you started this unit? Discuss with a partner or small group. Be prepared to report what you have learned to the class.

Activity B | Look back at the Unit Inquiry Question you developed at the start of this unit and discuss it with a partner or small group. Then share your answers with the class. Use the following questions to guide you:

1. What ideas did you encounter during this unit that contributed to answering your question?
2. How would you answer your question now?

Activity C | Use the following checklist to review what you have learned in this unit. First decide which 10 skills you think are most important—circle the number beside each of these 10 skills. If you learned a skill in this unit that isn't listed below, write it in the blank row at the end of the checklist. Then put a check mark in the box beside those points you feel you have learned. Be prepared to discuss your choices with the class.

Self-Assessment Checklist	
☐	1. I can talk about corporate social responsibility.
☐	2. I can write a persuasive inquiry question.
☐	3. I can use a T-chart to explore arguments for and against a proposition.

☐	4. I can use appropriate language to signal my own stance on an issue.
☐	5. I can evaluate a peer's writing and give feedback for improvement.
☐	6. I can use peer feedback to improve first drafts.
☐	7. I can use a dictionary to correct my grammar mistakes.
☐	8. I can use AWL and mid-frequency vocabulary from this unit.
☐	9. I can plan my arguments and counterarguments by considering my audience.
☐	10. I can concede and/or refute opposing views.
☐	11. I can avoid plagiarism by collaborating responsibly with peers.
☐	12. I can cite my sources using APA or MLA style.
☐	13. I can write a debatable thesis statement.
☐	14. I can write a turnaround introduction.
☐	15. I can write an effective conclusion that ends with a call to action.
☐	16. I can use nouns and quantifiers correctly.
☐	17. I can write a persuasive essay of four or more paragraphs.
☐	18.

Activity D | Put a check mark in the box beside the vocabulary items from this unit that you feel you can now use with confidence in your writing.

Vocabulary Checklist	
☐ accustomed (adj.) 4000	☐ dubious (adj.) 5000
☐ aspiration (n.) 4000	☐ establish (v.) AWL
☐ beneficial (adj.) 4000	☐ ethical (adj.) 4000
☐ code (n.) AWL	☐ harassment (n.) 4000
☐ commit (v.) AWL	☐ morale (n.) 5000
☐ community (n.) AWL	☐ multinational (adj.) 5000
☐ concept (n.) AWL	☐ objective (n.) AWL
☐ consumer (n.) AWL	☐ potential (adj.) AWL
☐ corporate (adj.) AWL	☐ purchase (v.) AWL
☐ dissatisfied (adj.) 5000	☐ redress (n.) 7000

Appendix 1: Vocabulary

Unit 1

AWL Vocabulary

automatically (adv.)
culture (n.)
encounter (v.)
exposure (n.)
illustrate (v.)
media (n.)
process (n.)
sequence (n.)
task (n.)
trigger (v.)

Mid-frequency Vocabulary

accomplish (v.)
aggressively (adv.)
barely (adv.)
chaos (n.)
filter (v.)
fraction (n.)
navigate (v.)
routine (n.)
saturated (adj.)
temptation (n.)

Unit 2

AWL Vocabulary

access (n.)
adjustment (n.)
assess (v.)
emphasis (n.)
generate (v.)
implement (v.)
individual (n.)
promote (v.)
technology (n.)
theory (n.)

Mid-frequency Vocabulary

dependency (n.)
destined (adj.)
discord (n.)
disorientation (n.)
impatience (n.)
impetus (n.)
irresistible (adj.)
obey (v.)
premature (adj.)
recharge (v.)

Unit 3

AWL Vocabulary

area (n.)
define (v.)
dispose (v.)
economic (adj.)
environment (n.)
impact (n.)
migrant (n.)
portion (n.)
revolution (n.)
sustainable (adj.)

Mid-frequency Vocabulary

cater (v.)
classification (n.)
destination (n.)
hiking (n.)
likewise (adv.)
necessity (n.)
overnight (adv.)
rafting (n.)
receipt (n.)
vacation (n.)

Unit 4

AWL Vocabulary

acquired (v.)
affect (v.)
chemical (adj.)
component (n.)
contract (v.)
physical (adj.)
rely (v.)
respond (v.)
survive (v.)
target (v.)

Mid-frequency Vocabulary

acidic (adj.)
antibiotic (n.)
antibody (n.)
artificially (adv.)
fungus (n.)
invade (v.)
membrane (n.)
mutate (v.)
nutrient (n.)
vaccine (n.)

Unit 5

AWL Vocabulary

factor (n.)
occur (v.)
predict (v.)
release (v.)
shift (v.)
significantly (adv.)
somewhat (adv.)
source (n.)
trend (n.)
whereas (conj.)

Mid-frequency Vocabulary

adversely (adv.)
drought (n.)
ecosystem (n.)
erode (v.)
greenhouse (n.)
hemisphere (n.)
infrared (adj.)
nourish (v.)
precipitation (n.)
vapour (n.)

Unit 6

AWL Vocabulary

code (n.)
commit (v.)
community (n.)
concept (n.)
consumer (n.)
corporate (adj.)
establish (v.)
objective (n.)
potential (adj.)
purchase (v.)

Mid-frequency Vocabulary

accustomed (adj.)
aspiration (n.)
beneficial (adj.)
dissatisfied (adj.)
dubious (adj.)
ethical (adj.)
harassment (n.)
morale (n.)
multinational (adj.)
redress (n.)

Appendix 2: Sample Paragraphs

Unit 1

Automatic Routines

In *Introduction to Media Literacy*, Potter (2016) notes that we **see and hear** (*encounter*) hundreds of media messages per day, but we actually only pay attention to **a few of them** (*fraction*). We **are able to do** (*accomplish*) this because we have automatic routines to help us **block out** (*filter*) most of the messages. An automatic routine is a **series** (*sequence*) of steps we take to do something **without thinking about it** (*automatically*). When a routine is automatic, it saves us time and energy and lets us concentrate on other things. That is how we are able to ignore a lot of information **around us** (that we are *exposed* to) and focus only on the messages that are important to us. If we had to think about every message that we **came across** (*encountered*), we would never be able to do anything else! Also, we would feel very confused, because there is a lot of information coming from different places that **doesn't seem to fit together** (*chaotic*).

Reference

Potter, W. J. (2016). *Introduction to media literacy.* (pp. 3–4). Los Angeles, CA: SAGE.

Unit 2

Society's Reaction to New Technologies

Society often reacts negatively when new **technologies** first come into use. This reaction is not necessarily due to a negative attitude toward technology, but rather can be explained by fear—the fear that people experience when they consider the changes new **technologies** might bring. First, people may fear the loss of certain skills. For example, when the printing press was first invented, it brought many people the opportunity to learn more through books; however, it also meant that fewer people actually spent time memorizing and reciting text that they had memorized (Bain, Colyer, DesRivieres, & Dolan, 2002). Another thing that people may fear is the loss of employment due to new technological inventions. We can see this reaction in the so-called Luddite movement of the 1810s, which saw new textile machines destroyed in order to preserve the jobs and skills of traditional weavers (Bain et al., 2002). Because fear is a natural human reaction to **technological** change, people's emotional reaction to such change has to be taken into account when new **technology** is introduced.

Reference

Bain, C. M., Colyer, J. S., DesRivieres, D., & Dolan, S. (2002). *Transitions in society: The challenge of change.* (pp. 104, 110). Don Mills, ON: Oxford University Press.

Unit 3

Sustainable Tourism

Visiting one of Canada's national parks is a much more **sustainable** way to observe nature than lounging on a cruise ship on the St. Lawrence River, because visiting a park is much better for the **environment** than travelling on a cruise ship. Canada's national parks in Alberta and British Columbia have been highly rated for their **sustainable** tourism practices and site management. If visitors follow the park's rules, such as not leaving garbage behind, not removing plants and animals from the park, and staying on marked trails, their **impact** on the surrounding environment is minimal. In contrast, cruises have been criticized for polluting the water with waste and polluting the air with exhaust fumes (Watson, 2015). While some cruise ship companies have improved their waste water treatment, other companies have not made any improvements in this **area**. Furthermore, many cruise ship companies have not reduced the amount of exhaust their ships release into the atmosphere. For that reason, the majority of these companies receive a D or an F on the Friends of the Earth 2016 Cruise Ship Report Card. Moreover, when travellers spend their **vacations hiking** or biking through a national park, they are in much closer contact with nature and thereby appreciate it much more. On a cruise ship, the traveller is always separate and at quite a distance from the landscape that can be observed. Hikers or cyclists, on the other hand, are part of nature when they move through the national park.

References

Watson, B. (2015, January 5). Murky waters: The hidden environmental impacts of your cruise. *The Guardian*. Retrieved from http://www.theguardian.com/sustainable-business/2015/jan/05/cruise-ship-holidays-environmental-impact

Friends of the Earth. (2016). *2016 cruise ship report card*. Retrieved from http://www.foe.org/cruise-report-card

Unit 4

Why People Do Not Get Vaccinated

People may choose not to be vaccinated for two main reasons. Some people are not vaccinated because of their unique health situation. Due to allergies to some components of the vaccine (e.g., chicken eggs in the flu vaccine), some people cannot receive the flu vaccine (Boulanger, 2014; Libster, 2014; Loving, 2016). Others may be very ill, and their immune system is suppressed due to the illness (e.g., AIDS) or medication that they must take (e.g., chemotherapy) (Boulanger, 2014; Loving, 2016). A second reason that some people are not vaccinated is fear. These people (or their parents, in the case of children) fear the vaccine itself more than the disease it can prevent. The first fear concerns the potential side effects of the vaccine. These people fear that the side effects could kill them or their children or have permanent effects. However, a child is much more likely to die from getting the chicken pox than from side effects of a chicken pox vaccination (Haelle, n.d.). Another concern relates to the ingredients in vaccines. Some parents are concerned about mercury or formaldehyde in vaccines. Although the substances are present in vaccines, the amount is significantly less than what humans are exposed to from other sources, and these substances are not accumulated in the body (Haelle, n.d.). Therefore, people are not vaccinated either because they cannot be vaccinated or because they have unreasonable fears of vaccines.

References

Boulanger, A. (2014). *Who should not be immunized and why.* Retrieved from http://www.healthline.com/health/vaccinations/immunization-complications

Haelle, T. (n.d). 8 reasons parents don't vaccinate (and why they should). *Parents.* Retrieved from http://www.parents.com/health/vaccines/controversy/8-reasons-parents-dont-vaccinate-and-why-they-should/

Libster. R. (2014, November). *The power of herd immunity* [TEDx Talk]. Available from http://www.ted.com/talks/romina_libster_the_power_of_herd_immunity#t-397029

Loving, S. (2016, April 14). *Herd immunity (community immunity).* Retrieved from http://www.ovg.ox.ac.uk/herd-immunity

Unit 5

Destruction of the Arctic Tundra

One of the most serious problems associated with global warming is the destruction of the Arctic tundra. The tundra is the most fragile biome on the planet. It is characterized by cold, dry winters and short summers. Because of the extreme conditions there, the ecosystems are simple and easily disrupted (Heithaus & Arms, 2013). A layer of permanently frozen soil, called *permafrost*, lies underneath much of the tundra. Rising temperatures cause the permafrost to melt, resulting in flooding and changes in the vegetation of the tundra. This in turn affects the birds and animals and their migratory patterns. Perhaps most concerning is the fact that the permafrost contains large stores of methane, a greenhouse gas that is more than 20 times as potent as carbon dioxide. If a large area of the permafrost melts quickly, huge amounts of methane will be released into the atmosphere, contributing to further global warming. Although the entire planet is threatened by global warming, unfortunately, the Arctic has experienced faster and higher rates of warming than other places in the world. Some experts fear that the Arctic tundra will be eliminated from the Earth forever, as a direct result of global warming (Rutherford & Williams, 2015).

References

Heithaus, M., & Arms, K. (2013). *Environmental science.* Boston, MA: Houghton Mifflin Harcourt.

Rutherford, J., & Williams, G. (2015). *Environmental systems and societies.* Oxford, UK: Oxford University Press.

Unit 6

Economic Benefits of Ethical Business Practices

A business should have ethical business practices. Some people argue that ethical business practices are not beneficial. This is because price, quality, and value are more important than ethical considerations (Carrigan & Attalla, 2001). However, Creyer (1997) found that consumers do consider ethics when buying something. Furthermore, consumers will only buy from unethical companies if the products are cheap. In other words, consumers punish unethical companies with low profits (Creyer, 1997). This shows that, in fact, there are few benefits to being unethical. Secondly, there is evidence that a corporation with ethical objectives is more profitable. Lin, Yang, and Liou (2009) found that companies with ethical policies generated more profits over time. Finally, the stock market values companies with ethical principles highly. Lo and Sheu (2007) discovered that stock of US companies with such principles was more expensive. For these reasons, businesses should establish and implement ethical objectives.

References

Carrigan, M., & Attalla, A. (2001). The myth of the ethical consumer—Do ethics matter in purchase behaviour? *Journal of Consumer Marketing, 18*(7), 560–578.

Creyer, E. H. (1997). The influence of firm behavior on purchase intention: Do consumers really care about business ethics? *Journal of Consumer Marketing, 14*(6), 421–432.

Lin, C-H., Yang, H.-Li, & Liou, D.-Y. (2009). The impact of corporate social responsibility on financial performance: Evidence from business in Taiwan. *Technology in Society, 31*, 56–63.

Lo, S.-F., & Sheu, H.-J. (2007). Is corporate sustainability a value-increasing strategy for business? *Corporate Governance, 15*(2), 345–358.

Credits

Literary Credits

Dictionary definitions in *Academic Inquiry* were taken or adapted from *Oxford Advanced Learner's Dictionary 8th Edition* © 2010 Oxford University Press and *Oxford Online Learner's Dictionary* © 2017 Oxford University Press (http://www.oxfordlearnersdictionaries.com/us). Reproduced by permission.

5 Republished with permission of SAGE, from Introduction to Media Literacy, by J. Potter (2106). Permission conveyed through Copyright Clearance Center, Inc.; 12 Republished with permission of SAGE, from Introduction to Media Literacy, by J. Potter (2106). Permission conveyed through Copyright Clearance Center, Inc.; 14 Based on ideas in: Bloom, B. S.; Engelhart, M. D.; Furst, E. J.; Hill, W. H.; Krathwohl, D. R. (1956). Taxonomy of educational objectives: The classification of educational goals. Handbook I: Cognitive domain. New York: David McKay Company; 15 Bloom, B. S., Engelhart, M. D., Furst, E. J., Hill, W. H., & Krathwohl, D. R. (1956). Taxonomy of educational objectives: The classification of educational goals. Handbook 1: Cognitive domain. London, UK: Longmans; 26 Republished with permission of SAGE, from Introduction to Media Literacy, by J. Potter (2106). Permission conveyed through Copyright Clearance Center, Inc.; 45 Bain, C. M., Colyer, J. S., Des Rivieres, D., & Dolan, S. , Transitions in Society: The Challenge of Change.© 2002 Oxford University Press. Reprinted by permission of the publisher; 51 Volti, R. (2008). Society and technological change (6th edition), pp. 171-174. New York: Worth Publishers; 81 Adapted from Oxford, R. L. (2011). Teaching and researching language learning strategies. Harlow, UK: Pearson; 83 Cartwright, F., Pierce, G., & Wilkie, R. Travel Quest: Travel & Tourism in the 21st Century. © 2001. Oxford University Press. Reprinted by permission of the publisher; 88 WWOOF connects volunteers with organic farmers by Nicholas Köhler. Published by Mclean's, September 17, 2009. Used with permisison of Rogers Media Inc. All rights reserved; 115 Based on Nation, I. S. P. (2001). Learning vocabulary in another language. Cambridge University Press: Cambridge; 118 Based on Oxford, R. L. (1990). Language learning strategies: What every teacher should know. Heinle & Heinle: Boston, MA; 122 From BIOLOGY, Student Edition. Copyright © 2012 by Houghton Mifflin Harcourt Publishing Company. All rights reserved. Reprinted by permission of the publisher, Houghton Mifflin Harcourt Publishing Company; 126 Asking for an outbreak of preventable diseases With vaccination rates plummeting, are anxious parents putting everyone at risk? By Kate Lunau and Martin Patriquin, published in Mclean's January 9, 2012. This is an edited version. Used with permission of Rogers Media Inc. All rights reserved; 155 Based on ideas in Oxford, R. L. (2011). Teaching and researching language learning strategies. Harlow, UK: Pearson; 157 From ENVIRONMENTAL SCIENCE, Student Edition. Copyirght © 2013 by Houghton Mifflin Harcourt Publishing Company. All rights reserved. Reprinted by permission of the publisher, Houghton Mifflin Harcourt Publishing Company; 162 Is geoengineering the solution to saving the Earth? by Brian Bethune, published in Mclean's January 12, 2016. Used with permission of Rogers Media Inc. All rights reserved; 196 Adapted from Lominé, L., Muchena, M., & Pierce, R. A. (2014). Business Management. Oxford: Oxford University Press; 201 Adapted from

Sehti, S. P. (2012, January). Two faces of apple [article]. Retrieved from http://www.carnegiecouncil.org/publications/ethics_online/0068.html; 202 Adapted from CBC News (2014, December 19). Apple on defence after BBC expose of working conditions in its factories. Retrieved from http://www.cbc.ca/news/business/apple-on-defence-after-bbc-expos%C3%A9-of-working-conditions-in-its-factories-1.2879208.

Photo Credits

1 Monkey Business Images/Shutterstock.com; 2 quka/Shutterstock; 13 Tashatuvango/Shutterstock.com; 14 06photo/Shutterstock.com; 16 (top) Olivier Le Moal/Shutterstock.com; (bottom) ventdusud/Shutterstock.com; 17 alphaspirit/Shutterstock.com; 18 © iStock/artvea; 23 (l–r) Photo by FDA via Getty Images; Mascha Tace/Shutterstock.com;35 luchschen/123RF; 36 rawpixel/123RF; 46 Bettman/Getty Images; 47 https://commons.wikimedia.org/wiki/File:FrameBreaking-1812.jpg; 48 (top) ESB Professional/Shutterstock.com; (bottom) Carolyn Ridsdale; 71 © iStock/bst2012; 72 (clock wise from top left) © iStock/aphotostory; © iStock/danilovi; © iStock/xijian; © iStock/Rawpixel; © iStock/pixdeluxe; © iStock/deimagine; 85 Robert Zehetmayer / Alamy Stock Photo; 88 Photo by Alvaro Canovas/Paris Match via Getty Images; 91 (l–r) ©Alex JW Robinson/Shutterstock.com; © iStock/TomasSereda; 107 nobeastsofierce/Shutterstock.com; 108 (clockwise from top right) Ramesh Lalwani/Getty Images; Davide Calabresi/Shutterstock.com; VOISIN/PHANIE/Getty Images; © iStock/belterz; 123 CNRI / Science Source; 124 E. Gray / Science Source; 127 MAGNIFIER/Shutterstock.com; 145 mikeledray/Shutterstock.com; 146 Photo by IISD/Kiara Worth (http://enb.iisd.org/climate/cop21/enb/images/30nov/3K1A8656.jpg); 148 Ben Good/123RF; 149 Watch_The_World/Shutterstock.com; 152 art-pho/Shutterstock.com; 158 FloridaStock/Shutterstock.com; 159 ©Vitoriano Junior/Shutterstock.com; 162 Kent Weakley/Shutterstock.com; 163 Photo by Kevin Frayer/Getty Images; 165 © ImageFlow/Shutterstock.co; 172 Ivan Kmit/123RF; 175 ©David Boutin/Shutterstock.com; 176 ©Darla Hallmark/Shutterstock.com; 178 © iStock/rtJazz; 185 ImageFlow/Shutterstock.com; 186 cleanfotos/Shutterstock.com; 201 pio3/Shutterstock.com; 202 AP Photo/Kin Cheung; 215 © iStock/AJ_Watt.

Index